THE JOURNAL OF WOMEN'S CIVIL WAR HISTORY

From the Home Front to the Front Lines

Accounts of the Sacrifice, Achievement, and Service of American Women, 1861-1865

VOLUME 2

edited by Eileen Conklin

This volume is dedicated to
Marge Estilow
historian, friend, and role model,
who, for the last eighty years,
has made the world a better place.

TABLE OF CONTENTS

Against All Odds:
Women Doctors Who Served in the Civil War

By Mercedes Graf

Introduction

The path for women in medicine has not been an easy one. Put simply, any woman who ventured beyond her domestic role as late as the 1830s was consider an anomaly.[1] While women had been welcomed as midwives, midwifery gradually came to be considered a subordinate branch of medicine.[2] At the same time, midwives were prevented from making inroads into the medical profession by male physicians who wanted to keep them in a separate sphere.

Opposition to females in medicine rested upon the presumed assumption that they were the weaker sex and thus were less able to stand the strain of practice. But it was the supposed mental differences that the opposition stressed. Women were "modest, dependent, retiring; they were lacking in courage and originality. They were, by nature, fitted for the care of the home, but disqualified for activities in more worldly spheres."[3] At a time when phrenology was still taken seriously, one author concluded with the telling observation: "She has a head almost too small for intellect but just big enough for love."[4]

By 1860, statistics regarding the historical patterns of female physicians indicated that there were about 200 women in the United States who had confronted the barriers and secured medical degrees.[5] Strong opposition to women practitioners, however, continued to be voiced by male doctors "who claimed that women were unfit for any profession, particularly one that required physical strength, strong nerves, and decisive judgment."[6] More precisely, the male establishment feared that female doctors challenged prevailing nineteenth-century gender roles. While it was acceptable that they should work side by side with their husbands, Victorian society left no doubt as to who was the true master in the relationship. Women were designated as inferior persons in law, education, and in matters related to political and property rights to say nothing of church affairs and theology. Given this state of affairs, only the most undaunted women were likely to pursue a medical career. If questioned, such women probably did not see themselves as challenging the status quo, but neither did they view themselves as dependent home-centered caretakers, although the majority did marry. Thus, in trying to gain insights about these early Civil War medical women, gender has to be used as a prism through which their experiences are filtered.

By the start of the Civil War, the nineteenth-century view of woman's proper place was still so deeply ingrained that the women who succeeded in getting the MD after their name faced the brunt of social ostracism from many quarters. Even if they had family support, they were betrayed by other females who regarded them as oddities of their own sex who had abandoned the feminine virtues of modesty and domesticity. In addition, women doctors faced the hostility of the general public as well as the enmity directed at them from their male colleagues. Elizabeth Blackwell, for example, had been voted in as a joke by the all-male student body prior to her acceptance at Geneva Medical College in New York. After her graduation in 1849, the doors of the school were immediately closed to women. Two years later, when Hannah Myers Longshore graduated from the Female Medical College of Pennsylvania, police had to guard the commencement exercises. By 1856, Marie Zakrzewska (better known as Zak) fared no better. While pursuing her degree at Western Reserve, she was spurned by guests at her boarding house and discouraged by some openly hostile male professors.

Despite such problems, women physicians threw their energy into training other females as nurses and doctors and they established hospitals and clinics for women, children, and the poor. Ann Preston, Dean of the Women's Medical College of Pennsylvania (originally called the Female Medical College and today known as MCP Hahnemann University) rallied support for the establishment of the Woman's Hospital of Philadelphia in the fall of 1861 while Marie Zakrzewska helped open the New England Hospital for Women and Children in July of 1862. The following year, Clemence Lozier founded the New York Medical College and Hospital for Women, and Mary Harris Thompson spearheaded the founding of the Chicago Hospital for Women and Children in 1865.

At the outset of the war, Dr. Elizabeth Blackwell was instrumental in founding the Women's Central Relief Association (WCRA), a group that aided in the recruiting and training of female nurses. While her contributions were enormous, her disappointments were many.[7] If she hoped that her efforts would allow her to help nurses overcome the problem of inadequate training, she was disappointed when the position of superintendent of nurses was created, and the job went to Dorothea L. Dix. One historian believed that Blackwell did not get the job because "most medical men were suspicious, hypercritical, or jealous of her."[8] By 1868, however, Elizabeth Blackwell and her sister, Emily, opened the Woman's Medical College of the New York Infirmary.

Yet the efforts of these pioneer women did little to legitimize the claim of female doctors to professionalism. The battle over women's entry into medicine was fought "between those who believed women should remain within the home—or at most should serve as nurses under male doctors—and those who felt that women could make a special and valuable contribution to the profession as doctors."[9] The latter position was maintained by the Female Medical College of Pennsylvania which insisted that the demand for well educated female physicians was on the rise, and that a high and honorable rank in the profession would be accorded to all who proved themselves worthy of it.[10]

While some women doctors were drawn to the larger setting of the hospital or clinic, quite a few opted for private practice. As it turned out, such a decision did not automatically guarantee acceptance by the community—and, of course, acceptance was quite often equated with worthiness. Louisa Shepard, who was reported to be the first woman to complete a course of studies from a southern medical school, became so totally discouraged by hostile public opinion that she soon decided to close her office.[11] Hannah Myers Longshore, as the first woman doctor in Philadelphia, also had her share of problems when local druggists would not fill her prescriptions and warned patients against her. She learned to fill her own prescriptions, however, and held her ground.[12] It is no wonder that one scholar observed that "any woman who became a physician in the nineteenth century can truly be considered a pioneer."[13]

The Impact of War on Women Physicians

With the outbreak of the Civil War, women began to expand their traditional domestic roles and were soon helping the war cause in sewing circles, church groups, and as members of the many relief societies that suddenly emerged. Other women followed their husbands to the battlefield, volunteered as nurses, and even disguised themselves as male soldiers.[14] There were also the cooks, laundresses, and prostitutes who followed the army while some women even aided their sectional causes by acting as spies or scouts.

Usually not mentioned by military historians is the group of women who were trained as physicians. Contributing perhaps to their obscurity is the fact that some of them served as nurses, unlike their male colleagues, as they could not secure official posts as military surgeons.[15] Furthermore, accounts regarding female physicians are usually scanty and fragmentary.[16] An added difficulty is the fact that women frequently change their surnames upon marriage which complicates a search for them in official records.[17]

In studying the early course of women in medicine, it is apparent that they shared a common goal in seeking a medical education, and their motivation was feminist in a very basic way since they wanted to improve the health care of their sex and of their children.[18] Still, they were a very diverse group and they differed from each other in many respects. As was mentioned earlier, some took on visible roles as exemplified by their founding hospitals or clinics while others devoted themselves to training and education. The majority, however, led productive but mostly anonymous lives when they remained on the homefront engaged in their private practices. Yet they had the satisfaction of knowing that by staying behind they enabled their male colleagues to be released for medical service on the battlefield.

In distinguishing Civil War women physicians for this article, I am referring to those doctors who took an active part in the war effort—active meaning that they tended directly to the needs of the wounded whether in the hospital, field, or on a floating transport. This group is comprised of seven women doctors.[19] While a few of these women tried to volunteer as military surgeons, they were quickly given the message that their services were neither sought nor valued by the army's medical department. Female physicians bent on healing had to find alternate ways to reach their goal. One choice was to volunteer as a nurse.[20] Although this might seem the easiest route, even this path was strewn with difficulties since the public was not convinced that such work was for refined women.[21]

The bits and pieces of information that have emerged about these early women physicians, however, make it possible to view the various ways they committed themselves to the war effort at a time when the path to professional success was not easy. Even though the various accounts provide only glimpses of their experiences, one thing is certain about the seven women in this discussion—they were united by virtue of their medical training and their commitment to healing at a time when the country was in a violent upheaval.

Orianna Russell Moon (Andrews)

Mary Elizabeth Massey noted that "there were no women physicians in Confederate service."[22] From what we now know today, this statement is open to interpretation since at least one trained physician appears to have devoted herself to the southern cause.[23] She was born at the family estate known as Viewmont in Albemarle County, Virginia, on August 11, 1834. Orianna was the second of seven children and the oldest of five daughters born to Orianna Maria Barclay and Edward Harris Moon. When she was old enough to make up her own mind, she chose to attend a preparatory school, Troy Female Seminary, in New York. This was an unusual occurrence since it was customary for Virginia girls to attend finishing schools at home, where the studies were consistent with the prevailing ideals of a "woman's sphere." After her graduation, Orie announced that she wished to follow in her brother's footsteps and become a doctor. If the countryside was surprised at this unconventional choice, her broadminded parents did not seem in the least bit upset, and they were entirely supportive of their daughter's decision.

By the time Orianna graduated from the Female Medical College of Pennsylvania in 1857, she had also finished her thesis on the mutual relation between cardiac and pulmonary disease.[24] A short time later, she was off to Europe, where she devoted another year to her medical studies. After six months in Paris, she visited her uncle, who was a missionary in Jerusalem. "Especially was she touched by the prevalence of opthalmia among the Arabs and she gave herself tirelessly to alleviating this disease of the eyes."[25]

By the start of the Civil War, Orianna was determined to use her skills in the war effort despite the fact that "only men were permitted to serve as surgeons."[26] Barely twenty-seven years old, she rushed to Charlottesville, Virginia to volunteer her services when the wounded started pouring into the town from the battlefield of Manassas.[27] She supervised a ward in the local hospital, and she began to turn university buildings into hospital units. Her ability and energy did not go unobserved, and it was rumored that she was commissioned as a surgeon in the Confederate army.[28]

In that first frantic week of July, when all the available doctors were working with the wounded, a young doctor from Alabama sent out a desperate call for assistance. Dr. John Andrews was one of three brothers who had fought at Bull Run. His brother William had been killed, and his younger brother, Robert, lay seriously wounded in the home of a relative in Charlottesville. When a consulting doctor responded to the call, he brought Orie with him. She remained, "and her sympathy was drawn to the man, who after doing all that medical skill could do, must watch his brother die. He was grateful for her help and sympathy, and as the two of them continued to work together in the days that followed, love blossomed even amid those dreadful scenes."[29]

In November of 1861, Orie married Dr. John Summerfield Andrews, and soon she was working with her husband treating the wounded, most likely as a nurse rather than as a physician. After the fall of the Confederacy, she and John practiced medicine together, first in Tennessee and then in Scottsville, Virginia, where they established a hospital. Orie had a large family that consisted of twelve sons, one of whom became a well-known senator. On December 21, 1883, she died at the age of forty-nine from cancer of the womb, and she was buried in the local cemetery in Scottsville.

During her lifetime, it had been difficult for Orianna to gain professional acceptance by many of her male colleagues who had little use for southern women in the world of work outside the home, let alone the practice of medicine. One doctor maintained that she was "a lady of high character and fine intelligence" who failed to distinguish herself as a physician although she had been an excellent nurse.[30] Present-day writers, however, are less biased; one writer has maintained that Orianna was "certainly among the best representatives of the Confederacy's 3500 physicians."[31]

Mary Frame Myers (Thomas)

The next physician, Mary Frame Myers, was born on October 28, 1816. The second of two daughters born to Samuel and Mary Frame, she lost her mother when she was only a few months old. Her Quaker father then married Paulina Iden and to this union were born five daughters and two sons.[32] Around 1833 Samuel felt compelled to move his family from the Maryland area to Ohio because of his strong feelings regarding slavery. Three years later, at the age of twenty, Mary started to teach in the district school, "but was told that she must teach for less than men, because she was a woman . . . [and] she was thoroughly aroused to the injustice."[33]

Mary wed Owen Thomas in 1839 and settled down in Fort Wayne, Indiana, where she started raising a family of three daughters. In 1852 Owen began studying medicine with a preceptor, and he enrolled at Western Reserve College in Cleveland, Ohio. When Mary decided to become a physician as well in 1853, Owen supported his wife's decision although she was in her late thirties by this time. (Unofficially she attended classes with her husband at Western Reserve, where Emily Blackwell was also enrolled.) It took several years for Mary to complete a formal program owing to interruptions due to the prolonged illness and subsequent death in 1855 of the couple's oldest daughter. But in 1856 Dr. Mary Myers Thomas finally graduated from Penn Medical University. Her interest in the medical problems of women was reflected in the subject of her thesis, "Ovarian Dropsy."[34]

Mary Frame Myers Thomas ca. 1870.

Courtesy Archives & Special Collections on Women
in Medicine, MCP Hahneman University.

Chloe Annette Buckel, M.D. (WMC, 1858).

Courtesy Archives & Special Collections on Women
in Medicine, MCP Hahneman University.

During part of the Civil War, Owen was a contract surgeon stationed at the Army Hospital at Nashville, Tennessee. "Dr. Mary Thomas accompanied him, but since a woman could get no status as a surgeon she was listed as a nurse, but did medical service."[35] Serving at different times as a volunteer nurse and superintendent under the auspices of Governor Oliver P. Morton of Indiana, Mary spent the war years collecting and delivering supplies to military camps and directing the hospital for refugees in Nashville where her husband worked. In the summer of 1863, she took supplies to Indiana soldiers at Vicksburg. At one point, when Mary was returning to Indiana, "she had responsibility for nursing fifty of the two hundred wounded and sick soldiers on board the steamship."[36]

In describing her courage and strength aboard this vessel, one writer observed:

> Of these, forty-seven were in her personal charge, and nine were so helpless that she fed them like babies with a spoon. One was crazed from sunstroke, and so violent that the officers were about to put him under restraint, when she took him in charge, controlled him and saw that he was safely forwarded to his home in New York. At some stopping-place . . . the boat caught fire, and for a short time destruction and a panic seemed inevitable. A frightened officer called to Mrs. Thomas to hurry and leave the boat while she could, but she indignantly reminded him of the helpless soldiers and declared her intention to stay on the boat till the last man was carried off.[37]

In postwar years, Dr. Thomas was concerned about the plight of insane women in her state, and she urged that capable women physicians be appointed in hospitals for such women. Credited with being the first woman physician in her home state of Indiana, she was also the first woman admitted to the Indiana Medical Society. Unfortunately she left no written record of her Civil War experiences. As her biographer noted: "She alone could tell it, and she was reluctant to talk of her share . . . there were other women who did so much more, she said, her share was but a small one."[38] She died on August 19, 1888 at the age of 72 in her home in Richmond, Indiana.

Chloe Annette Buckel

Chloe Annette Buckel, who liked to sign herself C. Annette, was born August 25, 1833, in Warsaw, New York. She graduated from the Female Medical College of Pennsylvania in 1856 and probably knew Orie Moon as she graduated one year behind her. She started to practice in Chicago, but when it looked like the war was going to last longer than anyone first thought, Annette, like Dr. Mary Thomas, volunteered her services to Governor Oliver P. Morton of Indiana.

While she had a difficult childhood, Annette's early experiences contributed to the strength of character she displayed throughout her life.[39] Her parents died when she was three months old, and she went to live with her grandparents. They, too, died when she was a young child, and she lived first with one aunt and then another. At age fourteen Annette began to teach school for $1.25 a week plus board. Determined to study medicine and desperate to save money quickly, she went to work in a burnishing factory. When she was still short of funds, she borrowed money against her life insurance policy so she could enter medical school.[40]

After she received her medical degree, Annette worked with both Drs. Elizabeth and Emily Blackwell in the New York Infirmary and Dispensary. Toward the end of the second year of the Civil War, she gave up her medical position, determined to offer her services to the government as a nurse. She "joined a company of nurses and surgeons which Governor Morton of Indiana sent south with sanitary stores; that upon arrival at Memphis she, with others, assisted in establishing hospitals in stores and warehouses."[41]

Because of her training and ability, Annette was appointed to help in the selection of women who wanted to become nurses. Governor Morton sent a letter to this effect to General Ulysses S. Grant. He pointed out that "having graduated at a Medical School she is admirably adapted to the labor and arrangement of Hospitals and giving attention to the distressed. I respectfully ask for her every facility in your power for the furtherance of her mission in your Army."[42] Dorothea L. Dix concurred with this appointment and appointed "Miss" Annette Buckel as her representative for the State of Indiana.[43]

Soon Dr. Buckel's work expanded and she was placing applicants in Louisville hospitals, instructing women nurses at Jefferson General Hospital in Jeffersonville, Indiana, and supervising Indiana nurses in Nashville and Chattanooga, Tennessee, as well as Huntsville, Alabama. During the spring of 1863 she provided direct service to the wounded on one of the hospital ships. Because of her distinguished service, she became known as the "Little Major," a title she carried with pride for the rest of her life.

The next year, one government nurse, Elvira J. Powers, who worked with Buckel, wrote about her experiences at Jefferson Hospital. In her narrative, she remarked that on Tuesday, September 27, 1864, she first "met Miss C. A. Buckel, M.D., agent of Miss Dix." For the remainder of the year, she worked under the "superintendence of Miss Buckel." When she referred to the doctor elsewhere in her account, Powers referred to her as "Miss. B." She was following the customary practice of shortening names or protecting the identity of associates in nurses' postwar reminiscences. Conversely, male military officers and surgeons were willing to acknowledge the link between women's role and nursing since such work was consistent with Christian duty and feminine self-sacrifice. Conferring titles on women doctors, however, seemed at odds with their hierarchy of job classifications.[44]

In considering her work with the wounded, one biographer observed: "Dr. Buckel seldom mentioned this subject, as the experiences were too heart-breaking to be spoken of lightly. I simply know that after conflicts she went onto the battlefield with the stretcher-bearers to succor the dying and give relief to as many as possible. This was in addition to her duties as chief of nurses in the tent hospitals, where often the work required unremitting duty days and nights on end."[45]

After the Civil War, Buckel spent the next ten years working as a resident physician at New England's Women's Hospital in Boston. When she decided she wanted to deepen her knowledge and skills, she went abroad to study for two years. On her return to the United States, she relocated to California. In 1889 she applied for a government pension and submitted a letter to the Committee on Invalid Pensions to substantiate her Civil War services. This letter is a thirty-two-page handwritten account that starts with a rationale for her volunteering, details her nursing experiences, and ends with her reason for applying for a pension.[46]

> Women, as well as men, sought in every possible way to be of use to the Government. Soon came calls for help from the sick and wounded. Many women in all parts of the North left their homes to rush to the front. Most of them had no experience in even home sickness. Still less did they know of hospital nursing and nothing at all of the horrors of war. No provision had been made by government for their transportation or maintenance. Military Surgeons had no authority, even if they had the desire, to assign them to duty . . . At that time, I felt I was most needed by my own sex, at home and waited, until I heard the tales of suffering and distress from the disappointed, returned women. . . .
>
> There were no trained nurses, and no means provided anywhere for organizing trained nurses, and no means provided anywhere for organizing or training the numerous women who volunteered in answer to the numerous calls for their help which came from friends of the soldiers, through the [U. S.] Sanitary Commission, and Governors of States.
>
> I decided to accept one of these calls, and go to the front, and see if I could not help organize the women so that there could become an efficient part of the U.S. Hospital Corps.

She then described some of her experiences.

> I learned that a large river steamer, the Nashville, was about to sail South to act as a floating receiving hospital for those on their way out of the malarial districts to the North. . . All the engines and propelling machinery had been removed from the Nashville to make room for hospital use. So we were towed to Milliken's Bend and fastened to the wharf. . . The dying would seize our hands or even our dress skirts, and beg us not to leave them to die alone. . . I am comforted by the belief that I was instrumental after the war in helping to establish homes for soldiers' orphans. It would be impossible to give details of my work in this hospital. . . .

The arduous work started to take its toll, and Annette became exhausted and ill. Although she did not feel sick enough to leave, a Sanitary Commission agent marched her to a steamer and sent her home. She later recalled that when she walked into her house, "my friends did not recognize me until I began to talk, I had changed so much, both in color and weight during my four months' absence. I was lemon color."

When Annette felt recovered enough to go back to nursing, she went down the Mississippi to Vicksburg, where she found another nurse, Miss Miller, still at work on the Nashville and "worn to a shadow, but proud of being the only one of the original attendants who had remained on duty." Finally making her way to Louisville, the young doctor took on another task. With the consent of the Assistant Surgeon General, she introduced women into several of the military hospitals on condition that she should be responsible for them. At Jeffersonville, Annette found a large hospital that was ready to be occupied and was exactly what she wanted for a training school. Although the Surgeon in charge, Dr. Goldsmith, had said he "would not have a woman about" he finally consented. About fifty women nurses were placed under her supervision in Louisville and Jeffersonville for nearly two years.

Annette concluded her account with this explanation. "All these women who worked nobly and unselfishly in the hospitals were recognized by Government as 'Female Nurses' but my name was never presented to the paymaster, and I hoped I would never need to ask any recognition from Government. Now that our nation is so prosperous, it seems easier to petition for help in time of need." In support of her pension claim, she submitted thirteen documents. Included were orders from General Grant permitting her to go "through lines at pleasure and on railroads and Government steamboats" as well as several testimonials from surgeons who had supervised her work.

On April 18, 1904, the Committee on Pensions was authorized to grant a pension of twelve dollars a month to C. Annette Buckel, late nurse, Medical Department United States Volunteers.[47] The bill did not use her title in referring to her, and during her Civil War years "she was referred to as Miss (not Dr.) Buckel."[48] She died on August 17,1912, leaving her estate to help mentally retarded children.

Hettie K. Painter

While very little is known about the next physician, Hettie K. Painter, even less is known about her before she saw service as a volunteer.[49] Since she was the niece of John Brown, there could be no doubt as to her allegiance to the northern cause. Shortly before the Civil War broke out, she lived in Kansas where she saw her husband dragged from his bed and murdered before her eyes.[50] Despite the fact that the house was set on fire, Hettie and her adopted daughter managed to escape in their night clothes. Although she was about forty years of age at the time of the incident, she was not too old to go on and render "valiant service" as a spy.[51] "By removing all her teeth, with an old pipe in her mouth and wearing...glasses, and patched dresses, she appeared quite aged."[52]

Hettie graduated from Penn Medical University in 1860 (four years behind Mary Thomas), and as part of her degree requirements submitted a thesis entitled "Electricity as a Remedial Agent."[53] Like Buckel, she received her medical degree before the Civil War and was willing to serve as a sanitary agent and nurse. The simple tasks of distributing clothes and delicacies for the Penn Relief Association of Philadelphia, however, were not enough to challenge a woman of her energy and background.[54] It was not long before she saw service as a hospital and field nurse. After the first battle of Bull Run, she nursed the sick and wounded for three months. Her efforts were so intense that she lost the use of her right hand and had to return to her home in New Jersey on furlough.

When Major General Philip Kearny urged her to return, she was soon back in the field, taking charge of the Georgetown College Hospital in Washington, DC.

From there she went to another DC site, the Armory Square Hospital, and then proceeded to join the army at Frederick, Maryland. For months Hettie was constantly on the move as she was ordered to visit DC to report on conditions there and supervise hospitals cars at Brandy Station, Virginia. She also nursed at the vast hospital sites at Aquia Creek, Fredericksburg, and City Point, Virginia.

At this last site, Grant had established a base camp where nearly two hundred women gathered from June 1864 to April 1865. At City Point, Painter worked alongside such women as Sophronia E. Bucklin, Julia S. Wheelock, Helen Louise Gilson, Cornelia Hancock, and Adelaide Smith. In describing Painter's services in her postwar reminiscences, Smith recalled that the New Jersey state agent "was a living example of the usefulness of a lady in the army, who can frequently effect more good by personal influence than would be allowed through regular channels."[55] But Painter was also a good friend to many of her sister nurses, and on one occasion she "stepped in as the bride's surrogate mother when the clergyman who was to give her away could not attend."[56]

In postwar years, "Mrs. Painter was afterwards widely known as one of the most efficient and humane nurses of the Army of the Potomac. Thousands of scarred veterans, scattered abroad through the country, remember with gratitude her tender ministrations to their comfort in hospital and camp."[57] By 1887, however, she was in need of financial help, and she applied for a government pension. It was pointed out that "but for the death of Grant, Lincoln, Kearny, [Major General Gershom] Mott, and others she would have received their warm commendations" in support of her application.[58] Fortunately, the Pension Committee was favorably impressed with her service record and noted: "Mrs. Painter was a graduate in medicine, a circumstance which made her services doubly valuable."[59] As in the case of other women physicians, the title "doctor" was not used.

Esther Jane Hill (Hawks)

Esther Jane Hill was born in Hooksett, New Hampshire, on August 4, 1833 (the same month and year as C. Annette Buckel). She was the fifth of eight children born to Parmenas and Jane Kimball Hill, and the family ancestry could be traced back to her paternal grandfather, who fought in the American Revolution.[60] Not much is known about her early life, but following her marriage to Dr. John Milton Hawks, she decided to enter medicine like her husband. She graduated from the New England Female Medical College in 1855, having attended two seventeen-week sessions in two successive academic years.[61] While in school, she met one of the lecturers, Dr. Marie Zakrzewska, and the two became lifelong friends.

With the start of the Civil War, Esther applied as a doctor to the federal government, but she was turned down because of her sex. Another rejection followed when Dorothea Dix refused to consider her as a nurse because Esther was too young, having not yet reached thirty years of age. Despite these two disappointments, Esther remained in Washington for several months as a volunteer in the hospitals.

After her husband accepted a position with the National Freedmen's Aid Association, she followed him to South Carolina. John eventually terminated his civilian contract and accepted a commission as an U.S. Army Acting Assistant Surgeon on Major General Rufus Saxton's staff in October of 1862, and he began treating wounded African American soldiers. Esther was soon working at his side, and she performed many medical services that included assisting in surgery. In addition, Esther helped organize the first general hospital established in Beaufort for colored soldiers. In her diary, she commented: "I went about for weeks with a soaped rag in hand, overseeing and instructing in the cleaning. . . I circulated among them with the greatest freedom—prescribing for them, ministering to their wants, teaching them, and making myself as thoroughly conversant with their inner lives as I could."

When her husband had to go on an expedition to the coast of Florida, no one was sent in his place. As a result, Esther took charge of a military hospital for black troops for nearly three weeks. She explained: "I am left manager of not only the affairs of the Hospital, but have to attend Surgeons' call for the 2nd [S. C. Volunteers]." After her husband's return, she was happy to devote herself to her church duties and teaching. In July of 1863, however, the news came that the hospital was to prepare immediately to receive five hundred wounded men. "150 of the brave boys from the 54th Mass. Col. Shaw's Regt. were brought to us and laid on blankets on the floor all mangled and ghastly. What a terrible sight it was . . . in 24 hours the poor fellows were lying with clean clothes and dressed wounds in comfortable beds"[62]

Esther Hill Hawks continued to work with her husband managing the Beaufort, South Carolina, Negro Hospital, and "she gave her services and medicines as physician and as teacher without money and without price." In fact, she ran the one of the first racially integrated free school in Florida during the Federal occupation of Jacksonville, and late in the war she helped operate an orphanage there for black children and became administrator for the Freedmen's Bureau.

On one occasion, she went to Hilton Head: "Offered my services to Surgeon in charge at Hospital and am to go up to-morrow to assist among the wounded."[63] Some of the patients Hawks dealt with during these period were from the First South Carolina Volunteers, the regiment in which Susie King Taylor had also served as laundress and nurse.[64]

In summarizing her varied war experiences, her biographer noted: "At times Esther went for days without sleep while treating the wounded in field hospitals. She did a tremendous amount of work caring for the wounded black soldiers of the Fifty-fourth Massachusetts Infantry after that regiment's ill-fated assault on Fort Wagner in Charleston Harbor. Later she did the same after the Battle of Olustee, or Ocean Pond, the only major engagement of the war fought in Florida."[65]

By 1870 Esther began to fell lonely and isolated, so she returned to New England and entered into a thriving practice with another woman physician. In Lynn, Massachusetts, her practice flourished although most of her patients were women and most of her cases were gynecological. In 1874 Esther began to practice on her own. (Her husband later resumed his practice there as well.) She was "an increasingly successful practitioner and revered public figure in her adopted city. . . . In recognition of her medical service during the Civil War she was elected unanimously an honorary member of the New Hampshire Association of Military Surgeons when that organization was formed in 1899 . . . [she] could not let a single progressive reform cause intended to better the human condition go by without making some contribution."[66] She died on May 6, 1906, and numerous tributes were paid to her in recognition of her humanitarian and civic work. Schwartz observed that "the Civil War gave Dr. Hawks the opportunity to transform her idealism into action. At great sacrifice and risk to life and limb she served freed men and black troops of the Union army as both healer and teacher in Federally occupied areas of the south.[67]

Sarah Ann Chadwick (Clapp)

Sarah Chadwick was born July 17, 1824, in Windsor, Kennebec County, Maine. She was the third of seven children born to Lot and Sarah Linn Chadwick. Sometime in her youth she moved with her family to Lee County, Illinois. She attended school here and later married James Milligan on March 9, 1847. After giving birth to a daughter, it appears that the young wife was deserted by her husband. In any case, she managed to marshal her resources and enter Cleveland Medical College in October of 1854 as "Mrs. Sarah Chadwick."[68]

Since it was a common practice for aspiring female doctors to show that male physicians of good standing supported them in training, she listed her brother-in-law as a sponsor. Because she apparently chose not to reveal her real status as a wife and mother to anyone, her classmates believed she was a widow. She graduated in 1855 and wrote a thesis entitled, "An Essay on Contagion."[69] One of her classmates was the German-speaking Prussian, Marie Elizabeth Zakrzewska.

Following graduation, Sarah appears to have practiced briefly in the Cleveland area. On November 15, 1861, she began her army service, and references to her medical work begin to appear in the literature. She is referred to as Clapp, her second husband's name, rather than Chadwick, which may account for some of the confusion regarding her identity. Bell Irvin Wiley noted that Sarah Clapp served as an assistant surgeon, and Richard Hall indicated she was with the Seventh Illinois Cavalry. One account noted that "though not commissioned," she served first as surgeon of a volunteer cavalry regiment and then as an assistant surgeon and that her services "may be recalled by survivors of the 7th Illinois Cavalry stationed at that time in Cairo, Illinois."[70]

The setting in which Sarah served should not be underestimated, however. "Cairo, Illinois, from which the Union armies were to start down the Mississippi and up the Tennessee, was a veritable hellhole, a muddy, mosquito-infested point between the converging Ohio and Mississippi rivers. Garbage heaps and pools of fluid waste were everywhere . . . Cairo until then a reasonably healthy river town, was now plagued with malaria and typhoid. Children's diseases ran wild through the army of farmer boys, who were utterly ignorant of personal care"[71]

Fragmentary evidence suggests that in addition to working with an Illinois regiment, she served on the hospital transports. After the battle of Shiloh, Belle Reynolds, wife of a lieutenant in the Seventeenth Illinois Regiment, referred to a woman, Mrs. C., who arrived to help. She related that while on board the steamer *Emerald*, which was headed to Cairo, "we were rejoiced to find that Mrs. C., one of our nurses, had arrived from Illinois, with quite a large supply of hospital stores. . . Soon the wounded came pouring in upon us, and for thirty-six hours we found no rest. At night we had three hundred and fifty wounded on board our boat."[72] It seems likely that Mrs. C. was really Sarah Chadwick since most of the women physicians performed the work of nurses, and they were frequently not referred to by their proper titles.

At the time of her resignation in August of 1862, Sarah had served ten month of rigorous medical duty, having spent most of her time in the regimental hospitals in Cairo, where casualties poured in continuously from some of the bloodiest confrontations of the war. "Unheralded, unrecognized, Dr. Sarah Ann Chadwick returned to Lee County, Illinois . . . her only verifiable medical practice having been in the most brutal and demanding settings."[73]

Sarah's pension application contains affidavits that confirm that she was formerly married to James Milligan on March 8, 1847, and divorced October 5, 1855 (the same year in which she graduated from medical school). Following her return home after the war, she married Henry Clapp, a former private in the Seventh Illinois Cavalry (recently widowed with four children) on October 11, 1866. After her marriage, Sarah does not appear to have practiced medicine. She led a quiet life until Henry Clapp died in 1887. Then the need for money seemed more urgent, and Sarah decided to document her service as a surgeon so she could apply for some financial relief. Fortunately, a private bill was introduced in the U.S. Congress on January 6, 1890, which substantiated her service record both on a volunteer and for hire basis.[74] Part of this bill read:

> This bill is of the payment of Sarah A. Clapp, nee Chadwick, for services as surgeon of the Seventh Illinois Cavalry. . . The documents accompanying the bill . . . show conclusively that Sarah A. Clapp (nee Sarah A. Chadwick) served successfully in the capacity indicated, as surgeon of the regiment from November 15 to December 27, 1861, and as assistant surgeon from December 27 to the following August; but that, owing to the refusal of the State medical examining board to examine for this service one of her sex, she could not be commissioned or paid. The testimony that the services were faithfully and intelligently rendered under trying circumstances and resulting in the saving of valuable lives is ample and apparent of a thoroughly reliable character.

Although the bill continued to be introduced every year thereafter, no action was taken. In 1905, however, she was finally awarded a small widow's pension of eight dollars a month. Finally, on June 18, 1906, Sarah penned a note on the bottom of a letter sent to her by Representative R. R. Hitt, and forwarded it on to President Theodore Roosevelt. In her note, she begged for relief, pointing out that her bill had been in Congress for a long time, and at eighty-two years of age, she was suffering for the common necessities of life. Her strategy worked, and on February 7, 1907, a bill for her relief was finally approved, and she received a lump sum payment of $850 for her medical services rendered forty-five years earlier.

Still in dire circumstances by 1907, Sarah pressed for an increase in her widow's pension. "I write this," she explained, "to ask you to raise my pension to the age of others of my age. I am now eighty-three years old. I was born July 17, 1824." She went on to state that she had only received a pension of eight dollars a month for about a year. "I did not apply for a pension sooner as I was given to understand that I would be pensioned at the time that my bill passed Congress for services rendered as Surgeon in Hospital. I received my pay from the Treasury at Washington the 12th day of last March as Surgeon and Assistant Surgeon, $850 being the amount."[75]

Other than this short letter in the pension file, Sarah did not record much about her services as a physician. When the Bureau of Pension replied to her request, it indicated that she was eligible for a pension based on her own individual service or "present pension as a dependent widow, the law prohibiting the payment of more than one pension to a person for the same period." Under her own service record, she could only apply "for pension as an army nurse" as there was no provision for women doctors. The Committee, however, decided to grant the increase and her widow's pension was raised to $12 a month.

Dr. Sarah Clapp died on December 1, 1908, at the age of eighty-three, just one year after her request for a higher pension. She was buried in the local cemetery at Lee Center, Illinois. An obituary printed in the local paper contained the following information:

> Mrs. Ann Clapp of Lee Center, widow of the late Henry Clapp, died Tuesday at her home. She was a daughter of Lot Chadwick, one of the early settlers of Inlet grove, and a man of prominence in public affairs and highly respected throughout this section during his lifetime, and postmaster during Lincoln's administration. The funeral will be from the home of her sister, Mrs. A. L. Haskell of Lee Center Thursday Afternoon at 12 o'clock.[76]

No acknowledgment of her Civil War service as an assistant surgeon was made. Her biographer observed that "her survivors were convinced that Dr. Sarah Ann Chadwick would be remembered neither as a woman with a life and a name unto herself nor as one of the pioneer woman regular physicians."[77] Her grave is marked with a plain stone that reads: Sarah Ann Chadwick, July 17, 1824, December 1, 1908.[78]

Mary Edwards Walker

The last of the seven women physicians to be discussed is Mary Edwards Walker, well known for being the only woman to have been awarded the Medal of Honor. She also garnered quite a reputation for appearing in trousers on the battlefield with a green surgeon's sash tied around her waist so there could be no doubt as to her profession. Born November 26, 1832, in Oswego, New York, she was one year older than Esther Hill Hawks but not yet thirty when war erupted. With the support of parents who valued health, religion, and education, she graduated from Syracuse Medical College in 1855. She married a classmate, Arthur Miller, but the relationship was unhappy and short-lived, although she did not secure an actual divorce for several years.

An early advocate of dress reform, Walker dressed in her modified bloomer costume with its long tunic and trousers even as she sought an appointment as an army doctor following the first shots at Fort Sumter. When she was unsuccessful, she decided to volunteer her services at the Indiana Hospital housed in the United States Patent Office in DC. In a letter to her brother and sister, she wrote: "I . . . am assistant Physician and Surgeon in this Hospital. We have about 80 patients now. We have 5 very nice lady nurses, and a number of gentlemen nurses."[79] Following this assignment, she made her way to the Army of the Potomac and provided medical aid after the battles of Fredericksburg and Chickamauga. Some of her experiences are described in a short narrative she wrote sometime after the war.[80]

Throughout the conflict, Walker continued her campaign for official recognition, even writing to President Lincoln for help. She pointed out that "she has been denied a commission, solely on the ground of sex, when her services have been tested and appreciated without a commission and without compensation and she fully believes that had a man been as useful to our country as she modesty claims to have been, a star would have been taken from the National Heavens and placed upon his shoulder."[81] Her request was denied based perhaps upon Lincoln's unwillingness to interfere with the Medical Department's hierarchy.

Around the same time that winter of 1864, Walker was authorized to report to the assistant surgeon-general, Chattanooga, Tennessee, for an evaluation of her medical qualifications. On March 8, 1864, she met with the board of medical officers. Dr. Perin, the director, ordered a medical board to examine her qualifications, but the medical staff of the Army of the Cumberland was unwilling to entrust a surgeon's work to an unqualified woman doctor. After meeting with Walker, they found her so inadequate "as to render it doubtful whether she has pursued the study of medicine." The board was "of the further opinion that her practical acquaintance with diseases and the use of remedies is not greater than most housewives possess. The board would except obstetrics, with which she seems to be more familiar. As a nurse, in a general hospital the Board believes her services may be of value and respectfully recommend her for that position."[82]

The fact that her medical degree could only qualify her for nursing duties, according to her learned male colleagues, made Walker furious. Much later, in a letter to Andrew Johnson, she voiced her sentiments in no uncertain terms. "I felt that the examination was intended to be a farce, and more than half the time was consumed in questions regarding subjects that were exclusively feminine and had no sort of relation to the diseases and wounds of soldiers."[83] As in the case of Sarah Chadwick Clapp, her sex was used against her.

Walker finally received a contract as an assistant surgeon in the winter of 1864, although she had already been sent by Major General George H. Tho-

Mary Walker wearing an Assistant Surgeon pin and Medal of Honor.

mas, who was overseeing her appointment himself, to Gordon's Mills, Tennessee.[84] Here she treated civilians in the countryside. On one occasion she treated a teenage boy with typhoid fever. "He resided several miles outside of the lines. . . I carried medicine with me and gave as prescription sufficient to last some little time, perhaps until his recovery. It was dangerous going out there. . . I had two revolvers in my saddle as well." Despite the danger that was involved, Walker explained: "The people expressed so much gratitude that I lost all fear of anything being done to myself."[85] On one of her trips, however, she was captured as a spy by the Confederates and confined for four months to Castle Thunder, Richmond, Virginia.

Despite the harsh conditions within the prison and the privations and suffering she endured, Walker offered to care for the wounded there, but her offer was refused because "the authorities would not trust her.[86] There is no doubt that her experiences as a POW, however, extracted their toll on her. When she applied for a pension, she cited the conditions at Castle Thunder as the source of the many health problems she experienced following her release.

> The effect of such confinement in prison, and the impossibility of obtaining sufficient food to properly sustain life, so injured my whole system as to make me incapable of practicing my profession to such an extent as to properly support myself. But aside from this general debility, my eyes have been severely injured. At the time of my exchange in the middle of August 1864, I could not read a dozen lines in an ordinary newspaper and ever since that time I have suffered with my eyes when attempting to practice my profession or to do the reading essential to a practitioner of medicine and surgery; rendering it difficult and in many instances impossible for me to attend to my duties.[87]

Although Walker never received the coveted army commission she desired, she was awarded the Medal of Honor on November 11, 1865. When she was questioned years later as to what she had done to merit the award, she responded: "The special valor, was for going into the enemy's grounds, when the inhabitants were suffering for professional service, and sent to our lines to beg assistance, and no man surgeon was willing to respond, for fear of being taken prisoner, and by my doing so the people were won over to the Union. We could not be ordered out of our lines without our consent and the dental, obstetrical, surgical, and medical distresses were such that I consented to respond."[88]

While Walker did not mention her status as a woman army doctor in this explanation, she always maintained that she was a singular exception. Apparently, she did not know of Sarah Chadwick Clapp's service although, in her defense, Walker had made efforts to prove her claim by writing to the Surgeon General. "Please give me," she requested, "a statement that my name is the only woman's name that appears among the A. A. Surgeons." Two weeks later, she received this response:

> In reply to your letter of the 11th, I am instructed by the Surgeon General to inform you that no record can be found at this office of the service of any woman as an Acting Assistant surgeon U. S. Army, other than that of Mary E. Walker.[89]

Fifty-two years after the war in 1917, Walker was among the 911 medal recipients who were disqualified. The Medal of Honor Board stipulated that the citation should go only to a member of the armed services who had distinguished himself in actual combat . . . above and beyond the call of duty. Her efforts to have the medal (and its replacement) restored were useless. She was not going to give up wearing the medal so easily, however, and she wrote a strong letter to that effect.

> I am the only woman who was a surgeon in the Army and was the only one who has received medals of honor from the United States Congress, both of which I have; and notwithstanding such an infamous regulation that I am not to wear it if I am not on the roll, "I shall wear it, and one of them I will wear every day, and the other I will wear on occasions." And for this Government, with the services of such a woman as I am, and have been, to do anything that is deplorable! And I cannot believe that an honorable board of ex-generals will deprive me of what honor there may be in this matter, and of the petty ten dollars a month that goes with it.[90]

And so she continued to wear her Medal of Honor every day until her death at the age of eighty-six on February 21, 1919, in Oswego, New York.

Persistence was a trait, however, that seemed to run in Walker's family. In 1976, Mrs. Helen Hay Wilson proved that she was a descendant of the Walker family—a granddaughter of one of Mary's sisters and, therefore, grandniece to the doctor. She filed papers to that effect and then proceeded to petition that her aunt's Medal of Honor be restored as she proclaimed: "Dr. Mary lost the medal simply because she was a hundred years ahead of her time and no one could stomach it."[91]

At the time of the review, however, the Board maintained that under the law, only Walker's actions while under official contract as an Army surgeon could be considered for award of the Medal of Honor. But they also conceded that the circumstances of the case were very unique.[92]

> ...it took place during a period of our Nation's history when a female was not tendered a commission in the Army; that the Board takes note that the deceased volunteered her services as a doctor during the initial stages of the civil War and feels that, had it not been for her sex, she would in all probability have been tendered a commission in 1861; that particular note is made of the fact that she freely gave her time and services as a doctor, to the benefit of the sick and wounded of the army, both in the field of battle and in hospitals, despite having been denied a commission, and prior to the award of a contract as a surgeon.

The Board admitted that when consideration is given to "her total contribution; her acts of distinguished gallantry, self sacrifice, patriotism, dedication and unflinching loyalty to her country, despite the apparent discrimination because of her sex, the award of the Medal of Honor appears to have been appropriate; that the award was in consonance with the criteria established by the Act of 17 April 1916 and in keeping with the highest traditions of the military service." In view of the foregoing findings and conclusion, the members decided that the action taken in 1917 to remove the deceased's name from the Medal of Honor Roll was unjust. Therefore, The Board recommended:

> That all of the Department of the Army records pertaining to MARY E. WALKER be corrected to show that she was validly awarded the Medal of Honor by President Johnson in 1865; that her name was selected to be entered on the Medal of Honor Roll, in accordance with the Act of 3 June 1916, and that the action taken in 1917 to remove her name from the Medal of Honor Roll is void and of no force, or effect.

On June 10, 1977, the official records regarding Walker's case were corrected. Fifty-eight years after her death, Walker's medal had finally been reinstated.

Looking back, it can be seen that women physicians in the Civil War were an elite band of women who demonstrated their ability to make choices. They confronted the prejudices of their day by electing to study medicine when it was considered a male prerogative. They volunteered their medical services willingly at a time when the government hospital system was in confusion, and some chose to do so as nurses when the barriers erected against them as female doctors made it difficult for them to secure official posts as surgeons. Even though they were not given the same kind of respect that was accorded their male colleagues, they were bent on practicing the art of healing in whatever ways that were open to them.

The stories of these women doctors add a great deal to the body of evidence on the life courses of females in the early years of medicine. Unlike their male colleagues who were in a position to assume leadership roles as military surgeons, they had to set different goals for themselves. Constrained as they were by Victorian attitudes, they had to pursue a "female" agenda that was consistent with the model of service and self-sacrifice accorded to women of that era. This meant that, for some of them, nursing was the means to an end. Their presence during the Civil War in whatever capacity, however, testifies to the fact that trained women physicians were willing to do their share on the battlefield.

In trying to tease out the similarities among these women, it can be seen that at least four of them were in their late twenties when they volunteered their services (Buckel, Hawks, Moon, Walker), and most of them had the encouragement of middle-class families. These women also knew how to use male support when necessary. Buckel and Thomas worked for the governor of Indiana, Walker and Painter relied on army generals to help them in the field, and Hawks and Andrews (as well as Thomas) had physician husbands to stand by their sides. It is a curious fact that six of these seven women (Buckel was the exception) married, since there was a tendency for a greater percentage of women doctors to remain single as more of them studied medicine. The postwar struggles of four of these women (Buckel, Clapp, Painter, and Walker) with the Pension Bureau further demonstrate that pensions were not easily awarded to them because of their past worth or proven potential as physicians or even nurses—although this was to be expected given the rules that governed the system at that time. The women also studied at the same schools or had aligned themselves with Drs. Blackwell, Preston, and Zakrzewska at one time or another. This suggests that there was a growing awareness of the need for professional and emotional support among women physicians.

As the late nineteenth century came to a close, there was a dramatic increase of women doctors in America. From 200 women physicians, their number rose to 2,423 in 1880 and to more than 7,000 by 1900.[93] More important, several Civil War nurses went on to study medicine when the conflict ended. Among these were two women who served in Illinois. Mary Safford (called the "Cairo Angel") graduated in 1869 from the New York Medical College for Women and went abroad for study. For nearly three years she took advance training in surgery, first in the General Hospital of Vienna and then at medical centers in Germany. At the University of Breslau, she was credited with the first ovariotomy performed by a woman. After finishing her studies, the renowned Belle Reynolds, who was awarded the rank of major because of her exploits at the Battle of Shiloh, became the resident physician in the Home for the Friendless in Chicago.[94] Following their service at City Point, Frances M. Nye studied in New York City while Mary Blackmar (who had interrupted her medical studies to serve as a nurse) finally completed her degree at the Philadelphia Medical College for Women in Philadelphia.[95] Vesta Swarts became a physician like her husband, and at the urging of the surgeon in charge at Armory Square Hospital, Nancy M. Hill went on to study under Dr. Zakrzewska before graduating from Michigan University at Ann Arbor in 1874. Last, Harriet Dada graduated from the Women's Medical College in New York in 1868.[96]

While it was probably not the intention of Civil War women physicians to serve as role models to others, they seemed to have achieved that goal in spite of themselves. Clearly they paved the way for medical women in the military although female physicians were not appointed to the Army and Navy Medical Corps until the middle of the Second World War.[97] If it had once been thought that women doctors were freaks of nature with heads "too small for intellect," these early pioneers proved that they were uncommon women instead.

Parts of this work appeared earlier as "Women Physicians in the Civil War," *Prologue*, Vol. 32, No. 2, summer 2000). I would like to thank several people for their help in gathering information for this article: Joanne Grossman and Barbara Williams, Archives and Art Program, MCP Hahnemann University, Philadelphia; Terry Prior, Director, Oswego Historical Society, NY; Terry Keenan, Syracuse University, NY; George Heerman, Illinois State Historical Library; Dennis Harrison, Case Western Reserve University; Linda Lilles and Patricia White, Stanford University Libraries; Margaret M. O'Bryant, Albemarle County Historical Society; and Stephen E. Towne, Indiana State Archives. In addition, I would like to thank DeAnne Blanton and Kristen Wilhelm, NARA. I am also grateful to Mary Ryan, editor, Prologue, College Park, Md., for her comments and editing with the first publication.

Endnotes

1. Regina Markell Morantz-Sanchez, *Sympathy and Science: Women Physicians in American Medicine* (New York, 1985), 63.
2. Mary Roth Walsh, "Doctors Wanted: No Women Need Apply": *Sexual Barriers in the Medical Profession, 1835-1975* (New Haven, 1977), 5.
3. Richard Harrison Shryock, *Medicine in America: Historical Essays* (Baltimore, 1957), 183.
4. *Ibid.*, 184.
5. If one considers that there were approximately 55,055 physicians in the country prior to the Civil War, this means that only 0.5% of them were women. See Virginia Penny, *The Employment of Women: A Cyclopedia of Woman's Work* (Boston, 1863).
6. Joyce Marie Butler Ray, *Women and Men in American Medicine, 1849-925: Autobiographies As Evidence*, (Ph.D. diss., University of Texas at Austin, August, 1992), 23.
7. Walsh points out that while Elizabeth Blackwell is usually credited with being the first woman to have received a medical degree In America, Lydia Folger Fowler was the first to study at a regular medical school, and Harriet K. Hunt was the first woman who completed a medical apprenticeship and practiced medicine successfully in the United States.
8. Massey, *Women in the Civil War*, 1994 (orig. publ. Bonnet Brigades, 1966), 46.
9. Ray, 23.
10. "Eighth Annual Announcement of the Female Medical College of Pennsylvania (now MCP Hahnemann), for the Session of 1857-58," (Philadelphia, 1857), 5.
11. See Shepard's account in Massey, 10; Elizabeth Bass, "Pioneer Women Doctors of the South," *Journal of the American Medical Women's Association*, 1947, 559.
12. Bass discussed the Myers women in "It Runs in the Family: Three Sisters Who Were Physicians," *Journal of the American Medical Women's Association*, 9 (February 1955): 45-47. This article refers to Hannah Myers Longshore and Jane Viola Myers, the half-sisters of Dr. Mary Frame Myers Thomas of Indiana who is discussed later.
13. Quoted in Ruth J. Abrams, ed., *Woman Doctors in America, 1835-1920* (New York, 1985), 57.
14. See De Anne Blanton, "Women Soldiers of the Civil War." Prologue, National Archives and Records Administration (NARA), 1992. She indicated that well over four hundred women from the North were successful in impersonating men. Also see Lauren Cook Burgess, *An Uncommon Soldier: The Civil War Letters of Sarah Rosetta Wakeman, alias Pvt. Lyons Wakeman, 153rd Regiment, New York State Volunteers, 1862-1864* (New York, 1994). This is the only known collection of letters from a disguised woman soldier.
15. Peggy Brase Seigel makes the point that it was difficult to learn information about Indiana Civil War nurses as historians excluded them from published accounts and because few biographical sketches of nurses published after the war include them. See "Indiana Women Nurses in the Civil War," *Indiana Magazine of History*, Vol. LXXXVI, No. 1, March 1990.
16. There is so little information available concerning Civil War physician, Dr. Hettie K. Painter, for example, that in postwar years her granddaughter's husband wrote to the Pension Bureau requesting a birth date noting: "We want the date for a tombstone on her grave. We are not able to get the date from family sources..." See "Letter from John Slaker" dated November 20, 1917, in Painter Pension File, RG 15, Application #663928, Certificate #405628, National Archives, Washington, D.C. NARA.
17. Dr. Sarah A. Chadwick (Clapp), Civil War physician, married Mr. Milligan, but after he left her she entered medical school under her maiden name of Chadwick. She practiced medicine under this name following graduation. After the war she married Mr. Clapp, and her pension records can be found under this name. See Pension File for Sarah A. Clapp, WC601330, RG 15, NARA. Also see Henry Clapp, RG 15, Application #831086, Certificate #601330. In the case of the famous nurse, spy, and scout, Harriet Tubman, her pension records (widow) are located under the name of Davis who was the Civil War veteran she married. See Harriet Tubman Davis: Accompanying Papers (HR55A-D1), 55th Congress, Record Group 233, Records of the House of Representatives, NARA, Washington, D. C.
18. This was the point made by Barbara Miller Solomon in "Historical Determinants in Individual Life Experiences of Successful Professional Women," *Annals of the New York Academy of Sciences*, 208, March 15, 1873, 170-178.
19. While the histories of seven women have been uncovered at this point, admittedly there may be others whose work has not yet come to light.
20. By the time of the Spanish-American War in 1898, a bias against women doctors in the United States Army still existed and the same

pattern was noted. Thus, several women listed themselves as graduates of medical schools rather than nursing schools, and women physicians who entered the war effort had to volunteer as nurses. Records of these women physicians (in six boxes) are documented on the "Personal Data Cards of Spanish-American War Contract Nurses, 1898-1939," RG #112, E149, NARA.

21. It was commonly held that the qualities of true womanhood by which a woman were judged were the four cardinal virtues: piety, purity, submissiveness, and domesticity. Another author concluded that submission consisted of behavior which was "timid, doubtful, and clingingly dependent; a perpetual childhood." Barbara Welter, "The Cult of True Womanhood: 1820-1860," in Jane Friedman and William G. Shade (eds.), *Our American Sisters* (Boston, 1973), 104.

22. Massey, 62.

23. File Regarding Orianna Russell Moon Andrews, Albemarle County Historical Society, Charlottesville, VA. Rebecca D. Larson pointed out that another women, Ella Cooper, finished her course of medical studies at the Medical College of Cincinnati but was not allowed to graduate. She then moved south to serve the Confederacy. "She nursed the wounded and dying, and cooked and cleaned for the military hospitals." In *White Roses: Stories of Civil War Nurses* (1997), p. 22.

24. Orianna is listed as a graduate in the "Eighth Annual Announcement of the Female Medical College of Pennsylvania, for the Session of 1857–58," Archives and Special Collections, MCP Hahnemann University, Philadelphia, PA (formerly the Female Medical College of Pennsylvania), hereinafter referred to as MCP Hahnemann. The title of her thesis is also listed in the same announcement, p. 15.

25. Una Roberts Lawrence, *Lottie Moon* (1927), pp. 31–32. Lottie was Orie's younger sister and a renowned Baptist missionary who served in China. See also Catherine B. Allen, *The New Lottie Moon Story*, 2nd ed. (1980).

26. "These Were the First," *Journal of the American Medical Women's Association* (March 1959), 248.

27. See Kay Collins Chretien: "Scottsville Doctor Pioneers New Role for Women," *The Observer*, July 15–21, 1998. She maintained that Orie presented herself to the authorities to enlist as a military doctor and that the enlisting officer was so surprised that he told her to go home and wait for further notice. Not long after, she received a message from Gen. J. H. Cocke asking for her services. "She replied in the affir-

mative, asking for an appointment in a field surgical hospital." But before this plan could go further, she had already volunteered her services. Also see Chretien's "Scottsville Produces First Southern Female Doctor," *The Observer*, July 1–7, 1998. Another view is provided in "Gutsy Ladies, Courageous Women People Albemarle's History," *The Observer*, Aug. 30-Sept. 5, 1984.

28. Shields Johnson, "Mother of Late W. L. Andrews was Surgeon of Confederacy," *Roanoke World News*, July 12, 1940. Up to this time, there has been no hard evidence to support the claim of a commission.

29. Lawrence, *Lottie Moon*, pp. 14–31. The family history as well as Orie's meeting with John Andrews is recounted in the first chapter.

30. Edward Warren, *An Epitome of Practical Surgery, for Field and Hospital* (1863), pp. 279–280. He was of the firm opinion that women should never become doctors.

31. Ervin L. Jordan, Jr., *Charlottesville and the University of Virginia in the Civil War* (1988), p. 60.

32. As noted above, two of Mary's half-sisters later became well-known physicians. Hannah Myers (Longshore) graduated from the Female Medical College of Pennsylvania in 1851. She became demonstrator of anatomy in this school of male instructors, and she was the first "female doctor" in Philadelphia. Jane Viola Myers never married. She graduated in 1853 from the Penn Medical College and opened her office next door to Hannah.

33. Florence M. Adkinson, "The 'Mother of Women,'" *Woman's Journal*, Sept. 29, 1888 (pages unnumbered). For a brief biography, see Clifton J. Phillips, "Mary Frame Myers Thomas," in *Notable American Women 1607-1950*, vol. 3 (1971), pp. 450–451.

34. Harold J. Abrahams, *Extinct Medical Schools of 19th Century Philadelphia* (1966), p. 230. The name of her medical school and the title of her thesis are listed here.

35. Frederick C. Waite, "The Three Myers Sisters—Pioneer Women Physicians," *Medical Review of Reviews 39* (March 1933): 119. See her daughter's account: Pauline T. Heald, "Mary F. Thomas, M. D., Richmond, Indiana," *Michigan History Magazine*, 6 (1922): 369–373.

36. Peggy Brase Seigel, "She Went to War: Indiana Women Nurses in the Civil War," *Indiana Magazine of History* (March 1990): 24.

37. Adkinson, "The 'Mother of Women.'"

38. *Ibid.*

39. In her later years, Dr. Buckel was deeply concerned about the welfare of children. She es-

tablished a group of cottage homes for orphan girls in Oakland, CA, and advocated for the establishment of separate departments for defective children in schools. See Joan M. Jensen, "Chloe Annette Buckel," *Notable American Women, 1607-1950*, vol. 1 (1971), pp. 265–267. Also see Elizabeth Mason-Hohl, M.D., "Early California and Its Medical Women," *Women in Medicine* (October 1942): 14–16.

40. "Chloe Annette Buckel," *The Medical Woman's Journal*, January 1924, p. 15.

41. "Committee on Pensions," 58th Congress 2d Session, S. Rept. No. 2325 (To accompany H.R. 8790) for the relief of C. Annette Buckel.

42. Copy of "Letter of O. P. Morton, Governor of Indiana to General U.S. Grant Notifying Him of the Appointment of C. Annette Buckel to Look after Conditions and Wants of Indiana's Sick," Aug. 4, 1863. Records from the U.S. House of Representatives, 58th Cong., Committee on Invalid Pensions, RG 233, NARA; hereinafter referred to as Buckel's Committee Papers.

43. Copy of "Appointment from D. L. Dix, Superintendent of Women Nurses," Dec. 22, 1863, Buckel's Committee Papers, RG 233, NARA.

44. Margaret Elizabeth Martin, "Dr. C. Annette Buckel, the 'Little Major,'" *California Historical Society Quarterly* (1940): 75. Elvira J. Powers, *Hospital Pencillings; Being a Diary While in Jefferson General Hospital, Jeffersonville, Ind., and Others at Nashville, Tennessee as Matron and Visitor* (1866), p. 95.

45. Mary Bennett Ritter, M.D., *More than Gold in California: 1849–1933* (1933), p. 171.

46. Brief Statement of Services of Miss C. Annette Buckel during the Civil War," notarized Dec. 7, 1889, Buckel's Committee Papers, RG 233, NARA.

47. "The Committee on Pensions," S. Rept. No. 2325, 58th Cong., 2d sess., Apr. 18, 1904, to accompany H.R. 8790. The original pension request for $24 had been turned down as the committee felt "there appears to be no reason why an exception should be made in this case and greater original relief granted than in former cases." Such an amount was that generally awarded soldiers.

48. Joan M. Jensen's account in *Notable American Women*, p. 266. While attention has been given to the fact that nurses had problems relative to gender stereotyping, it is quite clear from Buckel's experiences that women physicians encountered similar difficulties in government service. For more on nurses and similar issues, see Jane E. Schultz, "The Inhospitable Hospital Gender and Professionalism in Civil War Medicine," *Signs* 17 (1991): 363–392.

Morantz-Sanchez makes the point that although women doctors remained a small minority, "they were conspicuous because they violated nineteenth-century norms for female behavior" (p. 50). Hence, the title "doctor" would not be easily bestowed on them, and such recognition was not accorded to Buckel for her services.

49. See note #16 above regarding date for her head stone. Her first name is spelled two ways in early narratives.

50. "Dr. Hetty K. Painter, Niece of John Brown," *Nebraska History Magazine*, 23:1, January, 1942, 72-73.

51. *Ibid.* No documentation is offered regarding her spying activities.

52. *Ibid.*

53. Abrahams, 226. The name of her medical school and the title of her thesis are listed here.

54. Frank Moore, *Women of the War: Their Heroism and Self-Sacrifice* (1866), p. 585. He noted that she had a teenage son who worked as a telegraph operator during the war.

55. Adelaide W. Smith, *Reminiscences of an Army Nurse during the Civil War* (1911), pp. 116–117.

56. For a charming account of Painter's help at the makeshift wedding of one of the City Point nurses, see Jeanne Marie Christie, "'Performing My Pain Duty': Women of the North at City Point, 1865–65," *Virginia Cavalcade*, 46 (Summer 1996). A fuller account is provided in Smith's Reminiscences, 167–184.

57. John Young Foster, *New Jersey and the Rebellion: A History of the Services of the Troops and People of New Jersey in Aid of the Union Cause* (1868), p. 29.

58. Quoted in "The Committee on Pensions," 49th Cong., 2nd sess., S. Rept. 1716 (to accompany bill S. 2834), Jan. 25, 1887, for the pension relief of Hettie K. Painter.

59. There is also a copy of the original House Bill, which is not numbered but dated July 12, 1886, in Original House Bills, Nos. 9748-10017 49th Congress, 1st Session, bound volume, NARA.

60. See Gerald Schwartz, *A Woman Doctor's Civil War: Esther Hill Hawks' Diary* (1984), pp. 3-26. Also see the *Milton and Esther Hawks Papers*, Library of Congress, Washington, DC, and the Compiled Military Service Record of John M. Hawks, RG 94, NARA.

61. Eighth Annual Report of the New England Female Medical College (1856, 1857).

62. Schwartz, pp. 48-49, 51.

63. *Ibid*, p. 96.

64. See also Susie King Taylor, *Reminiscences of My Life in Camp* (1902, reprint 1968). Her account, which fills a void in the narratives of

black women in Civil War literature, is significant as it is one of the few existing first-person records written by a former female slave; and actual military life (served with the Thirty-third U.S. Colored Infantry) is rarely described from a woman's point of view while working side by side with men in the field. She was later found ineligible for a pension as an army nurse. See letter from Col. C. T. Trowbridge, Apr. 7, 1902, in preface to *Reminiscences*.

65. Schwartz, 20.

66. *Ibid*, 26.

67. *Ibid*, 1.

68. She is listed as S. F. Chadwick in "Catalogue of the Officers and Students in the Medical Department of the Western Reserve College, Session 1854–55, Cleveland 1855" and in the "Catalogue of the Officers and Students in the Medical Department of the Western Reserve College, Session 1856-57, Cleveland 1855." The authorization for her graduation appears in "The Minutes of the Medical Department of Western Reserve College at a Meeting in Cleveland on February 29th 1856," p. 290. She is later frequently referred to as Sarah Ann.

69. A copy of her thesis resides in the Archives, Howard Dittrick Museum of the History of Medicine, Allen Memorial Library, Case Western Reserve University, Cleveland, Ohio.

70. See Bell Irvin Wiley, *The Life of Billy Yank* (1952), p. 337; Richard Hall, *Patriots in Disguise* (1993), p. 200; and *Medical Woman's Journal*, March 1895. Also see brief sketch in *Pan American Medical Woman's Journal*, March 1952, pp. 34–35. Lee Middleton erroneously stated that Clapp served in the Seventeenth Illinois Cavalry in *Hearts of Fire: Soldier Women of the Civil War* (1993), p. 33.

71. George Worthington Adams, *Doctors in Blue, The Medical History of the Union Army in the Civil War* (1952), pp. 20–21.

72. Belle Reynolds's account in Moore, *Women of the War*, p. 262.

73. Linda Lehmann Goldstein, *Roses Bloomed in Winter: Women Medical Graduates of Western Reserve College, 1852-1856* (Ph.D. diss., Case Western Reserve University, May 14, 1989), pp. 224-225. Goldstein also details the early family history of Chadwick.

74. U.S. Congress, House, Private Bills, H.R. 10801, 51st Cong., 1st sess., 1890, p. 5760, and H. Rept. No. 2933.

75. Clapp's "Handwritten letter," Sept. 9, 1907 in pension record for Sarah A. Clapp, Certificate #601330, RG 15, NARA.

76. Quoted in Goldstein, *Roses Bloomed in Winter*, pp. 402–403.

77. *Ibid*, p. 402. Goldstein also theorizes that the

family" and the village" did not recognize Sarah's achievements because they may have felt embarrassment and shame over her divorce from Milligan years earlier.

78. *Ibid*.

79. "Letter to Brother and Sister," Nov. 13, 1861, Walker Papers, Oswego County Historical Society, Oswego, NY. For her military record, see Mary E. Walker Papers, Records of the War Department, RG 94, NARA.

80. There is a collection of her papers housed at Syracuse University, Department of Special Collections, Syracuse, NY, hereinafter referred to as Syracuse Papers. Among these papers are thirty-eight pages of notes typed by Mary E. Walker on legal-size paper and entitled "Incidents Connected with the Army." The pages are not arranged in any particular order, and they are unnumbered. Included with these papers is an untitled two-page section that may have been part of an introduction to a planned history of her life.

81. "Walker to Abraham Lincoln", Jan. 16, 1864, War Department Records, RG 94, NARA. A copy is also in the Syracuse Papers.

82. "Handwritten letter of F. H. Gross, Surgeon," Mar. 8, 1864, War Department Records, RG 94, NARA.

83. "Walker to Andrew Johnson", Sept. 30, 1865, War Department Records, RG 94, NARA.

84. She received an official contract on October 5, 1864, although she had been acting unofficially as a result of an arrangement between her and General Thomas since February of that year. See copy of "Walker's Acting Assistant Surgeon Contract" in War Department Records, RG 94, NARA. The first entry shows that she was to have been paid starting March 11, 1864.

85. "Incidents Connected with the Army," Syracuse Papers.

86. Lida Poynter, *Dr. Mary Walker, The Forgotten Woman*, unpubl. typescript, pp. 89–90, Archives and Special Collections on Women in Medicine, MCP Hahnemann University, Philadelphia, PA.

87. Walker's "Letter to the Committee of Pensions," July 14, 1876, in Walker's pension file, RG 15, NARA. She had also been exchanged for a Confederate officer, something she could never forget or allow others to forget.

88. Italics mine. Walker's "Letter to the Honorable Adjutant General," Apr. 22, 1916, War Department Records, RG 94, NARA.

89. Walker's "Letter to the Surgeon General," Feb. 11, 1888, and "Letter to Mary Walker," from the Surgeon General's Office dated Mar. 1, 1888. Both in Walker's pension file, RG 15, NARA.

90. Walker's "Response to Having the Medal of Honor Rescinded," May 24, 1916, War Department Records, RG 94, NARA.

91. "The Case of Dr. Walker, Only Women to Win [and Lose] the Medal of Honor," *New York Times*, June 4, 1977, 20.

92. Copy of the "Transcript of Hearing Case of: Mary Edwards Walker" 4 May 1977, Army Board for Correction of Military Records (ABCMR), The Pentagon, Washington, D. C. Complete transcript is 34 pages in length. Also see "Proceedings in the Case of Mary E. Walker (Deceased)" ABCMR, Docket Number: AC-76-07656.

93. Abrams, "Send Us a Lady Physician," p. 108.

94. Le Roy H. Fischer, "Mary Jane Safford," *Notable American Women*, Vol. 3, 220–222. Also see Fisher's "Cairo's Civil War Angel, Mary Jane Safford," *Illinois State Historical Society Journal*, 54 (Autumn 1961). "Miss Mary J. Safford," in L. P. Brockett, M.D., and Mary C. Vaughan, *Womans' Work in the Civil War: A Record of Heroism, Patriotism and Patience* (1867), pp. 357–361. Belle Reynolds: See Massey, p. 353; Moore, *Women of the War*, pp. 254–277. For a recent account, see Elizabeth D. Leonard's *All the Daring of the Soldier, Women of the Civil War Armies* (1999), pp. 125–131.

95. Adelaide W. Smith reported that some years after the war she spoke with Dr. Frances Nye, who had married a Confederate soldier she met in medical school. Oddly enough, he bore the same name, Francis M. Nye. "The identity of names, perhaps, induced a lasting friendship, and when they married Miss Nye changed only one letter in her name." See Smith's *Reminiscences*, p. 95. Smith also kept up a correspondence with Mary Blackmar, who had returned to her former medical school and then married Mr. Bruson. In a letter she wrote to Smith dated April 1910, Mary noted that after graduation she "led a strenuous life as a practicing physician in Florida." *Ibid*, pp. 232–233. A brief biography of Bruson's life is summarized in *The Woman's Medical Journal*, 26 (April 1916).

96. See pension record of Dr. Vesta M. Swarts, #1006l53, RG 15, NARA. For more on Vesta's army service, see Mary Gardner Holland, *Our Army Nurses* (reprint 1998), pp. 264–265; Mary Logan, *Reminiscences of the Civil War and Reconstruction* (1970), p. 373. Nancy Hill is noted in Holland, p. 139. For information on Dada, see Brockett & Vaughan, pp. 431–434; for a recent account, see Eileen F. Conklin, *Women at Gettysburg-1863* (1991), pp. 272–274.

97. This occurred on April 16, 1943, when President Roosevelt signed into law the Sparkman-Johnson Bill.

About the Author

Mercedes Graf is a professor of psychology at Governors State University (which is thirty miles south of Chicago, Illinois) where her favorite course is the psychology of women. In the last few years, she has shifted her interest from conventional themes in psychology testing to looking at women's issues from an historical perspective. Her article on women POWS in the Civil War led her to write about female physicians in that conflict after she learned that Dr. Mary E. Walker had been confined to Castle Thunder during the war. It seemed natural that a book, *A Woman of Honor: The Civil War Experiences of Dr. Mary E. Walker*, would soon follow. Currently she is studying the role of women physicians in other wars, but her interest in Civil War women is her primary interest.

"Into the keeping of a trustworthy woman"[1]

THE PRIVATE ARMY OF ELLA LOUISE WOLCOTT

By Meg Galantes-DeAngelis

When she arrived at the Hammond General Hospital at Point Lookout in late October of 1862, Ella Wolcott was not sure she had made the right decision. The hospital was new and there were only a few convalescent patients, most of whom were quite self-sufficient. Ella had been sent by Dorothea Dix to nurse; she was not comfortable doing little more than keeping the men company.[2] Discouraged, she wrote to her dear friend Julia Beecher[3] back home in Elmira, New York:

> But I can't tell you what an arrant humbug I feel myself to be! With all my glowing patriotism, self denying devotion, heroic choosing of the most difficult place, here I am with almost nothing to do. My ward was given to me this morning — I have given one man a flannel wrapper, another a handkerchief & dressing[4] one blister![5]

While waiting for the real work to begin, Ella began to take note of what might be needed in the future, when the cold weather set in and when the patients were wounded and ill rather than convalescent. From this point on, in every letter she wrote, whether to family or friends, Ella asked for supplies for the soldiers. And one letter at a time, Ella Louise Wolcott began to recruit her own private army, an army that would support her though three years of hospital work.

Ella Louise Wolcott was a prolific correspondent[6] and to our great fortune an archivist of much of that correspondence. A descendent of the illustrious Wolcott family of New England, Ella was born in Connecticut in 1828. Her parents, Elihu and his second wife Julia, were cousins. Both were great-grand-children of Roger Wolcott, Governor of the Colony of Connecticut (1750 – 1754.) Their shared grandfather, Erastus Wolcott, was a Brigadier General of Connecticut troops in the Revolutionary War and the brother of Oliver Wolcott, signer of the Declaration of Independence, Revolutionary War Brigadier General, Lieutenant Governor of the State of Connecticut (1786 – 1796) and Governor of Connecticut (1796 until his death in 1797).[7] Ella's father, Elihu, was a graduate of Yale University, a successful merchant, a well-respected churchman and an ardent abolitionist who ran as the Free Soil Candidate against Abraham Lincoln in the congressional election of 1846.[8]

In 1830 Elihu, Julia, and eight of their nine children left Connecticut where generations of the Wolcott family had lived since the arrival of Henry and Elizabeth Saunders Wolcott in 1635.[9] Their move to Illinois was precipitated by Julia's declining health. It was hoped that the move to the prairie would rejuvenate Julia and cure her of consumption. Julia rode to her new home in a wagon specially equipped with a full bed for her comfort.[10] Their long journey took them to Jacksonville, Illinois, then a small town of nearly 450 people.[11]

Over the next several years, Jacksonville grew exponentially and would probably have become the capital of Illinois had it not suffered a cholera epidemic in 1833.[12] Although the Wolcott family prospered financially and politically, young Ella suffered many emotional losses. In 1831, three-year old Ella's seven-year old sister, Helen, died after a bout with scarlet fever. The Illinois weather did not revivify Julia Wolcott's health and she began to decline rapidly. It was her sincere wish to see her two oldest stepdaughters married before she passed. So on November 28, 1832, Ella's two oldest sisters were married in a double wedding ceremony. Elizabeth, age 25, married Carlton H. Perry of Keokuk, Iowa. Hannah, age 21, married the Reverend William Kirby of Jacksonville. Two days later, on November 30, 1832, Julia Wolcott succumbed to her long battled consumption.[13] In that period of three days of joy and sorrow, the three most important women in the life of four year old Ella were gone from her home.

Luckily, sister Hannah stayed in Jacksonville. Her new husband, the Reverend William Kirby, was a member of the "Yale Band," a group of seven young graduates of the Theological Department of Yale College, who took as their mission the founding of a Presbyterian college. On Monday, January 4, 1830, instruction at Illinois College began. At the time of his marriage to Hannah, Reverend Kirby was an instructor at the college.[14] The Reverend Edward Beecher, second son of the legendary Beecher family, left his position as the Pastor of the prestigious Park Street Church in Boston, Massachusetts to become the College's first president.[15] Illinois College provided its students, instructors, the "Yale Band" and citizens of Jacksonville with the opportunity for a close intellectual community. With her mother gone, Ella spent a great deal of her time in the company of her sister Hannah within this intellectual community. Her intellectual curiosity was nurtured here. It is in this community she probably met a young man who would play an important part in her later life as her minister and friend, Edward Beecher's younger brother, Thomas Kinnicut Beecher.

By her sister Julia's account, Ella and Julia began their education early. Julia remembered her mother, who died when Julia was six, intervening with an especially strict teacher.[16] Ella called her education "irregular." From age four to seventeen, Ella sometimes attended Miss Spencer's School and was sometimes schooled at home. Later, as a student at the Jacksonville Female Seminary, she preferred the study of Geometry, Natural Philosophy[17] and Natural History. Ella loved to read — everything from poetry to politics. She was an accomplished musician and "love[d] Music best of any ëoccupation, play or pleasure."[18]

Ella's father married for a third and final time, to Sarah C. Crocker on September 17, 1835. Sarah became stepmother to the five children still living in Elihu's care: Arthur — age 20, Elizur — age 18, Frances Jane — age 16, Julia

Ann — age 9 and Ella — age 7. Soon, there were two new siblings, Sarah Elizabeth, who lived only eighteen months and Richmond, twelve years Ella's junior. Ella's sister, Julia, remembers life with their stepmother with regret: "In the fall after I was nine years old, my stepmother came into the home bringing many changes, and over this period I drop a mantle of silence. She was a thoroughly conscientious woman, unfaltering in her ideas of duty; and in her management of us I am sure she did the very best she could according to the light she had. As I look back now over the long years I believe that I remember this time without bitterness, but it is also without love."[19]

If these years were without conventional maternal love, Ella's relationship with her older sister Hannah was intimate and strong. Her relationship with her father was warm and solicitous. Julia's letters from the Monticello Female Seminary and her memoir are full of warm references to their father and their new baby brother, Richmond. Elihu's letters to Ella show us a doting father, full of concern and counsel. Elihu was loved by his family and was held in high regard in the community, in their church and in the abolitionist movement. When their Presbyterian church was rent over the issue of slavery, the Wolcott's were among the Free Soilers and abolitionists who founded a Congregationalist Church. Ella remembers the new congregation meeting in her family kitchen, using heavy planks on kitchen chairs to make pews for the congregants.[20] These connections to family, community and faith would help sustain Ella through her search for health in her more than ten year battle with scrofula.[21]

Ella speaks only once about her illness. In a 1858 letter written to the Reverend Thomas K. Beecher as a formal introduction to the congregation of The Park Church, Ella wrote: "I have for many years suffered from scrofula caused or developed by taking mercury. Two years ago I was very near dying — since then have in some respects improved much but have not firm health — a recent experiment of one weeks steady household labor has caused me bitter tears as I find how worthless I am — I am generally regular in eating and sleeping."[22]

It is not clear when Ella first began suffering from scrofula, but in 1848 Ella's family began to look for alternatives to allopathic[23] medicine. Her father journeyed with her to Brattleboro, Vermont to admit her as a patient at Dr. Robert Wesselhoeft's Water Cure Establishment.[24] The water cure, or hydropathy, was considered by some a viable alternative to allopathic or homeopathic[25] medicine, but by others, quackery. Using a variety of baths and water treatments, fresh air, exercise, comfortable loose-fitting clothes,[26] vegetarian diet and rest, the hydropathic physician treated the whole patient — mind and body. Ella spent much of the next ten years as a resident of various water cure establishments in several states. In this environment, Ella's interest in natural philosophy was nourished.

Life in the water cure establishments allowed Ella entrance into a society populated by interesting people from all over the country. Although her health was uncertain and she often felt lonely for her family or despairing when she relapsed, Ella also enjoyed this intellectually stimulating environment. Here,

Ella Wolcott.

as in her father's home, she was able to discuss politics, world affairs and engage in intellectual debates. Part of the philosophy of the water cure movement included providing patients and residents with an atmosphere where music and horticulture and living simply allowed them to relax and heal. It is not clear when Ella transitioned from a patient to a practitioner, but as early as 1854 Ella moved from Wesselhoeft's Water Cure to the Brownsville Water Cure[27] in Pennsylvania run by Doctor Clemens Baelz.[28] Letters from sister Julia and her husband, William "Chauncey," Carter recount their pride in Ella's knowledge and practice of medicine. Ella's sisters and friends took Ella's medical advice and used the medical practices and manuals that she suggested.

In 1856, Ella moved to the Elmira Water Cure in Elmira, New York, run by Silas and Rachel Gleason, both physicians. Ella's residence there was alternately as a patient and a practitioner. Here Ella was cared for by women who were physicians.[29] Her health continued to trouble her and her family circumstances soon changed. Ella's father passed away in December of 1858. Now, if she returned to Jacksonville she would return not to the home that she had shared with her father but to the home of one of her siblings. As an unmarried woman in her thirties, she had relied upon her father for a portion of her financial support. Now, she had to depend in part on her small inheritance from her father's estate to survive. This inheritance was, initially, advanced to her in the form of an allowance administered by one of her older brothers, Elizur. Ella had lived independent of the control of others for more than ten years. Ella decided, after consultation with her family, to make her home in Elmira.

Although this decision kept her far from her family, Ella had begun a life for herself in Elmira. In her stays at the Water Cure, she had become acquainted with many people and had begun to think of Elmira as her home. She became an active member of The Park Church and a close family friend of the pastor, the Reverend Thomas Kinnicut Beecher, and his second wife, Julia Jones Beecher. Her mother's sister, Helen Wolcott Hooker, and her family lived in Rochester, New York and their home had become a home away from home for Ella when she was well enough to leave the various water cures. Probably most importantly, Ella's family supported her settling in Elmira, a city where she could live economically, happily, and within a wide circle of friends.

But many things conspired against Ella's peaceful existence in her new found home. The Wolcotts were a family with a rich history of putting the service of country and to others above oneself. Ella doubted herself in this aspect. Although she gave of herself in her work at the Water Cure, in her church and in her family, Ella felt that she was not talented. In 1848, she spent some time at the "Cure" writing poetry but felt it was not worthwhile. In an almost prophetic letter, Ella's father wrote to the then dangerously ill Ella about her connection to the family's tradition of service and their propensity to be late bloomers: "It is an old remark — as old perhaps as our family — that the Wolcotts do not become 'of age' until they are forty, and as you are a 'full-blooded' Wolcott, you have yet, if you live, a long time in which to improve yourself."[30]

Ella's membership in The Park Church, which was founded in 1846 by congregants who had left the First Presbyterian Church over the issue of slavery and who were strongly supportive of the Union cause, echoed her familial experience with their own church schism and abolitionist beliefs back in Illinois. Ella's life in and out of Water Cure establishments had left her with a strong interest in natural philosophy and knowledge of medical care. Ella's age and marital status gave her an unusual mobility enhanced by her family's influential social and political connections. She was committed to doing her part as a Christian and an American. The confluence of these factors and the onset of the Civil War combined to propel Ella into the work that would become her life for three years. And somehow in her coming "of age," Ella overcame her physical difficulties and her self-doubt and plunged into a situation that she had unknowingly been preparing for her entire life.

At the outset of the war, Ella was living in Elmira and attempting to contribute to her own upkeep. Her inheritance had become less and less certain as her brother Elizur, executor of their father's will, refused to sell the property to be distributed because of the depression in real estate prices that were concomitant with the Civil War.[31] The war had brought Elmira unprecedented growth, its position at the crossroads of the major railroad lines and its location on the Chemung River had made it a hub of wartime activity. In fact, Elmira, Albany and New York City became the three major military depots in New York State. The Water Cure had many residents and there was much to do. Ella was, by this time, renting a small cottage on the grounds of the "Cure"[32] and was earning extra money selling items that she had knitted. Still, her inheritance was her chief support and as the possibility of it sustaining her much longer diminished, Ella was urged by her siblings to live as frugally and cautiously as possible.

It was, then, without their counsel that Ella made the decision that would change her life. She wrote from Washington, D.C. with evident delight and trepidation of her surprising news to her sister Julia Carter:

> If you have not looked at the Post mark you will not guess where this letter is written — I said I would not let anybody know until I had proved myself in my new situation but a few hours of leisure — (the first I have known for years,) tempt me to betray my secret — I am in Washington, at the house of Mrs. M. L. Bailey — formerly of the National Era[33] — I became acquainted with her this summer at the Water Cure. Miss Dix authorized her to send for me to work in the Hospitals[34] — I dare not refuse to trust those who have trusted me — and so will do the best I can — but do not be surprised if I make an ignominious failure — I arrived her yesterday — but cannot see Miss Dix Until tomorrow.[35]

Her brother, Elizur, finds out in mid-letter. His astonishment is evident but he pledges his continued support: "Nov. 5th — When I had written the above, Mr. King happened to call & said you were gone to Point Lookout Hospital... Let us hear from you & how you are satisfied with your employment, which must be tedious and disagreeable and let me know your necessities & if possible I will meet them or at least endeavor to do so."[36]

Ella was not immediately sent to her assignment at Hammond Hospital, Point Lookout, Maryland. While she waited in Washington to be transported to Maryland, Ella had the opportunity to see the city, visit with family and friends, and inquire after family members in the Army who were stationed elsewhere. The 141st New York[37] was encamped in Washington and Ella visited with them and helped distribute their mail. It is likely that Ella knew some of these men, the 141st New York had recruited two full companies in Elmira and two other companies also had Elmira men among their recruits. It is certain from her letters that Ella visited the Reverend Thomas K. Beecher, her longtime friend and minister, who was there with the 141st as their Chaplain.

Miss Dix gave Ella a letter of introduction so that she could visit the Columbia College Hospital and acquaint herself with the duties that would face her in her work as a nurse. Visiting other hospitals with her cousin, Alice Ellsworth Hall,[38] gave Ella a chance to see that there was more to hospital work than medical care:

> Then cousin Alice Hall sent for me to go with her to see some released prisoners at the Hospital — Poor fellows! How sick they were! How they lifted their languid heads to see Alice's beautiful face! One showed us the handcuffs with which he was confined — another a bit of the bread they were fed — it was of corn ground up cobs grain & husks together without sifting — the meal given them to make their own bread — One showed us the battered daguerreotype of his wife — I said ëHow glad she will be to learn of your release' — He burst out sobbing — Cousin Alice is a very angel among all the Hospitals here — She goes daily & more than daily carrying her little pail of arrowroot or jelly or goodies of some sort with an arm full of shirts, drawers, socks, towels & etc. which she distributes from bed to bed — feeding with her own hands — writing letters — & cheering with her low voice and beautiful presence — She is lovely.[39]

Transportation to Point Lookout was available irregularly and Miss Dix tried to secure Ella's passage several times before she actually succeeded. Even though Ella had lived simply and without excess, Miss Dix felt that Ella's personal baggage, one large trunk, was too much to take with her to the Hospital. Although she ultimately did take the trunk with her, Ella's exchange with Miss Dix reveals to us Dix's philosophy that the nurse is a soldier on a different kind of battlefield.

> Set it down! Don't bring it into the house!" (hastily as if it contained the plague) It is deposited on the side walk & I follow Miss Dix into the house — She leans both hands on the table in an attitude of her own and addresses me — I consider it Miss Wolcott as extremely desirable that my nurses should have as little luggage as may be — You may have observed that in the hall — it is what I consider sufficient for four nurses — Nurses should properly need no more than soldiers carry in their knapsacks — You should have no superfluities and many things that we are accustomed to are — entirely — superfluous — We live in war times — Things that at other times might be appropriate are now wholly inappropriate — for instance I should be ashamed to ride in a hired carriage or a carriage of my own — Government has offered

me a carriage and my friends have offered me one — and I am able to provide myself one — but I choose to ride in an ambulance. A Christian woman must feel that her money and her labor and her comfort are not her own.[40]

Finally, transportation on a boat on the Potomac was arranged. Ella traveled with Miss Sophronia Bucklin[41] who was also assigned by Miss Dix to a nursing position at Hammond Hospital at Point Lookout, Maryland.

Arriving in October of 1864, Ella soon realized that getting supplies at the isolated Point Lookout would be difficult. In her first letter after arriving at Hammond Hospital, she writes, "My candle is burning low and I cant have any kerosene — there is nothing to be bought here & in Washington things cost much more than in Elmira."[42] Ella wrote about what she thought was needed and her begging letters, as she called them, received immediate and enthusiastic responses. By December of 1862, Ella was already acknowledging the receipt of items from friends in Elmira.[43] The work at the hospital had changed substantially by this time. Wounded from the Battle of Fredericksburg were brought to the hospital and the horrors of the wounds made by the minie ball became a harsh reality to Ella. What she saw strengthened Ella's resolve and assured her that she was where she should be.

> ...dear Julia at last I know what I have come for — & am perfectly satisfied that I am doing what ought to be done —1073 men have come from the battle of Fredricksburg — We are all very busy with the care of them — My ward is small compared with those the Sisters of Charity have — but I go the rounds the oftener — I had the pleasure of hearing my Dr. whisper to his associate 'you see they have better care here than they can get over there' — One man's arm I believe will be saved partly by the constant poulticing I have given it. Another poor fellow I fear must lose his — I dread it more than anything else — more than I should have done at first — for I have tried so hard to save it — The first day they arrived we all went to the new wards & did what we found to do — without advice from the Drs. As they were too busy to speak — Oh what sights — I must not describe them to you — but I can think & dream of nothing else — The Minie balls are horrid — What does possess men to fight so! Oh what a burden somebody will have to shoulder when account is taken of this — But I still say 'it is a good cause' — fight on to the very end for it is right to save the bitter suffering that will surely come if the wrong is allowed to triumph now — & above all let not this suffering already past, be in vain.[44]

Here, finally, she was truly needed. But the isolation of the hospital and the paucity of supplies made it difficult to care for the men. Ella's begging became more specific and even encouraged her correspondents to enlist others in her army.

> I want to beg for the Hospital — I know the ...same cry goes up all over the land — but here we are so isolated —& the winds across the waters are so bleak — & we need so many things — & I know just where every item could be put in to do genuine necessary service — Would the ladies of Bridgeport through your mother give us a box? Bridgeport is richer than Elmira and there are many New England boys here — I want a box of lemons prodigiously to make a cooling drink for this wound fever — I want fruit of all

kinds to keep off the tendency of scurvy they have contracted in camp — it corrupts their wounds — I want wine to keep up their fainting strength when their wounds are probed and dressed — I want flannel shirts almost without number — for the rheumatic — the consumptive — the thin bloodless men who stand for an hour in line before they can get their meals — I want shirts and sheets and pillowcases to make even a single change for them — I want double gowns that those who are wounded may sit up without taking cold — Slippers I hope to have from Elmira — Our Matron has just said to me 'haven't you some friend who would send a barrel of crackers? We need them so much.' Now this is great deal to beg from those who have been giving constantly since the war begun — but I know if they could see what I see they would give continually — I have spent every cent I dare spend — & I hope to be able to give my wages — Dear Julia you needn't say I am extravagant — If you were here you would do the same — And if the ladies at home could see the grateful looks of the men — Is it very presuming of me to ask for a box from Bridgeport? Thro' you? If I did not see how I could use it well I would not — but I have so few rich friends to ask.[45]

Ella's correspondents shared her letters. Passed around to friends, relatives, church congregations, and ladies aid societies, Ella's letters had a wide appeal and provoked enthusiastic responses. "Write common place diary letters to us — say five minutes a day. Common place to you is of intense interest & freshness to us."[46] "Write us more such letters, that we may share with you in this blessed work."[47] Friends who knew her well were in awe of her stamina, so uncharacteristic of her physical strength in recent years. Julia Beecher wrote, "...you are working so hard — Oh Ella think of what you are doing — Cooking with green wood, in a crowd — from 6 AM to 12 PM — You could not work two hours in the water cure dining room — without getting sick — You must indeed be sustained from above... How fascinating your letters are — wonderful!"[48]

The women at home were giving their all to the war effort and Ella's letters provided the proof that their efforts were needed and appreciated. Her responses recognized that her work would be impossible without their work. Ella's correspondents write of their wholehearted devotion to the patriotic work. Ella's letters to her "army" renewed their purpose:

I am happy to say that we have, today, sent you two boxes, containing various articles, a list of which I enclose. For our ability to do this, we are greatly indebted to your interesting letter, which has produced a great effect on every one who has read it; by the detailed accounts you have given of the use of each article we sent, you have enabled us more fully to realize the good we were permitted to do, and excited every one to new efforts; hoping that some noble man, suffering for our beloved country, may through our means, receive even a temporary alleviation of his pain. We have followed you in imagination from bed to bed, of them, our brothers, seen you in the long watchings, through the weary hours, yet our pity becomes envy, when we consider the happiness you must derive from the consciousness that you are able to relieve so much pain perhaps to save a limb, or even a life of one of those men, to whom we all owe such a debt.[49]

The nursing service was not without it own politics. Ella was considered invaluable by the soldiers and many of the Surgeons with whom she served. Still, when hospital administration staff changed, changes in the nursing staff were inevitable. Ella admired and trusted Miss Dix and preferred to work in hospitals under her auspices. In late February 1863, Mrs. A. H. Gibbons, the long-time matron of Hammond Hospital, applied to Surgeon General Hammond for an independent appointment as the supervisor of Hammond Hospital's nursing staff.[50] Ella wrote to Miss Dix to tell her about the developments at the hospital:

> Mrs. Gibbons came to my room I think Tuesday evening — said that the control of the female department of the hospital & the selection of nurses was now entirely in her hands — that you would receive official information of this fact on your return to Washington — that we might remain here or return to you — but that she should stipulate that if we remained here we should have no correspondence with you on Hospital affairs — that is, the management of this Hospital — that we might have till the next morning to decide — Of course this took us greatly by surprise — I thought anxiously and prayerfully over my decision — I would on no account be disloyal to you or to the truth or to our good cause — I cannot suppress my sense of discourtesy to yourself — calling it by the softest name — Yet it seemed to me that if ever I could do good it was here and now — that I am wonted to this place — deeply attached to it — and to some of my patients — To leave it and go to another hospital would be to serve a new apprenticeship — time lost — To go to you without warning might embarrass you...By the whole tenor of your life and teachings so far as I have known, I believed that you would yourself set the faithful performance of a duty at hand, before any personal demonstration toward yourself — Therefore on the next morning I told Mrs. Gibbons that I would remain — I submitted to her stipulations about a correspondence with you, telling her you would not wish to hear details of what you could not control, but that I must assure you that I mean no disloyalty to you — Dear Miss Dix please let me say here that with every interview I have learned to love and respect you more, and I deeply regret all which must now grieve you.[51]

Ella ultimately left Point Lookout to nurse under the supervision of Miss Dix at Chesapeake Hospital at Fortress Monroe, Virginia. But with each move and change in circumstance, Ella's army of support remained constant. When she wrote that she had left the Hammond Hospital and had been working among the contrabands while awaiting her next hospital assignment, Ella's supporters in Elmira, New York wrote "do as you will as to the things sent you. As long as you continue economic & honest & strong enough to use resources — they shall not fail you."[52]

With every letter, no matter where she was assigned, Ella continued to lobby for the needs of her boys. As her confidence built, so did her contacts. She confided in Miss Dix that she had begun a fruitful correspondence with many kind benefactors. "My friends have become interested thro' my letters and I am daily expecting valuable supplies."[53] The ladies of The Park Church in Elmira, New York were the core of Ella's army, her unfailing and faithful workers who supplied her with everything from blackberry cordial, the hospital elixir of life, to every type of clothing that the men would need. The congregation sent her a monthly allowance of between $50 and $100 to be spent on the care of the men.[54] When Ella needed clothing made or personal items sent, friends at the church or the water cure went to work to meet her needs. Friends also took care of Ella's affairs in Elmira. Reverend Beecher kept Ella's accounts but she rarely followed his conservative monetary advice. Ella often required him to send her money from her small inheritance when the allowance and her wages were not enough, in the end depleting her savings completely for the cause.

Other residents of Elmira also took up Ella's cause and sent supplies directly to her for distribution to the boys in the hospital. Several of the young women at Elmira Female College attempted to affect the lives of the soldiers in the hospital not only with their gift of clothing, but with their supportive, patriotic messages. Among them was M. E Rennie who wrote, "Think not for a moment that the brave who have gone forth to battle for the right in the cause of union are forgotten by those left behind, No! Many are the prayers offered to our creator for your safety and success; none speak but to praise the gallant soldier. Let your motto be there is no such word as fail."[55] Patients at the Elmira Water Cure Establishment also joined Ella's "army." Miss S. A. Emerick made socks for the soldiers and sent a note of encouragement. Miss Emerick had great hopes for the power of her socks:

> The knitter of these socks though not a soldier in the Union Army but a member of the Invalid Corp of the Water cure, and wishing to do something for the cause of our country, employs busy fingers in working for our noble and heroic soldiers. Take these socks, and wear them, and may they protect you from cold, wet and disease, and become the means of defending you from all missiles of war coming from rebel hands. And may the time be very near when our brave defenders will no more need supplies as soldiers, but return to the dear ones at home, where they can find hearts, hands and socks, ready to receive them, is the earnest wish of the knitter, and the wish of all the friends of the soldiers.[56]

Through Ella's family connections, individuals and groups became frequent contributors to the hospital stores. Julia Wolcott Carter, Ella's only full sibling, and her family sent regular contributions to be administered with Ella's capable hands. Julia's letters furnished both monetary support for the work and emotional and moral succor for Ella's sometimes flagging spirit. "But truly it is a blessed privilege to do the work you are now doing. My dear sister 'be not weary in doing well,' & the Lord give you strength to hold out until there shall be no need of hospitals. We are very glad to contribute directly to the soldiers & the greater the need, the more willing are we to give, so, it be used wisely and well. If the other was opportune, perhaps the enclosed will not be less so; & my dear child we are not afraid to trust you...And dear Ella I am even more willing to give when it goes to the men, then when it went to the officers, for my sympathies greatly with the privates."[57]

Although the Wolcott sisters were first cousins of Major General James Wadsworth,[58] who fell while leading the men of the 4th Division 5th Corp of the Army of the Potomac into the fray at the Battle of the Wilderness on May 6, 1864, many of their loved ones served as enlisted men. Several cousins served in regiments from a number of states. Their youngest brother Richmond Wolcott and their nephew William Kirby were both enlisted men in the 10th Illinois Infantry. Two of their brother Samuel's sons, Henry and Edward Wolcott, served in the 140th and the 150th Ohio respectively.

Julia knew the power of Ella's letters and the enormity of the need. Friends in the Wolcott hometown of Jacksonville, Illinois, frequently inquired after Ella and her work. Julia exploited this interest to support Ella's work. "Mrs. Bancroft has been asking me to come & read some of your letters to the Society. So just after New Years I went in one afternoon & read part of all three of the letters you have written since you were at the Point. They all seemed very much interested & as the result they voted after I left to send you fifty dollars...It shows a confidence in you which must be gratifying to you."[59]

Although less supportive than Julia and her husband, William C. Carter, Ella's elder brother, Elizur, was interested in Ella's work but was less confident of her physical strength for the work. Elizur sent her inheritance allowance to her and often cautioned her about her need to be frugal and save some money for her future. We learn of the support extended by her eldest brother, Samuel, through a letter published in the *Cleveland Leader* on June 24, 1863. Apparently, Samuel shared one of Ella's "begging" letters with the ladies of his adopted hometown, Cleveland, Ohio. The letter was published and the ladies responded generously and were warmly thanked by Ella who encouraged them to continue to send more supplies to the hospital. Never missing an opportunity to enlist more recruits to her "army," Ella wrote eloquently of the unrelenting needs at the hospital. The column from the newspaper is printed here in its entirety.

> Our friends will doubtless remember the eloquent and touching appeal for hospital supplies, from Miss Wolcott, of Hammond hospital, published some weeks ago in our city papers. The liberal stores of choice articles of diet, wines &c., called forth by that letter have been for many days awaiting the necessary directions for shipment and the ladies who so freely gave these delicacies will read with interest a second letter from this faithful attendant upon the sick and suffering at Point Lookout:

> Hammond Hospital, Point Lookout Md.
> January 14th, 1863
> Secretary Soldiers' Aid Society –

> Dear Madam: Your favor of Jan. 8th, I just received. Your prompt and favorable reply to my hasty appeal excites surprise, pleasure and gratitude. I wrote to my brother by night, in haste and weariness. Just so do I now address you, and since you so kindly accepted that with all its shortcomings, you will pardon this though it be brief and confused.

> By recent changes, I have been thrown for a day or two upon double duty in a strange ward, full of confusion and negligence. From six o'clock this morning until eight this evening. I have been seated but one half hour and that was when reading aloud by a bedside which abundantly repays all my

labor. I think of it now for if the watches of the night are short to me, they are long for the brave lad who lies there. Shot by a poisoned bullet, the gangrened wound nearly as large as my hand, loathsome to every sense, he lies in a darkened room, never making a moan or uttering a complaint, or asking a favor — always the same steady, low voice and quiet eyes. Eating little and losing strength, he must be fed. Lack of time alone prevented my walking a mile to buy some eggs for him. Do you wonder that I long for stores of all kinds at hand? I wrote to my brother at a venture, hardly expecting an answer, as I feared you were too far off to reach us. The publication quite startled me, but if it aided your — our — good cause I will put aside the shrinkings of vanity and thank God that he wrought through my feebleness. Had I known of the great battles in the southwest, I should hardly have dared apply to you. With kindred and friends, as I suppose, engaged in that fearful strife, I may not be jealous of supplies sent westward, but if you can also spare for us, I repeat the assurance that your gifts shall be faithfully used. Our hospital receives its regulation supplies from the Government, and also, in some degree, the gifts of the Sanitary Commission and Aid Societies of the North. They are well used and fill their place; but in so large an institution they must be dispensed by strict rules. We receive them through the surgeon, the wardmaster, the steward, the great cookhouse that serves from 1,500 to 2,000 rations. Rarely can an order be reached within twenty-four hours. This is as it should be for economy's sake among men who can wait, but for the very sick, when every hour counts, we rely upon our matron's store-room, and her stores are running low. This is my excuse for begging. Of clothing also, as well as food, I will only say we are in great need.

One article I will speak of as being more likely to be obtained in Cleveland than anywhere else where I have the opportunity of asking, viz: German books. So many Germans are here, and they are eager for reading. Perhaps their countrymen in Cleveland, (and I believe they are numerous) would give for them.

I am directed by our Chaplain, Rev. Dr. Spooner, of Baltimore, to say that if you will direct them to the care of the Christian Commission of Baltimore, they will be promptly re-shipped to Point Lookout. Please mark the box (not on a card) 'Hospital Stores, Miss Wolcott, Hammond Hospital, Point Lookout, Md., care of Christian Commission, No. 77 Baltimore street, Baltimore Md.' Please also to write to me my mail when they leave Cleveland, giving a list of the articles sent. The officers of the Commission are G. S. Griffith, Chairman, Geo. P. Hays, Treasurer, J.N.M. Tilton, Secretary. — Send as freight by all means, if you can do so with economy and any degree of promptness. To suggest caution in the packing is doubtless superfluous, yet, our matron tells some sad stories of broken bottles and wasted wine.

After all, my letter is not brief, for my excited sympathy will speak. Hoping to hear from you again, I am, with grateful acknowledgement,

Yours truly,
Ella L. Wolcott[60]

Support for Ella's work came from Massachusetts, Ohio, New York, Connecticut and Illinois,[61] from small towns and large cities. Sarah Bostwick of

New England Soldier's Relief Association in New York City wished to join Ella in her work in the hospitals but knew she did not have the personality for it. Instead, she worked for the soldiers at home. The work at home required a particular skill and determination and Miss Bostwick was worried she was not up to the task, "I only wish I had more to send but I have begged so much I was almost ashamed to start out again and yet I am ashamed not to have courage always to ask for help for our brave boys."[62] The Reverend Thomas K. Beecher and friends from Elmira recommended Ella and her work to the Women's Central Association of Relief in New York City. Soon, supplies from this New York City branch of the United States Sanitary Commission were being sent to Ella regularly. This was a particularly important accomplishment, as the application for Sanitary Commission supplies normally required a requisition from a Surgeon-in-Charge. Ellen Collins of the WCAR cautioned Ella about this policy, yet sent eleven boxes of supplies[63] in a period of two weeks. Miss Collins wrote, "We were glad to respond to your application, and could not hesitate to do so, when we read the very hearty and cordial endorsement of your friends in Elmira. It gave us pleasure, too, to gratify them."[64]

But there were long periods when requests to the Sanitary Commission went unanswered and unfilled.[65] This was especially trying for Ella when she was appointed the Sanitary Commission Agent for Point Lookout.[66] Over a period of months, Ella bemoans the difficulty of getting supplies and information from the Sanitary Commission. "I have not heard directly from the San. Com. And began to fear that as well as some other Depts was a humbug — for the clerk promised to send me stores, and did not — to return my papers and write to me, but did not — to inquire whether such & such things were furnished by the San. Com. — & did not."[67] Sometimes Ella's soldiers had very specific needs that were not being met from the standard Sanitary Commission stores. Martha Chace and friends knew slings were desperately needed and made as many as possible. Their diligence caused a problem, "I have exhausted supply of buckles in Norfolk and so made buttonholes instead."[68] Other friends went into production of slings that Ella designed for maximum comfort.[69] Cushions and pads for injured limbs were desperately needed to make the soldiers comfortable. Ella and her "army" tried many types of stuffing — hair, oakum,[70] excelsior,[71] sea grass and found that washable stuffing was best. They experimented with different grades of firmness and types of covering. After several tries, they achieved what Ella felt was the perfect cushion. "Now for the cushions...They were evidently prepared with great care — They are much more even & smooth than any lot we have received from the Christian or San Commission — showing how prevalent is ignorance concerning their use — You must remember that on these cushions an inflamed surface, tender as any boil, is to rest in all the weight of utter helplessness — What your cheek could not bear in health for one night a swollen arm or skeleton back cannot bear for day and night."[72]

Ella's true gift was using her gift as an expressive writer to thank her benefactors and to tell them about the importance of their labors. Even as her work increased, Ella faithfully acknowledged each gift.[73] She knew each gift was vital and she made sure that the donors felt the urgency of need. "My thanks in behalf of our Soldiers are in an especial manner due to the donors of these articles — The shirts arrived at the very moment when the last one obtained from other sources was given away — the coldest day we have yet had, saves our men blue and shivering — The articles of food and drink are apparently superior to any in our possession...Thanking you now with a full heart, that ëthe blessing of him who was ready to perish' with God's blessing, will abide upon your labors. I remain yours in our holy cause."[74]

Several individuals and families became self-appointed field agents for Ella. Not working with any particular ladies society or church group, these ladies lobbied their neighbors and worked with family members to supply small but frequent contributions to the hospitals. Hattie Marsh's mother and neighbors helped her fill the boxes she sent. "In fact I have done very little, mother has worked and fussed and I have only had to tell folks what I wanted and thank ëem for it when it came. I do feel so glad to think they have done so well."[75] E.W. Wills, unable to visit and gather supplies from her neighbors and friends because of the birth of a son, contacted others to continue her work while she was confined. "I invoke the liberty to send your letter on to our Connecticut friends...I will speak to the Aid Society here as soon as I can get out and I hope you will receive some things from some of the various sources."[76]

Helen Sterling of Springfield, Massachusetts worried that the packages her family sent were not enough. "It is purely a family affair. All of our neighbors and friends do a great deal for the Christian and Sanitary Commissions...otherwise we might have sent more."[77] Yet, she mentions some of the contents of the box: pillows, slippers, cologne, comfort bags, fruit and promised copies of the Congregationalist to be sent as it is published. Sisters Lucy Tyson and Elizabeth Smith were Ella's agents in Baltimore, Maryland. They procured supplies for her, made contracts with merchants for milk and other essential perishables[78] and filled supply requisitions with the Christian and Sanitary Commissions.[79] They did whatever they could to support the work but also served as emotional benefactors for Ella, who late in the war served in the absence of other lay women nurses. "We have spoken often of you since your visit & wished it was in our power to make your self sacrificing devoted life more comfortable. Please do not stay there too long I think you look worn. I cant bear to think of you even being so wholly without what is due there when I suppose yr hospital ought to have the same resources as Annapolis."[80]

Ella's wide circle of friends responded regularly and enthusiastically to her letters. Although many letters to the Beechers and some to Ella's siblings exist, few of the "begging" letters to others survive. But her letter to family friend Mr. Kirk gives us an intimate look at Ella and her mission. She begins the letter with the intent of sending a short note to Mr. Kirk seeking a position for a young man. She had no intent to write a "begging" letter but the cause of her boys was always paramount. This letter, printed here in his entirety shows us in no uncertain terms why Ella's correspondence moved those who read them to work so tirelessly for the good of the soldiers.

U.S. Hospital
Point Lookout, Md.
Sept. 15, 1864

Mr. Kirk —
Dear Sir —

    I snatch a few moments from hospital duties to ask you, in behalf of a friend, if, with your wide business acquaintances in the West, you can tell me of an opening for a young man, 17 years of age of thorough integrity and sound principle, of fair talent, excellent family + every circumstance to learn and succeed in a large wholesale hardware business? His present salary would be a matter of small consideration to his parents compared with an opportunity for thorough business connection and fair chances for promotion in it. Also good social influences are greatly desired. If in these times when labor of all kinds is wanted, you can think of a good situation of this kind will you kindly inform me?

    I trust I have no need to say how fondly I remember your wife and the members of your family whom I have not seen for so long. I had a short but delightful visit with Alice in Pittsburg — I look anxiously thro the papers for news from Ben — But I have little time now to write or to speak of my own friends — And I know that, your hearts as well as mine are full of <u>one great Cause</u> before which even demonstrations of personal regard seem meager — I had no thought when I began this sheet to write a begging letter other than the request I named — But, when I would write one word of myself before all other considerations springs up <u>my work</u> & my wants. Who helps me now in the richest most sacred life I have ever known seems almost nearer than ties of blood can make. Therefore "drawing a bow at a bullseye" I will tell you what I am trying to do — and ask whether your neighborhood can or will help me. I am here especially to receive and distribute supplies received from personal friends — of from any quarter — I am the only Protestant lady connected with this hospital which has 15 Sisters of Charity in its wards as nurses. To this service I am especially appointed by Miss Dix with consent of the Surgeon in Charge and the Surgeon General — I visit all the wards of the hospital and know with my own eyes that the soldiers receive what I send to them — So far as my time and conveniences will permit, I prepare food for the most needy — now I will tell you what we need — and if my readiness to do so needs an excuse, let me tell you it comes from a scene which I can never forget — one morning in one of the wards I found, following the surgeon from bed to bed, a tall Pennsylvanian with eyes which showed his recent weeping and hands meekly folded together or trembling in vacancy — his citizen's dress and the vague helpless hopeless yearning in his face told me what he was. The father had come for his young son, but, did not find him — and the Dr. was protesting that if he had had suitable diet & medicine & drink, he need not have died of the scurvy a few days before — and now the heart broken father burying his grief in his sympathy for the yet living comrades of his son, followed in the surgeon's wake asking each sufferer what was the matter and what he needed — "Eggs?" "50cts a dozen!!" "Chickens!" "1.50 a pair" "Why we have all we want and more at home" and "Eggs are only 10 cents a dozen" "Butter 60 cents a pound" "Only 20 or at most 25 with us" "Milk?" " Potatoes?" "Vegetables?" "Fruit?" "Not to be obtained!" And the father knowing that all this his own hired servants had enough and to spare must now be told that his younger son, no prodigal but, a patriot who had spent the substance of his own body not in riotous living but in brave service for God and country had perished for need of them — as truly "perished with hunger" as if salt, meat and bread had not been set before his loathing eyes — This was several weeks ago — soon after I came here — + I was disposed to blame the hospital authorities — The season is more advanced now + we are able to have a little improvement — but there is more to be said in palliation than you would think — and our needs will continue. Our hospital accommodates 1400 patients, has now about 800 — but we expect all to be filled from the battles going on — It is on a muddy peninsula between the Potomac and the Chesapeake — The water is brackish + particularly needs some mixture to make it endurable or healthful. The adjoining country is "secesh" in feeling — and yields nothing or but little for use in the hospital. We are out of the way of all visitors + have nothing to attract sympathy from outside — We have a steamer three times a week from Washington — but as prices are enormous we procure but little. Our regular transportation is by steamer once a week from Baltimore. The mail is brought nightly by the steamer from Baltimore to Norfolk — sometimes express freight comes by the trains — The price of butter is 60cts a pound — eggs from, 35 to 50 cts a dos. Potatoes $2.00 per bushel. Cabbage or Beets $5.00 per barrel — Chickens I don't know now but last I bought were $5.00 per dos — Judge by this the increased prices of keeping one hospital! — and tell me you forgive me for not being able to write even a business letter without dropping a chance seed to grow for our soldiers.

It is not of you personally that I beg — But that you would if possible circulate my story to keep alive in country neighborhoods that spirit of devoted patriotism without which men will be as truly starved in our own hospitals as on Belle Isle — For the farms of Pennsylvania are unravaged <u>because</u> these men lie here — If they and their comrades had not set their strength against Lee's army, the great barns of Penn, if they reaped the flames, would this year have held no harvests — And now I beg a little of these harvests — Our men have not been paid for months — + nearly every one has lost his all upon the field — They are in need of everything — But I will not ask shirts & drawers and shoes of the country — only where sheep are raised & the old fashioned spinning wheel is found will they send us socks! And anything that can be raised on a farm and gleaned from a garden — Cider — Apples — Butter — Eggs — Tomatoes — in cans — pickles — catsup — Onions — Cheese — All kinds of fruits — dried or canned — also we need rags & lint & if filled up with freshly wounded men will be greater in need — Any Soldier's Aid Society will probably pay the freight on all that may be sent — Or if otherwise I will gladly pay for all sent to me —

Forgive my long raving about "my soldier boys —" To begin so long a letter by asking a favor & end by wholesale downright demands upon time and influence & purse!

Unpardonable! Except that Mrs. Kirk's kind heart will apologize for me — and whether these hours stolen from the night ever come back to me bringing their heart with them, "(sic) if they may but excite new diligence in some weary arms, and kind friends will forgive my own tears I shall forgive myself for lack of sleep and lack of manners. Many changes have taken place in your family & in mine since the days when Alice adopted me as sister & and her Mother sanctioned it — God notes all — & I pray his blessing upon us all — and remain,

Yours respectfully
Ella L. Wolcott[81]

And as they always did, Ella's letter touched something in Mr. Kirk and he sent her a contribution of $4.00.[82] It may not seem like much but with its donation, and possibly without his even really knowing it, Mr. Kirk had been recruited. He, like so many before him, had joined the private army of Ella Louise Wolcott.

Ella was stationed at the Hammond Hospital at Point Lookout, Maryland from October 1862 until April 1863, and again from July 1864 until August 1865. Miss Dix transferred her to Chesapeake Hospital at Fortress Monroe, Virginia, where she worked from May 1863 until June 1864. Ella also spent time working in contraband camps nearby the hospitals. At the end of the war, Ella stayed at Hammond Hospital with the convalescent soldiers, both Union and Confederate, until the close of the hospital in August of 1865. During her second tenure at Hammond, Ella's added role as the Relief Agent of the Sanitary Commission added many challenges but also allowed her to acquire items that she felt would buoy the spirits of the men. Replicating many of the morale building strategies of the Water Cure movement, Ella gathered books and periodicals for a library, instituted musical entertainments and even produced plays starring the convalescent soldiers.

Ella was offered work in several different hospitals at the War's end, including as the matron of the National Asylum for Disabled Soldiers.[83] Miss Dix wrote to Ella to tell her that the Surgeon in charge in Smithville, North Carolina requested her services.[84] But the work was hard on Ella. She had somehow withstood the physical and emotional punishment of the three years of nursing but as the war wore down so did she. Ella's long letters to her family and friends were reduced to short notes as she struggled to gather the strength to travel home. In July 1865, Ella wrote to Reverend Beecher about the hospital closing and her hopes to return to Elmira: "We are breaking up — & I am broken down — All our patients are gone — only a guard to pack up and finish — I expect to be at home next week — Unofficial proposals are made to me to be Matron of the National Asylum for disabled soldiers to be probably located here — If I live I may accept — but now I can only cry 'a wet sheet and a bath tub!' I am very much as I was twelve years ago — and I might doubt about getting home at all, as I sit now swathed in ice water — But next to Providence my faith is in ice & my good Mary."[85]

Ella did finally return home to Elmira. She moved into a cottage on Water Cure Hill, quite near her friends the Beechers, The Park Church, and the Elmira Water Cure. Ella returned to live a quite life as the librarian of The Park Church. There she was a lifetime member of the Advisory Board, established Shakespeare classes and directed theatricals. The Park Church Bulletin notes:

"Miss Wolcott is still the center of the intellectual life of the church if not the city. Everybody, from Pastor Eastman[86] to the sweet girl graduate, goes to her for guidance in literary works and historical investigation."[87]

Never married, Ella enjoyed warm, although often long distance, relationships with her many nephews and nieces. She continued, throughout her life, a prolific correspondence with her family and friends. Although there was community support for Ella to apply for a pension, it is unclear if she ever did apply. In fact, her later correspondence makes only rare mention of her work during the war. Nor did she often speak of her war work in her community. An undated newspaper column gives us insight into how Miss Wolcott felt about any fame that would arise from her war service:

> 'She ought to have a pension' that is what a friend of mine said to me the other day of Miss Ella L. Wolcott, Park Church librarian and conductor of the ladies Shakespeare classes.
>
> Miss Wolcott lately has been reading before her classes the letters she wrote to Thomas K. Beecher while she was a nurse in the army hospitals during the civil war. The letters have proved very interesting. My friend's remark was prompted by the story they told. They made up a narrative of devotion surpassed by the record of no woman who cared for the sick and wounded during that great conflict.
>
> With the rest appeared the sacrifice Miss Wolcott made of her little fortune, Mr. Beecher was the custodian of a thousand dollars belonging to Miss Wolcott. He was going to invest it in United States bonds. The suffering of the soldiers, however, made so great an impression upon Miss Wolcott that, much against the good man's protest, she drew on the fund little by little until it was exhausted. So Miss Wolcott did not own a United States bond but invested the little fortune in the alleviation of the soldiers' needs. She gave all she had which is all that was required of the rich young man desiring to be saved.
>
> Miss Wolcott does not know that she is a heroine. The next time I see her I am going to look the other way. She does not like 'newspaper notoriety.'
>
> But I think she should have a pension, too, if she'll take it. She has the record all right. And we have men in Elmira who could get her one if they would.[88]

Despite her chronic scrofula, Ella lived a long life. She died in her beloved cottage on Water Cure Hill in Elmira on April 29, 1912 at age 83. Ella's last wishes were that there be no funeral or church service. She asked that she be quietly cremated and that her ashes be scattered on Water Cure Hill. Although she did not leave much money, she wanted it to be divided among her over 100 nieces and nephews and their children. Every heir received a check for five or ten dollars. In a letter addended to her will, Ella wrote, "My love cannot count for much to the younger generation which knows me not. Such as it is, I give it to all."[89] Writing to his aunt Helen Kirby Dwight,[90] Ella's Executrix, Clement R. Kirby,[91] noted his surprise at receiving an inheritance. And in a few sentences he sums up the life of this most trustworthy and extraordinary woman: "Aunt Ella was a wonderful and very unusual woman for her time. She would stand out at any time and place I fully believe."[92]

Endnotes

1. Ella L. Wolcott to Reverend Thomas K. Beecher and Julia J. Beecher, October 26, 1863, Acquisitions, Harriet Beecher Stowe Center, Hartford, Connecticut. Cited hereafter as HBSC.

2. Ella L. Wolcott to Reverend Thomas K. Beecher, November 2, 1862, Acquisitions, HBSC.

3. Julia Jones Beecher was the second wife of Thomas Kinnicut Beecher, of the renowned Beecher family. The Reverend Beecher was the minister at the Park Church in Elmira, New York, where Ella was a member.

4. Quotations used in this article are printed verbatim. All syntactical, grammatical and spelling errors are found in the original quotations.

5. Ella L. Wolcott to Julia Jones Beecher, October 24, 1862, Acquisitions, HBSC.

6. Ella L. Wolcott's correspondence spans the seventy-two years from 1840 until her death in 1912. Her war years correspondence contains letters that are often 10 to 15 handwritten pages. These letters survive because of her foresight to ask her correspondents to save the letters that she wrote in diary fashion, some letters having entries written over as much as a week's time.

7. Stiles, Henry R., *The History and Genealogies of Ancient Windsor, Connecticut including East Windsor, South Windsor, Bloomfield, Windsor Locks, and Ellington. 1635 –1891*, Volume 2, Part 2, Hartford, Connecticut: Press of the Case, Lockwood, & Brainard Company, 1892, pages 798 – 826

8. Doyle, Don Harrison, *The Social Order of a Frontier Town, Jacksonville, Illinois 1825-70*, Urbana: University of Illinois Press, 1978, page 58.

9. Stiles, page 799.

10. Carter, Julia Wolcott, "Not An Autobiography," October 1905, Folder 10, Josephine A. Dolan Collection, Archives and Special Collections, Thomas J. Dodd Center at the University of Connecticut Libraries. Hereafter cited as Josephine A. Dolan Collection.

11. Doyle, page 21.

12. Olson, Greg, "Prague on the Prairie: The Cholera Epidemic of 1833 and Its Impact on One Illinois Town," *Illinois Heritage*, Volume 5, Number 1, January- February 2002, pages 6 – 9.

13. Carter.

14. Frank, Charles E., *Pioneer's Progress: Illinois College 1829 – 1979*, Published for Illinois College by Southern Illinois University Press, 1979.

15. *Ibid.*

16. Carter.

17. Natural Philosophy is the study of nature and natural phenomenon. Natural Philosophy textbooks of the early to mid 19th century might include a variety of topics including chemistry, biology, botany and physics.

18. Ella Wolcott to Reverend Thomas K. Beecher, April 20, 1856, Folder 27, Josephine A. Dolan Collection.

19. Carter.

20. Ella L. Wolcott, Dictated Genealogical Information, undated, Folder 6, Josephine A. Dolan Collection.

21. Ella suffered from scrofula, tuberculosis of the lymphatic glands, especially those in the neck. The disease develops into abscesses, multiple skin ulcers and draining sinus tracts. Debilitated by this invasive illness, Ella resided for several years before the Civil War in various Water Cure establishments in Vermont, Pennsylvania and New York in a quest to be restored to health.

22. Ella Wolcott to Reverend Thomas K. Beecher, April 20, 1856, Folder 27, Josephine A. Dolan Collection.

23. Allopathy is the practice of mainstream medical treatment, using drugs and treatments different than those that would stem from the homeopathic treatment of the disease.

24. Elizur Wolcott to Ella L. Wolcott, July 22, 1848, Folder 13, Josephine A. Dolan Collection. Dr. Robert Wesselhoeft was born in Saxony and was originally trained in the law but became interested in pathology after meeting a physician. In 1840 Wesselhoeft was treated for bilious and rheumatic fever by Vincent Priessnitz, the father of the revival of hydropathy. Trained as a homeopathic physician after his immigration to America, Dr. Wesselhoeft used more and more water treatment in his practice. On May 29, 1845, Wesselhoeft opened the Brattleboro Water Cure, one of the first in America. The water cure treatment became popular almost immediately. In the late summer of 1845, Harriet Beecher Stowe found the treatment and atmosphere at Wesselhoeft's curative. The Wolcott's, by then well acquainted with the Beecher family (Edward was the President of Illinois College and Thomas was a student at Illinois College at about this time), may have learned of Harriet's favorable treatments and may have reasoned that Ella might have favorable results there as well.

25. Homeopathic medicine is the practice of complementary treatment of disease. Based on

the idea that like cures like, the patient is given small doses of natural drugs that would in larger doses cause the disease.

26. For more about the "Dress Question" and it's connection to the Water Cure movement see Donegan, Jane B., *Hydropathic Highway to Health: Women and Water-Cure in Antebellum America*, New York: Greenwood Press, 1986. The debilitating nature of confining dress became a defining issue of women's health for the constituents of the water cure movement. Ella's exposure to the concepts of Reform Dress sometimes called "The American Costume," had a lasting effect on her attitudes towards women's clothing. In her letters she mentions the freedoms of wearing bloomers and requests and enjoys wearing clothing that is comfortable and utilitarian for the task at hand. This even allows her to disregard to strict age boundaries of fashion for her own pleasure, comfort and ease.

27. Julia W. Carter to Ella L. Wolcott, October 15, 1854, Folder 17, Josephine A. Dolan Collection.

28. Weiss, Harvey B., and Kemble, Howard R., *The Great American Water Cure: A History of Hydropathy in the United States*, Trenton, New Jersey: The Past Times Press, 1967.

29. For a discussion of female physicians and practitioners in the Water Cure Movement see: Weiss and Kemble, Donegan, and Cayleff, Susan E., *Wash and Be Healed: The Water-Cure Movement and Women's Health*, Philadelphia: Temple University Press, 1987. Rachel Brooks Gleason, co-founder of the Elmira Water Cure and wife of Doctor Silas O. Gleason, was a hydropathic practitioner for many years before she was permitted to study to become a physician. Her husband was instrumental in advancing a resolution for Central Medical College in Syracuse to admit female students. When she graduated in 1851, Rachel became one of the first four women in the United States to receive a formal medical degree. Other women doctors would also practice at the Elmira Water Cure including the Gleason's daughter, Adele, Rachel's sister, Zippie Brooks Wales, and several other pioneering female health professionals who went on to get their medical degrees.

30. Elihu and Richmond Wolcott to Ella L. Wolcott, December 16, 1848, Folder 13, Josephine A. Dolan Collection.

31. Elizur Wolcott to Ella L. Wolcott, October 26, 1862, Folder 15, Josephine A. Dolan Collection.

32. Julia W. Carter to Ella L. Wolcott, February 24, 1861, Folder 18, Josephine A. Dolan Collection.

33. The *National Era* was published in Washington D. C. It was the official weekly newspaper of the American and Foreign Anti-Slavery Society. Mrs. M. L. Bailey was the wife of Dr. Gamaliel Bailey, the editor of the *National Era* from 1847 until his death in 1859. "Uncle Tom's Cabin" by Harriet Beecher Stowe was first published as a serial in the *National Era*.

34. One cannot help but imagine that Ella was just the sort of woman that Miss Dix was looking for to become a nurse. In her thirties, religious, skilled in caring for others, with inner strength and a family that was supportive, Ella could be great asset if her health held out.

35. Ella L. Wolcott to Julia W. Carter, October 18, 1862, Folder 66, Josephine A. Dolan Collection.

36. Elizur Wolcott to Ella L. Wolcott, October 26, 1862, Folder 15, Josephine A. Dolan Collection.

37. The 141st New York Infantry Regiment was organized in Elmira New York and was mustered in on September 11,1862. After three years of service they were mustered out after the Grand Review on June 8th 1865. The regiment lost 4 Officers and 71 Enlisted men killed and mortally wounded, 2 Officers and 172 Enlisted men to disease, Total 249.

38. Cousin Alice Lindsley Hall was the daughter of Ella's first cousin Abigail Wolcott Ellsworth Hall and her husband David Aiken Hall. Abigail was the daughter of Sophia Wolcott Ellsworth and her husband Martin Ellsworth. Sophia was a younger sister of Ella's father, Elihu Wolcott. David Hall, Alice's father, was a lawyer in Washington, D.C. The Halls lived in Washington during the war. Alice was a young girl of 19 years when Ella was in Washington in 1861. Alice married Dr. Cornelius C. Wyckoff of Buffalo, New York in 1877. They had no children.

39. Ella L. Wolcott to Julia J. Beecher, October 24, 1862, Acquisitions, HBSC.

40. *Ibid*.

41. Sophronia Bucklin of Auburn, New York was unmarried and in her late twenties or early thirties when she entered the nursing service. Although Dorothea Dix felt she was too young, Miss Bucklin possessed all the other qualities that Miss Dix required. Miss Dix accepted her to the nursing service in late 1862. Miss Bucklin served first at Judiciary Square Hospital in Washington, D.C. In October of 1862, Miss Bucklin was reassigned to the new Hammond Hospital at Point Lookout, Maryland. She traveled there with Miss Wolcott and there they shared a room. Miss Wolcott's first description of Miss Bucklin: "My roommate Miss Bucklin is not refined but she is good." (See Ella L. Wolcott to Julia Jones Beecher, October 24, 1862, Acquisitions, HBSC.) Miss Bucklin served at Hammond Hospital from November 1862 until March of 1863 when she and all the Protestant lay nurses were reassigned to other hospitals. Miss Bucklin contin-

ued to nurse in many locations including in Gettysburg after the battle. She later wrote a memoir of her service as a nurse during the Civil War called *In Hospital and Camp: A Woman's Record of Thrilling Incidents Among the Wounded in the Late War*.

42. Ella L. Wolcott to Julia J. Beecher, October 24, 1862, Acquisitions, HBSC.

43. Ella L. Wolcott to Julia J. Beecher, December 21,1862, Acquisitions, HBSC.

44. *Ibid.*

45. *Ibid.*

46. Reverend Thomas K. Beecher to Ella L. Wolcott, November 1,1863, Acquisitions, HBSC.

47. Lydia R. Ward to Ella L. Wolcott, March 2, 1863, Folder 59, Josephine A. Dolan Collection. Lydia R. Ward was the Secretary of the Soldier's Relief Society of Bridgeport, Connecticut.

48. Julia J. Beecher to Ella L. Wolcott, February 25, 1863, Acquisitions, HBSC.

49. Lydia R. Ward to Ella L. Wolcott, March 2, 1863, Folder 59, Josephine A. Dolan Collection.

50. Brockett, L.P., M.D., and Vaughn, Mrs. Mary, *Heroines of the Rebellion; or Woman's Work in the Civil War: A Record of Heroism, Patriotism and Patience*, Philadelphia: Hubbard Brothers, Publishers, 1888. Pages 467 – 476.

51. Ella L. Wolcott to Dorothea L. Dix, February 27, 1863, Folder 59, Josephine A. Dolan Collection.

52. Reverend Thomas K. Beecher to Ella L. Wolcott, October 2, 1863, Acquisitions, HBSC.

53. Dorothea Dix to Ella L. Wolcott, February 27,1863, Folder 59, Josephine A. Dolan Collection.

54. In many letters sent over the course of her war service, Ella acknowledges, sends thanks and requests supplies from her faithful friends of The Park Church in Elmira. The Beechers wrote to Ella confirming shipments of goods and reporting on their work for the hospitals. Although these records are incomplete, Ella's surviving Hammond Hospital record books note multiple shipments of supplies and regular monetary donations from Elmira.

55. M.E. Rennie to a soldier, no date, Folder 59, Josephine A. Dolan Collection. Although undated, this note from M. E. Rennie of the Elmira Female College is stored with several notes dated between November and December 1863.

56. S. A. Emerick to a "Union Soldier", December 30, 1863, Folder 59, Josephine A. Dolan Collection. Miss Emerick was a patient at the Water Cure, Elmira, New York.

57. Julia Wolcott Carter to Ella L. Wolcott, September 19, 1864, Folder 19, Josephine A. Dolan Collection.

58. Brigadier General James Samuel Wadsworth was the eldest son of Naomi Wolcott Wadsworth, older sister of Ella and Julia's father Elihu. Born in Geneseo, New York, Wadsworth was a lawyer and businessman of great repute. A compassionate man, Wadsworth aided the starving Irish during the Potato Famine by sending a ship full of grain to Ireland. Wadsworth was killed in action on the second day of the Battle of the Wilderness. A monument was placed on the field there in his honor. The inscription reads,

James Wadsworth

Brigadier General and Brevet Major General United States Volunteers Commanding the 4th Division V Corps Army of the Potomac.

Was mortally wounded near this spot May 6, 1864 and died two days later in the field hospital of Hill's Confederate Corps. He fell attempting desperately to resist a Confederate advance that threatened the strategic Plank-Brock Road intersection.

59. Julia Wolcott Carter to Ella L. Wolcott, February 12, 1864, Folder 19, Josephine A. Dolan Collection.

60. Ella L. Wolcott to Secretary of the Soldiers Aid Society, Cleveland Leader, January 24, 1863.

61. Hammond Hospital account book of Ella L. Wolcott, 1864 - 1865, Folder 62, Josephine A. Dolan Collection. The account book, incomplete and unbound, lists many benefactors that sent supplies or monetary donations directly to Miss Wolcott to be used, as she felt necessary. Organizations inscribed as benefactors include the Sanitary Commission in Washington and Philadelphia, New Jerusalem Church in New York City, the American Unitarian Association, the Christian Commission, The Hartford (CT) Soldiers Aid Association, Elmira Church, and the Soldiers Aid Society of Jacksonville (IL). Other donor organizations included those in Elmira NY, Buffalo NY, East Windsor Hill CT, and Springfield MA. Individual donors listed in the account book are Miss Tyson, Miss Dix, Miss Dansell, Mr. Leonard, Sgt. Mitchell, Mrs. Hawley, Mr. Charles Morton, Mrs. Brewster (Hartford, CT), Mrs. Angell and Mrs. Purnell (Boston), Unknown, Olivia Langdon (soon to be Mrs. Samuel Clemens), Julia Carter, Mr. Beecher, John Kirk, and Miss Robinson.

62. Sarah Bostwick to Ella L. Wolcott, March 9, 1864, Folder 60, Josephine A. Dolan Collection. Although there is only one letter from Sarah Bostwick to Ella Wolcott the letter intimates that the women were well acquainted with each other and that there was continuing association between Miss Bostwick and her New England Soldier's Relief Association and Ella Wolcott.

63. Ellen Collins to Ella L. Wolcott, May 30, June 1 and 13, 1864, Folder 60, Josephine A. Dolan Collection. These three letters from Ellen Collins trace one of Ella's interactions with the Women's Central Association of Relief, New York City. Contents of some of the boxes are listed in the May 30, 1864 letter and show that the boxes shipped held many supplies: 119 pillows, 140 pillows, a box of lemons, a box of oranges, 200 sheets, 203 flannel shirts, two dozen Pap boats, 2 dozen pitchers, 81/3 dozen c.c. mugs. The June 1, 1864 letter notes 100 slippers sent. Pap boats were specialized feeders for invalids. C.C. mugs are measured mugs for medication and other liquids.

64. Ellen Collins to Ella L. Wolcott, Monroe, June 13, 1864, Folder 60, Josephine A. Dolan Collection.

65. Miss Wolcott notes in many letters that the hospital is not receiving supplies from the Sanitary Commission. Often, she says that this is because the Surgeon's have not made a request for supplies. In 1864, she was appointed the Sanitary Commission Agent at Point Lookout and in several letters written after her appointment she continues to note that supplies often do not come or are insufficient.

66. Relief Agent Commission Papers from the United States Sanitary Commission for Miss E. L. Wolcott, September 15, 1864, Folder 60, Josephine A. Dolan Collection.

67. Ella L. Wolcott to Julia J. Beecher, October 2, 1864, Folder 60, Josephine A. Dolan Collection.

68. M. H. Chace to Ella L. Wolcott, June 20, 1864, Folder 60, Josephine A. Dolan Collection.

69. Ella L. Wolcott to Reverend Thomas K. Beecher, June 21, 1864, Acquisitions, HBSC.

70. Oakum is loose hemp.

71. Excelsior is a stuffing material made of small, curly wood shavings.

72. Ella L. Wolcott to Reverend Thomas K., June 21, 1864, Acquisitions, HBSC.

73. Ella kept meticulous records not only of who sent supplies but also of who received articles of clothing, or which hospital wards used supplies.

74. Ella L. Wolcott to Mr. William G. Church and the Ladies of the New Jerusalem Church of New York City, not dated, Folder 59, Josephine A. Dolan Collection.

75. Hattie Marsh to Ella L. Wolcott, not dated, Folder 59, Josephine A. Dolan Collection.

76. E. W. Wills to Ella L. Wolcott, July 7, 1864, Folder 60, Josephine A. Dolan Collection.

77. Helen Sterling to Ella L. Wolcott, July 28, 1864, Folder 60, Josephine A. Dolan Collection.

78. W. L. James to Ella L. Wolcott, September 5, 1864, Folder 60, Josephine A. Dolan Collection.

79. Elizabeth B. Smith to Ella L. Wolcott, July 31, 1864, Folder 60, Josephine A. Dolan Collection.

80. Lucy Tyson to Ella L. Wolcott, August 14, 1864, Folder 60, Josephine A. Dolan Collection.

81. Ella Wolcott to Mr. Kirk, September 15, 1864, Folder 60, Josephine A. Dolan Collection.

82. Account book of Ella L. Wolcott, November 1864, Folder 62, Josephine A. Dolan Collection.

83. Ella L. Wolcott to Reverend Thomas K. Beecher, June 25, 1865, Acquisitions, HBSC.

84. Dorothea Dix to Ella L. Wolcott, July 26,1865, Folder 65, Josephine A. Dolan Collection.

85. Ella L. Wolcott to Reverend Thomas K. Beecher, July 26, 1865, Acquisitions, HBSC. Ella's reference to the wet sheet, bathtub and ice water refer to the treatments that were so successful in restoring her health at the Water Cure. Mary is Mary Peterson; a black woman who worked at Hammond Hospital and later went to Elmira with Ella.

86. Pastor Eastman could be either the Reverend Samuel E. Eastman or his wife, the Reverend Annis Ford Eastman. They came to the Elmira to be assistants to Reverend Thomas Beecher and after his death took over the pastorate of The Park Church.

87. Park Church Bulletin, no date, Folder 51, Josephine A. Dolan Collection.

88. Newspaper Article from an unknown paper, probably from Elmira, New York, no date, Folder 31, Josephine A. Dolan Collection.

89. Note by Ella L. Wolcott, July 30, 1892, Folder 46, Josephine A. Dolan Collection.

90. Helen McClure Kirby Dwight was the daughter of Ella's beloved sister Hannah McClure Wolcott Kirby who helped raise Ella after her mother's death.

91. Clement Rufus Kirby was the oldest son of William Arthur Kirby, second son of Ella's sister Hannah McClure Wolcott Kirby.

92. Clement R. Kirby to Helen K. Dwight, March 24, 1915, Folder 47, Josephine A. Dolan Collection..

THE ANATOMY OF A CDV:
ELLA LOUISE WOLCOTT

By Meg Galante-DeAngelis

When I first saw them, I felt a rush of excitement. Nestled in a folder with several other pictures, they sit unmarked. After spending weeks transcribing her letters, looking into her eyes was almost like meeting her face to face. I felt like I would have known her anywhere.

There are two pictures. The first has a formal look, a soft, kind face with a severe hairdo and the collar of a sacque. Even all these years later her warm eyes still tell us much about her inner self. But it is the second picture, intriguing at best and just plain odd at worst, that makes you want to know her more completely. There she stands in a distinguished pose, shared by women in countless carte de visites. It is not the ever so slight tilt of her head, or even the exceptional sacque she wears, so very long and luxurious that incites curiosity. It's the hat. It is incongruous, and wonderful and maybe even a little outrageous for a woman her age. The picture is delightful and intriguing. Who is she and why is she wearing that amazing, inappropriate hat?

Thankfully, this CDV is not among the innumerable portraits that will remain a mystery to us. Not only do we know the identity of this beguiling woman, we also know some of the story of her beautiful sacque and her quirky hat. Ella Louise Wolcott was an extraordinary woman. On the day these two pictures were made, she was away from the Hammond Hospital at Point Lookout trying to secure provisions for the soldiers in her care. She was often in charge of the fever ward — where many of the hospital's sickest soldiers were sent. Her workload was Herculean, her hours interminable. The physical and emotional strain was enough to break the strongest person but Ella somehow thrived. This was a surprise to her family and friends. Although Ella had always been independent and opinionated, she was never physically strong. In fact, she had spent the thirteen years before the outbreak of the war battling scrofula, a form of debilitating tuberculosis. After exhausting allopathic methods, Ella turned to hydropathy. Living in various Water Cure establishments offered Ella opportunities she would probably not have had in her family home. Well educated but unmarried, Ella may have lived out her life in the home of one of her many brothers or sisters. But at the Water Cures she was independent. She met men and women from all over the country — many of them well known and well educated. She enjoyed vegetarian food, fresh air and exercise. She learned about the healing power of water and the freedom of loose fitting clothing, even the controversial bloomers. Ella learned that comfort was important for her health. She also learned that conventions about clothing were not important to her.

Ella Wolcott.

Knowing all this, the outfit Ella wears in the full-length picture begins to make more sense. Ella's letters reveal her delight in refusing to sacrifice comfort or individuality for fashion convention. In her first face to face meeting with Miss Dorothea Dix, Ella confronted Miss Dix's questions about her health and her hat:

> Monday morning we were on time for Miss Dix — She protested against me as not strong enough and appointed me to what she calls her hardest place — Point Lookout — She said I must dress very warmly — & objected to my hat as unsuited to the service — wanted me to get a bonnet — but I chose rather to get six oz worsted and begin a hood — I have received various hints from her since respecting my poor modest little hat — but I wont[1] get a bonnet! Battle no.1 with Miss Dix![2]

Even though Ella was willing to stand up to Miss Dix, she recognized that her "little brownie"[3] was not considered by most to be appropriate headwear, "I dare not go to church in Washington in my hat."[4]

Apparently, there were other good-natured exchanges with Miss Dix about "brownie." In a letter to her friend Julia J. Beecher, Ella reminisces about the comforts of home and again sticks up for her little hat:

> All these good things which I have as it were <u>possessed myself</u> thro you are a 'joy forever' — like every 'thing of beauty' — so take comfort in your comfortable home — you so share it that you give more than you receive — But oh to think of your bonnet! You! While I so pertinaciously stick to my little brownie! It was rather out of season last month in Washington — & I heard things said in the street when I passed — and Miss Dix offered to give me a bonnet! But I told her I wouldn't wear one![5]

One wonders if the battles over "brownie" were on Miss Dix's mind when she wrote this note to Ella on March 3, 1863:

> You may recollect that the Nurses gave me a memorandum for the purchase of certain articles — shoes — bonnets &c — in yr uncertain state I had felt it so doubtful if you would need these that I have delayed the commission — I should like to oblige all but if there is no need I will not send — inquire & inform me if you please —[6]

The sacque Ella wears was specifically designed for warmth and comfort at her post at Point Lookout. Its loose fit, in place of the more closely fitted paletot, is reminiscent of the comfortable clothing worn at the Water Cure. Ella wrote to her friends in Elmira:

> This will be a very bleak exposed situation in winter — I shall send to you soon for a large box of things — One thing, which is a real bother I ask of you now — I want a cloak of black or brown shag or lion skin — just which you think is best & can easiest procure — I want — I want it nice and warm — you have 'carte blanche' as to price — but as my pocket was picked on Baltimore, I cannot pay for it for perhaps a month — Anybody will trust you or me — Let it be made sacque pattern — I think that which Sarah Young or Zippie has will answer if you can get no better — only it must come quite to the knees and below — If it fits you it will fit me — Let it be lined with flannel after your own taste — Let the outside pockets be large and deep — I have seen some which I liked, somewhat like the enclosed pattern — Let it

be bound or not as you may decide — I think it may be left with raw edge — Perhaps you can get a cloak maker to cut it and Mrs. Young would do the sewing, letting it go towards paying for my wringer.[7]

The extra length and the large pockets are evident in the photograph. The ladies of Elmira had made a particularly fashionable coat with an exceptional collar, cuffs and pockets. Ella was happy to receive the sacque; Point Lookout in early spring was still cold enough to make it necessary.

My cloak is <u>very</u> nice — & I have been glad to wear it even today — I want you to thank all the ladies for me — I found the names of Mrs. Carpenter — Mrs. Gallagher — Mattie Hawthorne, Mary Gleason — Mrs. Murdoch — Mrs. Baker — Sarah Young — & I doubt not many others had a hand in the work — You may be sure I remembered them all with love & gratitude.[8]

Stylish or not, appropriate for her age and station or not, "brownie" stood the test of time. It was important to Ella and it had become a part of her persona. Friends offered to replace it, but Ella held firm to her "brownie."

My little brown hat which I have worn all summer about twenty times a day, & which my men said they liked to see the light veil & the long ribbons fluttering on the one nail where I always hung it in the ward — I washed & turned the ribbons & it will do splendidly — so don't mind about the beaver & the feathers which I did bring with me.[9]

Thanks to Ella's letters, we can look at these photographs and meet, at least two dimensionally, this fascinating woman who looks at us with such warmth. We know her a little better now, independent, generous, and always committed to the cause of the soldiers. She was what many would call the salt of the earth, and she was, to our extreme delight, just a bit quirky.

Endnotes

1. All spellings, abbreviations, underlining, grammar and syntax in the here used quotations are those of the author and not the editor

2. Ella L. Wolcott to Julia J. Beecher, October 24, 1862, Acquisitions, HBSC.

3. Ella L. Wolcott to Julia J. Beecher, December 21, 1862, Acquisitions, HBSC.

4. Ella L. Wolcott to Julia J. Beecher, October 24, 1862, Acquisitions, HBSC.

5. Ella L. Wolcott to Julia J. Beecher, December 21, 1862, Acquisitions, HBSC.

6. Dorothea Dix to Ella Wolcott, March 11, 1863, Folder 59, Josephine A. Dolan Collection.

7. Ella L. Wolcott to Julia J. Beecher, October 31, 1862, Acquisitions, HBSC.

8. Ella L. Wolcott to Julia J. Beecher, April 7, 1863, Acquisitions, HBSC.

9. Ella L. Wolcott to Julia J. Beecher, November 15, 1863, Acquisitions, HBSC.

About the Author

Meg Galante-DeAngelis teaches in the School of Family Studies at the University of Connecticut. She is an Associate of the United States Civil War Center at Louisiana State University and a reviewer for the *Civil War Book Review*. Her lifelong interest in the lives of women and children during the American Civil War had led her to write on many topics of social history, including the patriotic work of children and the images of women in the Civil War era songs and ballads. She is currently editing the extensive papers of the hitherto unknown Civil War heroine, Ella Louise Wolcott.

IF A LADY CAN'T, A WOMAN CAN:
THE WOMEN OF SHARPSBURG

By Kathleen Ernst

When the Civil War began, the women of Washington County, in Western Maryland, were a complex population of white, free black, and slave; Unionist and Secessionist; activist and abstainer. These diverse women, however, were destined to share an overwhelming and horrific experience; the 1862 Maryland campaign, which culminated in the battle of Antietam Creek, or Sharpsburg.

Sharpsburg had been laid out in 1763 and named for the provincial governor of Maryland. In its first century the area attracted farm families, most of British and German descent, but also some French Huguenots, and some from Scotland, Switzerland, and the Alsace Lorraine. Many extended families settled in the area, inter-marrying and putting down roots that in some cases still survive to the present. In 1860 Sharpsburg was a little village of about 1,300 whites. Two hundred and three free blacks also made their home there, although only nine owned property. Sharpsburg was an agricultural service center where laundresses and tavernkeepers and physicians provided to the area residents' basic needs. The Antietam Creek powered several mills and an ironworks. The Potomac River rippled only 3 miles away, with a good crossing spot later known as Blackford's Ford, Boteler's Ford, or Pack Horse Ferry. Intended to serve as seat of Washington County, Sharpsburg lost to Hagerstown by one vote and seemed destined to settle quietly into rural obscurity.

As the national dilemma loomed, this little village in the border state splintered. J. Thomas Scharf, Confederate veteran and author of a history of Western Maryland published in 1882, believed that Maryland suffered more than most states with the coming of the Civil War:

> Public feeling was, perhaps, even more intense in Maryland than in other states, for the obvious danger to which she was exposed by her geographical position in event of conflict between North and South, and from the very strong counter-currents which existed in popular sentiment. This conflict of opinions and sympathies was nowhere more marked than in Western Maryland...[1]

And nowhere else was the geographic situation more pronounced than in Washington County, where it was possible to have breakfast on the Virginia border and lunch in Pennsylvania.

Slavery was not a subject generally discussed in terms of the looming crisis. Farm families in Western Maryland managed relatively small operations, and were much less likely to own slaves than the large-scale tobacco farmers in the south-eastern counties. But slavery did exist in this area, and slave catchers prowled the Maryland-Pennsylvania border plying their ugly business. According to the 1860 census, Washington County was still home to 398 slaveowners and 1,437 slaves. In the Sharpsburg district, 52 slaveowners governed 150 slaves. Seven of those owners were women, who governed from one to seven slaves. Evidence shows, however, that slavery was dying. For example, Sharpsburg's most prominent physician owned three slaves, all sixty-five years or older; he also employed a female domestic servant and a male farm hand.[2] Also, slavery did not necessarily denote political sentiments in Western Maryland. A number of staunch Unionists owned slaves, just as some prominent Secessionists did not.[3]

During the first year and a half of civil war, those women with personal interest had supported their cause, whichever it was, in traditional ways; sewing shirts and housewives, caring for sick soldiers. Unionist women gave their soldier-sons lavish send-offs; Secessionist women bade farewell more discreetly before their boys slipped across the Potomac to Confederate Virginia. Theresa Kretzer, a 21-year-old milliner living in her parents' house on East Main Street, stitched a huge Union flag and hung it from her bedroom window. When Secessionist neighbors tore it down, she suspended the flag over the street from a rope stretched from house to house, out of reach.[4] Federal troops were stationed in the area, so the war was a constant companion. But until General Robert E. Lee brought the Army of Northern Virginia across the Potomac in September, 1862, real war had not descended upon Maryland.

Lee came north for a variety of reasons. He hoped to "liberate" Maryland, and raise recruits. Maryland's agricultural bounty was appealing to men who went to sleep hungry as often as not. The Southerners also wanted to harass his enemy on their own soil, demoralize Northerners, and encourage support from abroad. They splashed into the Potomac River with high hopes and soon descended on Frederick, a prosperous little city east of the mountain ridges bisecting Western Maryland. After a brief stay they moved west toward Catoctin and South Mountains as a Yankee force commanded by Major General George B. McClellan marched from Washington, D. C. in pursuit.

Rumors flew among the tiny villages and hamlets nestled among the mountain ridges in the armies' path. Secessionists were overjoyed to learn of their army's approach. But for many others, the arrival of the Confederate Army was a much more serious affair. Every family faced difficult choices: should they flee to safety, leaving their homes unprotected? Should they stay and face occupation? Many men who had made no secret of their political sentiments feared that their presence might bring the wrath of the opposing army down upon their household. Some feared that they, or their servants or slaves, might be impressed into the Southern army. Others knew their livestock and horses were likely targets.

Consequently, even before the first column marched into view, hundreds of men skedaddled. Some took their wives along. Many did not. "This is a day long to be remembered," one Washington County man wrote in his diary on September 10. "…About 12 or 1 o'clock everything put for the mountain, and there are scarcely anything left but women and children…."[5] Hundreds of women abruptly found themselves alone with their children, left behind to face pending invasion and protect their homes. Many of these lived on isolated farms. They had no way to get news, no way to keep in touch with their loved ones, no way to know what was in store. Angela Davis, a Unionist who lived in a village north of Sharpsburg, felt terribly isolated as the Confederates marched through. "It seemed as if the men came out of the ground like locusts, and their terrible line of march would never cease," she wrote later. "….Soldiers were encamped all around us, and we were completely hemmed in and cut off from the rest of the world. You can have no idea what a terrible feeling this is. It seemed as if there were a dark, thick, high, impenetrable wall between us and the rest of mankind."[6]

For those wives and mothers with loved ones in uniform, the armies' arrival was bittersweet. Some Secessionist women saw their men for the first time in two years. The campaign gave Confederate Jake Heck, from the village of Boonsboro, the opportunity to visit his mother and sister, Sallie. He was enjoying a home-cooked meal the next morning when his brother John, who was serving in the Union army, arrived. After that startling reunion, Jake finished his breakfast and slipped through the lines to rejoin his regiment. Days later, Mrs. Heck and Sallie endured agonies of fear when the battle raged in Sharpsburg, knowing that the brothers were likely both engaged and facing each other.[7]

General Lee still hoped to win Marylanders' support, and his soldiers were under strict orders not to forage. Nonetheless, many families lost livestock and food supplies, and few of those were comforted by Confederate bank notes received in exchange.

And much to the dismay of Unionist civilians, the Yankee soldiers pursuing the Rebels were more troublesome. Despite outpourings of support, some of the Northern boys were uncomfortable with Maryland's divided loyalties, and suspicious of even friendly gestures. The Yankees also had less to gain by polite behavior, and foraged widely. One soldier described the wake left by two armies:

> Each side of the road in the fields was well tramped out by the infantry, the main thoroughfare having been left for the trains. The fences were down entirely. Debris, broken wagons and abandoned property were strewn about everywhere. Telegraph poles and wires were cut and destroyed, and it was quite apparent the only purpose of the pursuers and pursued was to get along as rapidly as possible, regardless of what was lost, mutilated, or forgotten.[8]

Farm families could ill-afford the destruction, but personal calamity was soon eclipsed by the first thunder of real war. The Union column caught up with the Confederates among the high passes on the long ridge of South Mountain. On Sunday, September 14th, the fight raged for hours among rocky terrain as each side tried to push the other down the mountain. Six miles west, Sunday services were interrupted by the distant crash of battle. Nervous Sharpsburg residents stared at the ridge, wondering.

The bloody struggle on South Mountain cost each army dearly: The Confederates lost 2,300 of the 18,000 men engaged and the Federals 1,800 of 28,000. The Southern force still held the high ground as darkness fell, but officers knew they could not hold the ground, and began a quiet retreat. They were under orders to march to Sharpsburg.

Stragglers roamed the countryside as columns splintered on narrow country lanes. The Southern troops treated women living west of South Mountain with less courtesy and discipline than they'd displayed in Frederick. They'd been bloodied badly on South Mountain, and were disappointed with Maryland's response to their arrival. Only a few hundred men had rallied to their cause, and even many Secessionist women they'd encountered—fearing the wrath of Yankee neighbors—didn't dare express their support. Countless Rebel boys still marched barefoot. Most still marched hungry.

September was a busy time of year in the agricultural communities. Women were busy clearing their gardens, and sweating over their stoves as they put up countless batches of preserves and jellies. Porches were piled with mounds of pumpkins and squash. Baskets of early apples and onions waited in root cellars. Women had spread peaches and plums on scaffolds to dry in the sun, and hung the final products in neat muslin bags in their attics. Even the village women kept chickens and cows, and the long back lots were dotted with orchards and gardens.

The soldiers descended like locusts, and quickly emptied abandoned homes of anything edible. A few women who'd stayed behind shrewdly offered meals or bread for sale, but many more fed the gaunt soldiers out of pity or helplessness. "They nearly worried us to death asking for something to eat," a Sharpsburg woman said. "They were half famished and they looked like tramps." A slave who worked at the Otto farm recalled, "The hill at our place was covered with Rebels. They'd walk right into the house and say, Have you got anything to eat? Like they was half starved. ...They ate us out directly. The Union troops, who come onto our place a few days later, wasn't so hungry. The Rebels was always hungry, and the men were miserable dirty."[9]

Some women muffled their horses' hooves with carpet scraps, and wrapped their aprons over the animals' eyes, and spent interminable hours keeping them quiet in their cellars and outbuildings as the columns passed. One wife hid her husband beneath her voluminous skirts when Confederates came searching for men to serve as local guides. Sporadic artillery fire sent families tumbling to their cellars, and did nothing to calm jangled nerves. "There was seven or eight of us [who took shelter in the cellar], white and black," recalled one slave, "and we was all so scared we didn't know what we was doin' half the time."[10]

When word of the Confederates' approach reached Sharpsburg, neighbors descended upon Theresa Kretzer, imploring her to take down her flag. Theresa, described by a contemporary as "fiery and impulsive," complied only reluctantly. She and a friend carefully folded the flag into a strong wooden box and buried it in the ash pile behind their smokehouse. On Tuesday, September 16th, several Confederates—tipped off by sympathetic citizens—arrived at the house and demanded the flag. By her own account, one threatened her with a gun. "It's of no use for you to threaten," she said. "Rather than have you touch a fold of that starry flag I laid it in ashes." Believing that she had burned the flag, the soldiers left.[11]

General Lee had originally planned to retreat back across the Potomac, but he changed his mind. To the residents' dismay, the Confederate force settled into a line about four miles long, stretching across gardens and cornfields and pastures. Soldiers banged on doors, urging people to leave. "The majority of citizens paid little attention to the order, believing it impossible that the roar of battle should disturb their usual quiet," recalled one soldier. "It was evident, though, to us who had been accustomed to seeing preparations made for a battle, that a storm was approaching."[12]

Elizabeth and Samuel Mumma lived with eight children just north of Sharpsburg, near the small church were local German Baptist Brethren (also called Dunkers) gathered for worship. Soldiers instructed the family to vacate their home, and the family quickly began to pack a few belongings. When some preliminary cannonading began, however, the family decided to leave at once. Daughters Lizzie and Allie, angry about their eviction—and about having to leave behind new silk dresses—refused any assistance from the Confederates. The family spent an uncomfortable night on a church floor.[13]

In the center of the Southern line Unionists Elizabeth and Henry Piper managed a busy farm household that included slaves, hired hands, and three generations of Pipers. Confederate Major Generals James Longstreet and D. H. Hill commandeered the home for their headquarters. That evening the nervous Piper daughters served the generals dinner and, in an attempt to be courteous, offered them wine. Longstreet initially refused, but changed his mind after Hill drank some without ill effect. After dinner the men urged the family to leave. Elizabeth buried her dishes in the ash pile and quickly packed what they could carry into a farmwagon. "We left everything as it was on the farm," Mary Ellen Piper recalled later, "taking only the horses with us and one carriage."[14]

Meanwhile, the Federal force was still trotting toward Sharpsburg in pursuit. Civilians living east of Sharpsburg saw the first two Federal divisions appear on Monday afternoon, September 15th. Elizabeth and Philip Pry family owned a prosperous 125-acre farm on a high bluff. According to local tradition, an officer who identified himself as George Armstrong Custer pounded on their door and announced that General McClellan had chosen their home for his headquarters. Soon staff officers hustled about the yard and couriers pounded up and down the dusty drive. Soldiers tore fences down to build a little redan around the command post, and infuriated Elizabeth by hauling her best parlor chairs outside. General McClellan ultimately provided an ambulance to take Elizabeth and children to safety, but the Prys suffered enormous financial losses, from which they never recovered.[15]

The main body of the army didn't arrive until after dark. The next morning, women peeped from their windows nervously. The distant sounds of bugles echoed oddly with the roosters' calls, and farm lanes were still busy with rumbling wagons and couriers pelting back and forth. Many people expected a battle to commence, but for most of that day the Yankees jostled into place on the hills east of Antietam Creek.

The opposing artillery sporadically exchanged fire, adding to the panic and chaos among area residents. According to one account, General Lee was eating breakfast at Delaney's tavern when a shell burst through the wall. The slave cook recalled later, "It busted and scattered brick and daubin' all over everything. There was so much dirt you couldn't tell what was on the table. I was bringing in coffee and had a cup and saucer in my hand. I don't know where I put that coffee, but I throwed it away, and we all got out of there in a hurry."[16]

A few late skedaddlers found the roads jammed and inns overflowing. Some found shelter in a shallow cave near the Potomac. Others begged lodging from friends and relatives who lived at least a few miles from the battle lines. A fierce artillery barrage erupted around dusk, and those civilians still in Sharpsburg crouched in their cellars, trembling with each deafening roar. That night, no one got much sleep.

The Federal assault began at first light on September 17th. Confederate gunners met the barrage with a blast of cannon from the Nicodemus farm near the Hagerstown turnpike. A group of women and children had sought shelter in the Nicodemus cellar, and they found the bombardment unendurable. In the midst of the barrage the door flew open and the terrified women flew outside "like a flock of birds, hair streaming in the wind and children of all ages stretched out behind," wrote Southern cavalryman William Blackford later. Snatching skirts high, clutching little ones, the women stumbled across the rough earth of a freshly-plowed field. "Every time one would fall," Blackford recalled, "the rest thought it was the result of cannon shot and ran the faster." Blackford galloped into the field, brought several of the children up behind him, and escorted the women to safety behind the Southern lines. Gunners on both sides, he noted with approval, held their fire during the rescue.[17]

The earliest phase of fighting swirled around the little Dunker Church and the nearby cornfields and barnyards. The Mumma family's home was so potentially enticing to Yankee sharpshooters that a Confederate general ordered it to be destroyed. A volunteer from North Carolina picked up a chunk of burning wood from a cook fire, carried it to an open bedroom window, and dropped it on the painstaking piecework of a quilt covering the bed. Soon a column of black smoke rose into the morning sky as the house burned. The family lost everything but a watch that had been snatched as they fled from their home before the battle.[18]

During the morning artillery barrage, Sharpsburg also came under heavy fire. One soldier described a few other late skedaddlers trying to scramble out of town:

> It was sad to see so many people deserting their homes, but in all the uproar and confusion I could not restrain a hearty laugh at the many ludicrous sights presented. ...I saw middle aged women running through the streets literally dragging their children after them; the little fellows had to take such tremendous strides that it seemed to me they hit the ground but seldom.

Then came a dozen young ladies, each with a stuffed sack under each arm, some of which in their haste they had forgotten to tie, and as they ran the unmentionables were scattered behind them.

With "cannon shot from the enemy literally rak[ing] the streets and batter[ing]...houses," and women and children "running, crying, and scream-ing so loud that their combined voices could be heard above the roaring battle," the resourceful soldier stopped to examine the ladies' undergarments. "I was in need," he concluded sadly, "but could get none that would fit."[19]

The slave cook who had fed General Lee breakfast the day before was so unnerved by the bombardment that she decided to flee. As she emerged onto the street the first thing she saw was an ambulance passing, with blood drip-ping through the floorboards. She could hear whimpering inside, and one man crying "O Lord! O Lord!" over and over. "We hadn't gone only a couple of houses when a shell busted right over our heads," she remembered later. "So we took back to the cellar in a hurry. The way they was shooting and going on we might have been killed before we was out of town."[20]

Countless women spent the day huddled in cellars or caves, trying to soothe to terrified children. Many found shelter in the Kretzer family's basement on East Main Street, where a natural spring provided water. The Kretzers carried what chairs were available down the stairs, and made additional benches from boards. Some of the younger refugees scrambled onto the bins and shelves used for storing potatoes and apples. "We were as comfortable as we could possibly be in a cellar, but it's a wonder we didn't all take our deaths of cold in that damp place," Theresa Kretzer recalled later. "By the end of the day, some of the people huddled there was on the edge of hysteria. A number of babies were there, and several dogs, and every time the firing began extra hard the babies would cry and the dogs would bark. Often the reports were so loud they shook the walls."[21]

The damp was particularly hard on a woman who had delivered a baby girl on September 10th. Her neighbors fretted about her delicate health, so she and her newborn were carried up into the kitchen. She had been there only a short time when a shell crashed into the house, sending debris flying and setting up a choking cloud of dust and smoke. The terrified mother begged to be returned to the cellar. Bundled into an armchair, she was carried back downstairs. "I'd rather take my chances on taking cold and dying," she said, "than to be killed with a shell or cannon ball."[22]

It was a long day for the hundreds of civilians trapped in their cellars. A few of the mothers had thought to carry enough food for their children, but most of them went hungry as the hours passed. "We had to live on fear," Theresa Kretzer remembered. Many of the women and children cowering in the dark cellars were further terrified that day when Southern soldiers, decid-ing they'd seen enough of the battle, crept down the damp stairs to join them. Six pushed their unwanted company on the group in the Kretzer cellar; one was wounded, his ear "nearly off." When Theresa and her mother slipped to their stable at noon to milk their cows, they found several more hiding in the haymow: "We're tired of fightin,'" one explained.[23]

A few women did brave the barrage. Savilla Miller, a young woman living with her father three doors up the street from the Kretzer home, was at home during the battle. The Millers were staunch Confederate sympathizers, and friends with Henry Kyd Douglas, a local young man now serving in the Confederate army. During the fierce shelling that day, Douglas was astonished to find Savilla calmly passing water to the Rebel soldiers as they retreated, under fire, down Main Street. Concerned for her safety, he urged her to seek safety. "'I will remain here as long as our army is between me and the Yankees,' she replied with a calm voice, although there was excitement in her face. 'Won't you have a glass of water?'" She was still at her post later, when a shell exploded in front of the house, killing one soldier. Savilla escaped unhurt.[24]

Four other young women were evidently staying with Savilla, and when an exploding shell set fire to a house on East Antietam Street, they "rushed to the scene and amidst flying shot and shell and whistling bullets, and armed with basins and buckets, carried water from the little spring in the lot adjoining the house and put out the fire. In a short time it caught again. These young ladies again repaired to the scene and this time was successful in thoroughly extinguishing it."[25]

Meanwhile, many local people from nearby communities were drawn to local hills to watch the battle unfold. Artist Edwin Forbes noted, "The Battle of Antietam was probably the most picturesque battle of the war... Thousands of people took advantage of the occasion, as the hills were black with spectators. Soldiers of the reserve, officers and men of the commissary and quartermasters departments, camp-followers, and hundreds of farmers and their families watched the desperate struggle. No battle of the war, I think, was witnessed by so many people."[26]

In the afternoon, heavy fighting centered around one of the graceful stone bridges spanning Antietam Creek near Sharpsburg. Waltons Grove Farm was located near the lower bridge, known locally as Rohrback's Bridge. In 1862 it was home to Henry Rohrback and his wife, and their daughter Jane Rohrback Mumma's family. That family included young Ada Mumma, just five years old. That morning the family hauled mattresses to the cellar, and Ada initially thought that staying there was great fun. But when Federal Major General Burnside and his staff arrived, curiosity impelled the child to creep up to the porch for a better view. The Yankee general was horrified to see her. "Your family is not in the house...?" he asked Ada's grandfather. "Send them away at once!" Henry refused to leave, but Ada's father decided to risk flight. He, Ada, her slave nurse, and Ada's mother and grandmother settled into their light carriage for their escape. "We had the orchard to cross first," Ada recalled. "The bullets were whistling all around us. One went through my father's hat and several went through the curtains on the carriage. Then I heard a terrible whistling and an explosion which sent the earth and stones in every direction, which I was told was a shell exploding. It was not very far from us and we were all terrified."[27] General Burnside lost five hundred men trying to get across Rohrback's bridge that day, known since as "Burnside's Bridge."

As the afternoon hours inched by, Federal troops slowly pushed the Confederate line back to the outskirts of Sharpsburg. "Sharpsburg was enveloped in the flames of burning buildings, while flocks of terrified pigeons, driven hither and thither by the screaming and bursting of shells, flew round and round in the clouds of smoke," a Confederate cannoneer wrote later.[28] One of Savilla Miller's sisters watched from high ground near the village, and later described the scene in a letter. "That night I thought the whole town was on fire. You may imagine my feelings, thinking of dear papa and all I left. I did not expect to see anything but embers when I returned next day."[29] The homes of two Sharpsburg widows burned down that day, and possibly others as well.[30]

The Yankees were on the verge of winning the day when Confederate reinforcements arrived from Harpers Ferry. Fighting died away around sunset. Sharpsburg Unionists were dismayed to realize that the Confederates still held their village. A few trembling civilians eased open their cellar doors, not knowing what they would find. The familiar landscape was gone, replaced with a ghastly scene. The Confederate gunner wrote in his diary, "Some of the enemy's shells set some of the buildings on fire in Sharpsburg, and the flames threw a red glare on the sky that reflected a pale ghostly light over the battle plain strewn with the upturned faces of the dead."[31] One pregnant woman, alone with her children, had spent the day in her cellar packing bandages and provisions. That evening the little band ventured onto the battlefield, lugging baskets and quilts. One of her daughters later recalled, "There was a red haze from the sunset…the brick of the church was red, and as far as I could see were suffering, crying, or dead men…red, red, red. It was a red stew. I can remember my mother laboring with three big baskets and I holding her skirt, pulling a large bundle along the ground, and all of us, my brothers and sisters, too afraid to cry."[32]

The next day, most civilians and soldiers alike expected a renewed contest. McClellan had over 50,000 troops at hand, many of them fresh; Lee could muster less than 33,000 spent men. But the Confederates didn't withdraw across the Potomac for another day. People who had sought refuge began coming home, and found complete desolation. Dead men and horses and debris littered the roads, and their houses, barns, outbuildings. Soldiers had ransacked the civilians' houses, leaving no food or provisions.

Refugees who had sought shelter at a nearby cave picked their way home through a gruesome landscape. One young girl later told her grandchildren of "stepping over bodies" as they walked.[33] The Grice family started for home on September 18th with old Logan, their pony. One of the Grice daughters recalled that "the dead lay so thick that old Logan would be very careful not to step on any of the dead." That grim debris was too much for Mr. Grice, who was riding Logan. "But [my] mother, a thoroughbred Irish woman of pluck, would shake [my] father and cause him to recover, and make fun of him and tell him to get back on the horse and continue the trip."[34]

When Ada Mumma returned to her home near Burnside's Bridge, she found her grandparents helping the surgeons with dozens of wounded. "I could not sleep," she recalled. "I could hear those poor men calling 'water… for God's sake, give me a drop of water.'"[35] Her grandmother had returned a day ear-lier and found the farmhouse so jammed with wounded that she had to climb in a window. At all·those houses where surgeons were working, residents found piles of amputated limbs heaped outside windows. The stench of death hung in the humid air.

There were over seventeen thousand wounded soldiers in the area. Women pushed aside their own shock in order to help meet those men's overwhelm-ing needs. By dawn on the 18th women were already binding wounds, hold-ing hands, making tea, distributing whatever provisions they could scare up. In some local churches women packed away prayer books while their hus-bands laid planks over pews to make more makeshift beds. In others the pews were ripped out altogether, and hammered into makeshift coffins. Dying men, terrified of being lost among the unknown dead, begged the women to write down their names.

And soon, a new flood descended upon the tiny village: frantic moth-ers and fathers and wives, come to look for wounded or missing relatives. They had few provisions, and nowhere to stay. Somehow the local women—already struggling to care for their children and the wounded—managed to feed and house the newcomers, too. One local woman sadly recalled a young wife who arrived and was met with the news that her husband had died and was already buried:

> Unwilling to believe the facts that strangers told her…she still insisted upon seeing him. Accompanying some friends to the spot she could not wait the slow process of removing the body, but in her agonizing grief, clutched the earth by handfuls where it lay upon the quiet sleeper's form. And when at length the slight covering was removed and the blanket thrown from off the face, she needed but one glance to assure her it was all too true. Then passive and quiet beneath the stern reality of this crushing sorrow she came back to the room in our house.[36]

Taking care of the wounded and their visitors took an enormous toll on the local women. Staunch Confederate Nancy Michael resisted a Federal surgeon's plan to turn her home into a hospital, but without success. The Michael fam-ily was given one room to stay in, and when typhoid fever swept through the crowded home, both soldiers and family members suffered. One Michael daughter died on October 24th; Nancy died a month later. The provost guard billeted across the street inexplicably added to the Michaels' grief by not im-mediately allowing them to remove their daughter's body for burial.[37]

It took months to clear the makeshift hospitals. One girl wrote of caring for wounded soldiers in her barn when everyone else in her family was ill. "[Fa-ther] showed me a chart of the barn which showed the position of each pa-tient on the floor and he indicated in that way which medicine I was to administer to each," she explained later. "I successfully performed this duty but it was not an agreeable one for after each visit I would be covered with vermin…The hospital made it sickly at our home. Although the greatest care was taken and disinfectants were used liberally all about the house, my little sister was taken with typhoid fever and was very ill."[38]

Many people of fragile health died in the dreadful weeks following the battle. Ada Mumma's mother was pregnant when she fled their home near Burnside's Bridge. She delivered a baby girl on October 10th;, the child died immediately and the mother within a month. Ada explained later, "My mother, due to the great amount of excitement, was taken ill and died."[39]

Hundreds of shells, guns, and ammunition lying about created more problems. Women exhorted their sons to leave them alone, but some of the boys could not resist. Several children were killed, and others maimed, while handling the weapons. Other grown men were killed trying to remove unexploded shells from their farm fields. Only one Sharpsburg civilian—a young girl—was killed outright during the 1862 campaign.[40] But in the weeks that followed, dozens of civilians died from bursting shells, one of the epidemics that swept through the crowded hospitals, or other trauma-related problems.

President Abraham Lincoln arrived in Sharpsburg on October 1st, and spent four days viewing the field, visiting hospitals, and meeting with General McClellan. One of the president's stops was Mt. Airy, Maria and Stephen P. Grove's beautiful farm just outside the village, where four hundred men were recuperating or dying. The Groves had sent their children to safety during the battle but had stayed to protect their property, despite repeated requests to leave by the Union soldiers establishing a signal station on their roof. According to family lore, when a well-intentioned officer told Maria that a lady couldn't stay at the house during the battle, she responded, "Sir, if a lady can't, a woman can!"[41]

After the battle of Antietam, the Confederate Army retreated back to Virginia. Some weeks later, the bulk of the Union Army moved on, too. Left behind were the civilians of Western Maryland, still coping with thousands of sick and wounded men, with empty pantries, with root cellars and farmfields stripped bare. Winter was coming, and typhus still lingered in the crowded homes.

The 1862 Maryland campaign was a turning point in the war. The Northern troops trudging through Western Maryland recognized that the civilians they encountered lived in neither the true North nor the true South, and because of the ambivalence, they viewed the Marylanders with both admiration and suspicion. Northern soldiers marching through Maryland experienced for the first time the confusing and painful experience of true civil war, forever blurring the distinction between friend and enemy.

But the South was disillusioned too. The 1862 campaign was the first of three that ventured north of the Potomac, and the last truly embodied with the idealistic chivalry so romanticized in popular culture. The Southern soldiers who splashed onto the Maryland shores were an eager, liberating Army, waiting for the chance to free Maryland, waiting for the promised hordes of new recruits. They forded the Potomac again two weeks later disillusioned, jaded, battered. The Rebels lost more than battles on the campaign. They lost some of their faith.

And the women of Sharpsburg lost their innocence. It was particularly difficult for the Confederate-minded women to spend four years of war living in a state that stayed loyal to the Union, under the eye of Federal troops and

Unionist neighbors. Their soldiers slipped south across the Potomac, out of touch and out of reach. And eventually, more Secessionist women were arrested for their sympathies and support. Some, including Savilla Miller, were detained and questioned and eventually sent home. Some were exiled to Virginia.

The Unionist women struggled too, however. One perceptive soldier from New York noted, "Patriotism in this border State was not confined to sentiment, it was a living principle—intensified by what it cost. It is an easy matter to be a patriot where all are patriots, but not so easy nor safe when surrounded by traitorous neighbors.[42] Echoed a female relief worker who arrived from Pennsylvania, "They felt, what we at the North knew nothing of, that loyalty meant life was at stake, homes deserted, property destroyed, and the friends of early, happier years, all given up,—for what? Devotion to the country, and the flag!"[43]

The 1862 campaign gave the women of Sharpsburg their first opportunity to test their political convictions against not just the noble ring of rhetoric, but the fire and brimstone of battle. They had lived through more than battle, as horrendous as that had been. The women whose war work in 1861 had been stitching flags and baking cakes were by the end of 1862 competently managing monumental relief efforts, and helping their farmer-husbands face complete devastation. The women left alone while their husbands skedaddled, who helped their children recover from witnessing carnage beyond comprehension, and huddled by candlelight in the late autumn to total up financial losses and wonder how they would survive the coming winter—like Maria Grove, they all dredged up a rare courage to confront what they must. And when they provided water to enemy soldiers, when they helped wounded boys say their prayers, and when they opened their homes to devastated mothers and widows, they managed to wring some goodness from overwhelming tragedy.

Endnotes

1. J. Thomas Scharf, *History of Western Maryland* (Philadelphia: L. H. Evarts, 1882), 194. Scharf served in the First Maryland Artillery, CSA, before being appointed to the Confederate States Navy.

2. Eighth Federal Population Census, 1860, Schedule 1 (Free Inhabitants) and Schedule 2 (Slave Inhabitants).

3. For example, Barbara Fritchie of Frederick, the vocal Unionist who became a legend when John Greenleaf Whittier wrote a poem depicting her defiantly confronting Confederate troops, appears on the slaveholders' census for 1860. According to the same census, Frederick lawyer Bradley Tyler Johnson, destined to become a brigadier general in the Confederate army, did not own his one black household servant. In Sharpsburg, Dr. Augustin Biggs, a "strong Union man," owned three slaves in 1860.

4. Fred Cross, "Story of Flag Woman Saved at Antietam" (1929), Antietam National Battlefield Archives. Kretzer family genealogical information courtesy Linda Irvin-Craig, of Hagerstown; and from the Eighth Federal Population Census, 1860. Main Street was known as Front Street by contemporary residents.

5. Otho Nesbitt diary, September 9, 10, 1862, Clear Spring District Historical Association.

6. Angela Kirkham Davis, "War Reminiscences: Letter," Western Maryland Room, Washington County Free Library.

7. John H. Bast, Sr., *History of Boonsboro*, Western Maryland Room, Washington County Free Library. The service records of these two men are not clear. Private Jacob Heck of Boonsboro is listed on the roster of Company G, Second Maryland Infantry, CSA; however, this unit did not form until after the battle of Antietam. Possibly Jacob Heck served in a Virginia unit during the first portion of the war. Federal rosters list two John Hecks.

8. The Survivors' Association, *History of the Corn Exchange Regiment, 118th Pennsylvania Volunteers, from the First Engagement at Antietam to Appomattox* (Philadelphia: J. L. Smith, 1892), 35.

9. Clifton Johnson, *Battlefield Adventures: The Stories of Dwellers on the Scenes of Conflict in Some of the Most Notable Battles of the Civil War* (Boston: Houghton Mifflin, 1915), 119 & 104.

10. Johnson, *Battlefield Adventures*, 110.

11. Johnson, *Battlefield Adventures*, 118-119. See also "A Rival for Barbara Fritchie;" "Story of Flag at Antietam," *The Daily Mail*, January 30, 1934; and "Story of Flag Woman Saved at Antietam," all in Antietam National Battlefield Archives.

12. NAT Letter (unidentified Confederate soldier), October 6, 1862, courtesy Al Fiedler, Jr.

13. O(liver) T. Reilly, *Battlefield of Antietam* (Hagerstown, Md.: Self-published, 1906), 20; Virginia Mumma Hildebrand Collection, Western Maryland Room, Washington County Free Library.

14. Appendix A, 141, Claim of Henry Piper vs. the United States, No. 445 Congressional Case December Term, 1886-87, Testimony of Mary Ellen (Piper) Smith, copy in Antietam National Battlefield Archives. Mary Ellen, one of the Piper daughters, was being questioned in conjunction with her father's efforts to receive compensation for the devastating financial damages the farm suffered at the hands of Union soldiers during the campaign. See also Reilly, *Battlefield of Antietam*, 54.

15. Gary Scott, Architectural Historian, National Park Service, *The Philip Pry House — Historic Structures Report*, November, 1980, copy in Antietam National Battlefield Archives.

16. Johnson, *Battlefield Adventures*, 110-111. Johnson did not identify by name any of the people he interviewed. The slave referred to her "boss" as Mr. Delaney and identifies herself as "cook at Delaney's Tavern," but neither the tavern or the inhabitants have been corroborated by secondary sources (unlike other subjects and stories in Johnson's book). The woman clearly dated the incident with Robert E. Lee as September 17th, but given what historians know of the general's movements, it seems likely that the incident happened on the 16th.

17. W(illiam) W. Blackford, *War Years with Jeb Stuart* (New York: Charles Scribners' Sons, 1945), 151.

18. Reilly, *Battlefield of Antietam*, 20; see also Hildebrand Collection, correspondence between James F. Clark and Samuel Mumma, 1906.

19. NAT Letter, October 6, 1862.

20. Johnson, *Battlefield Adventures*, 111.

21. Johnson, *Battlefield Adventures*, 120.

22. Reilly, *Battlefield of Antietam*, 23, story attributed to Theresa's older sister Anne Kretzer; The Obstetrical Records of Dr. Augustus (sic) Biggs, of Sharpsburg, Washington County, Maryland, 1836-1888, transcribed by Rosamund Ann Ball, Western Maryland Room, Washington County Free Library. Biggs recorded births only in the fathers' names.

23. Johnson, *Battlefield Adventures*, 120-121; Hildebrand Collection.

24. Henry Kyd Douglas, *I Rode with Stonewall*, (Chapel Hill: University of North Carolina Press, 1940), 170-171. See also Reilly, *Battlefield of Antietam*, 18; John P. Smith, "Reminiscences of Sharpsburg, Maryland," *Antietam Valley Record*, September 26, 1895.

25. Smith, "Reminiscences of Sharpsburg, Maryland." See also Jacob Miller collection, Antietam National Battlefield Archives. The girls were apparently staying with Savilla Miller. Although Savilla and Jeanette were close in age, correspondence in the Miller collection suggests that Jeanette was Savilla's older sister Elizabeth's daughter. Clara Brining was daughter of cabinetmaker and one-time militia captain John C. Brining of Boonsboro.

26. Edwin Forbes, *Thirty Years After: An Artist's Memoir of the Civil War* (Baton Rouge and London: Louisiana State University Press, 1993), 258.

27. Recollections of Ada Mumma Thomas, June, 1934, in Hildebrand Collection.

28. Edward A. Moore, *The Story of a Canoneer Under Stonewall Jackson* (New York and Washington: Neale Publishing Company, 1907), 154-155.

29. Elizabeth Miller letter, February 8, 1863, Miller collection. She added, "The shels were all from the yankies that made all this distruction and distress...."

30. Scharf, *History of Western Maryland*, 251-252; Thomas Ellis, M.D. *Leaves from the Diary of an Army Surgeon* (New York: John Bradburn, 1863), 297; Nesbitt diary, September 29, 1862.

31. George M. Neese, *Three Years in the Confederate Horse Artillery* (New York and Washington: Neale Publishing Company, 1911), 126.

32. Margaret Beltemacchi, letter to Rep. Goodloe Byron, June 3, 1971, Antietam National Battlefield Archives.

33. Maxine Campbell, May 1, 1997. The child was the daughter of Jenny Bragounier Lumm and Solomon Lumm. Solomon Lumm was a miller; he and his wife had a three-year-old and a five-year-old daughter in 1862.

34. Reilly, *Battlefield of Antietam*, 23; Hildebrand Collection.
35. Hildebrand Collection.
36. H(olstein) Mrs. (Anna), *Three Years in Field Hospitals of the Army of the Potomac* (Philadelphia: J. B. Lippincott Company, 1867), 13.
37. Samuel Michael letter, November 27, 1862, Antietam National Battlefield Archives.
38. Thomas J. C. Williams, *History and Biographical Record of Washington County* (John M. Runk and L. R. Titsworth, 1906), 361-362.
39. Hildebrand Collection.
40. Several accounts mention a Sharpsburg child dying, and an unverified account identifies that child as a girl; see Ellis, 297; David Hunter Strother, *A Virginia Yankee in the Civil War: The Diaries of David Hunter Strother* (Chapel Hill: University of North Carolina Press, 1961), 114.
41. Hildebrand Collection.
42. Isaac Hall, *History of the 97th Regiment of New York Volunteers (Conkling Rifes) in the War for the Union* (Utica; Press of L. C. Childs and Sons, 1890), 82-83.
43. H(olstein), *Three Years in Field Hospitals*, 24.

About the Author

Kathleen Ernst is a social historian and educator who writes and speaks often about civilian life during the Civil War. She has a Masters Degree in History Education and Writing from Antioch University and served for twelve years as a Curator of Education with the State Historical Society of Wisconsin at Old World Wisconsin Public Television.

Kathleen's first nonfiction book, *Too Afraid to Cry: Civilians in the Antietam Campaign*, was an alternated selection of the History Book Club. Publication credits also include *Civil War Times Illustrated*, *America's Civil War*, and *Columbiad*. Her work for young people includes a series of historical novels about the Civil War (*The Night Riders of Harper's Ferry*, *The Bravest Girl in Sharpsburg*, *Retreat from Gettysburg*, and the forthcoming *Ghosts of Vicksburg*) and two historical mysteries. *Retreat from Gettysburg* won the Arthur Toffle Juvenile Fiction Award in 2001 and one of her mysteries was nominated for the Edgar Allan Poe Award for Best Children's Mystery, 2001, by the Mystery Writers of America.

"They Called Her Captain"

THE AMAZING LIFE OF EMILY VIRGINIA MASON

By Karen Rae Mehaffey

Introduction

I was introduced to Emily Mason in 1997 by means of a little booklet published by The Jeweler's Daughter.[1] The booklet was a reprint of an *Atlantic Monthly* article published at the turn of the century. Penned for profit, it was a series of reminiscences conveying the story of Emily's life during the Civil War. Since then, Emily has always been with me, invading my research and pulling at my heartstrings. I finally gave into her last year and agreed to research and write her story.

Though from a prominent family and herself a published author, Emily has been publicly elusive. My research revealed that there had never been an article or book written about her. Yet here was a woman that came from a wealthy First Family of Virginia, counted the Lees and Monroes as close, personal friends, had a brother who was governor of Michigan, and had published the first, post-war biography of Robert E. Lee. Letters and trips to archives, libraries, and sojourns on the Internet have slowly revealed the elusive Emily. As is typical in researching many women of the 19th century, regardless of their significant contributions to society, they were still women and their allotted place was in the home. It was unthinkable to produce a biography of a woman of society, particularly one so well connected as Emily. Her place in history was as the capable and well-bred daughter, sister, and aunt of warriors and politicians of the 19th century. What is provided here is Emily as I have found her to date with anticipation that she will continue to evolve her tale.

Family History

The Masons of Virginia were one of the most respected families in the "Old Dominion." Thomson Mason, Emily's great-grandfather, came from England with his brother, George Mason, later the author of the first "bill of rights" of Virginia.[2] Two of her uncles and her paternal grandfather were U.S. senators from Virginia.[3] This same grandfather, Stevens Thomson Mason, was an aide to General Washington at Yorktown during the American Revolution. The family home, named "Raspberry Plain", was in Fairfax County, Virginia, and boasted James Monroe as a neighbor.[4] Into this illustrious family was born Emily's father, John Thomson Mason. Good-natured and educated as a law-

Emily Mason.

Collection of the Bentley Historical Library,
Univ. of Michigan, Ann Arbor.

yer at William and Mary, John married Elizabeth Moir who was from an affluent, Scottish family of Williamsburg.[5] Established at Raspberry Plain with the prospect of being a gentleman farmer and lawyer, Mason grew restless as was apparently his nature. He got involved in several financial schemes losing much of his fortune and decided to seek an appointment out West. Mason was given an opportunity to practice law in Lexington, Kentucky, moving his wife and new son, Stevens, there in 1812.[6] With a library of books and little money in hand, the family established themselves and continued to grow.

Emily Virginia Mason was born in Lexington on October 15, 1815. (The Masons would have thirteen children but only four would survive to adulthood.) In the same year, John Mason had done well enough to purchase a 300-acre estate and moved his family into the house he named "Serenity Hall". In 1819 Emily's father lost the money he had managed to earn through worthless financial schemes.[7] In 1824 Emily's paternal grandmother died leaving the Raspberry Plain estate to her father. This must have eased their financial distress and John Mason had the slaves he inherited from his mother sent to Kentucky to work at Serenity Hall plantation.[8]

Emily's early life was spent in relative comfort in Lexington and she was groomed to be a plantation mistress. By 1825 she was enrolled as a student at Colonel Denham's school and later, "in the French school of Madame Mantelli." Emily rode to school on a pony, chaperoned by her brother, and took dance and French lessons. Living in genteel society among other Southern families, her early life was carefree. Though Lexington provided a pastoral childhood for little Emily, her life was about to change.

John Mason grew restless in Kentucky and longed to be involved in the expansion of new territories. A friend aided him in getting an appointment to be Territorial Secretary of Michigan at $1200.00 per year. John and his son, Stevens, left Lexington in the summer of 1830 for the frontier atmosphere of Michigan territory. Emily, her mother, and her sisters had the household packed up and joined them in the fall.[9] After the Southern gentility of Lexington society, the Mason women were somewhat appalled at Detroit. Built on a river, it was a shipping, lumber, and mining town, with dirt streets, Indians, and an open sewer running through the center of the city. But the Masons rented a fine brick home and established residence. The elder Mason suffered public life in the hands of his political rivals in the city where territorial disputes were hot. Stevens, on the other hand, seemed to enjoy a good argument (and an occasional fist fight) and protected his father during the many heated arguments they encountered in public. John Mason only lasted a year in Detroit, much to his wife's relief, securing a political ambassadorship to Mexico. In the summer of 1831, John Mason and his wife headed for the Southwest, leaving the girls with their brother. In July 1831, Stevens was appointed in his father's place at the tender age of nineteen.[10]

While her parents flitted to the Southwest, Emily and her siblings continued their education in Detroit. In 1830-31, Emily and sister Kate attended a small academy run by Belgian Catholic sisters. In 1832 they were taking French lessons and various academic subjects from a Fr. Kundig and a Fr. Bowdoel.[11] (This time with the Catholic sisters and priests would have a profound effect on Emily. Though she was raised Episcopal, she would convert to Catholicism in the 1850's and remain a devout Catholic all of her long life.) Emily's formal education was briefly continued in Troy, New York, at the school of Mrs. Emma Willard. Though at a distance, her father supervised the education of his daughters and made sure that they were trained in the classics. Emily was now an adolescent and saw her education come to an end. As the eldest daughter, she oversaw the cooking and cleaning of the family home and entertained visitors and her brother's friends.

After her brief time in New York, Emily returned to Detroit in the summer of 1833. Now seventeen, Emily took on the full-time role of hostess for her brother while continuing to look after her sisters. Emily's brother became governor of the Michigan territory in the fall of 1833 at the age of 21. Suddenly, Emily was the mistress of the first governor's home in Michigan and helped lead local society. The next several years were spent looking after her brother's affairs, keeping the household books, entertaining, and maintaining their home in the midst of scandal. Known as a Unionist, Stevens felt strongly in a territorial dispute with Ohio, fighting for a strip of land that included Toledo. In spite of the political issues, Stevens raised money for the territory, helped see Michigan through a cholera epidemic, and raised troops to fight in the Black Hawk War. His fiery personality and strong views kept him in the local papers, but also made him popular with the frontiersmen of the state. He was reelected in 1837 and married a New York belle on November 1, 1838.[12]

By 1839 Emily's life of pleasant socializing and education began to unravel again. Stevens decided not to run for governor for a third term and left his office in political turmoil. That same year, their mother died after a brief illness. Stevens, his wife, and sisters, stayed on in Detroit and Stevens started what would be an unsuccessful law firm. In 1840 Emily's sister, Kate, married a man named Isaac Rowland and started a family in Detroit. In 1841 Stevens would remove his wife and new daughter to New York City. Emily and her sisters returned eventually to Virginia, though the exact date is unknown. Emily was still in Detroit in December of 1842 when she wrote her father and complained he had not come for Christmas. On January 5, 1843, Stevens Mason died of pneumonia in New York.[13] Emily returned to Virginia, but traveled extensively with her sisters, visiting friends and family in Washington, Texas, New Orleans, and Arkansas.

In 1845 Emily and her sister, Laura, accompanied their father to Fort Gibson which was in the territory that would become the state of Oklahoma. John Mason was appointed Commissioner to the Cherokees and would settle at the Fort while establishing his new role. Emily and Laura were two of only ten women at the Fort and the young women were caught up in a series of picnics, dances, carriage rides, and formal calls by enthusiastic soldiers. Emily remained unmoved by the attention, considering herself too old for such attentions. Emily did carry on a "friendship" with Detroiter Lewis Cass, Jr., the son of Governor Lewis Cass. Emily and Lewis knew each other since childhood and Cass was a good friend of Stevens Mason. Though there was never any confirmation of

Emily's love for Lewis, he spoke of his missing her and his great affections for her in his letters sent to Fort Gibson. (Year's later, Emily and Lewis would meet again in Europe, where he had been sent as Ambassador to Italy. Lewis died in Rome and Emily returned with his body to Detroit. She was executor of his will and inherited part of his estate.)

While still at Fort Gibson, Laura Mason met and fell in love with a dragoon from the Fort, named Robert Chilton. Her father disapproved of the union as the Chiltons and the Masons had at one time dueled and the Masons took the worst of the affair. But with persistence, Robert continued to see Laura and write her father for his approval. Consent was given for the marriage after Thomson Mason surprised his daughters and announced his own marriage. Robert and Laura planned a whirlwind wedding and traveled to Virginia for a brief honeymoon. During the Civil War, Robert became an aide to General Robert E. Lee.[14]

In 1850, John Mason died in Galveston, Texas, leaving Emily and her sisters in utter poverty.[15] This ended Emily's traveling and she returned to Virginia to assist with disposal of the family home. Emily was offered a home with several families but she refused to rely on others. With what little inheritance she had, she purchased a small farm in Fairfax County, Virginia, and moved her now-widowed sister, Kate, and Kate's children, (two sons and twin daughters) into the house.[16]

Now thirty-five years of age, Emily was responsible for a household of relatives and a small, working farm. She was known for being independent and took on the job of painting and wallpapering the inside of the farmhouse, redecorating it to her tastes. In a book published right after the war, Emily was listed as one of the "queens of society" and was remembered for her personal zeal at farming. It was noted that, "On one occasion a carriage full of elegantly dressed ladies, from Washington-only ten miles distant-came to the house. The visitors found Miss Emily in the stable loft, putting away and salting down the fodder; but she came in blooming from her work with a pleasant greeting for her friends, and, like true Southerners, they did not admire her less for doing what was needed with her own hands..." Another account in the same essay verifies Emily's practical attitude. "...A young gentleman of her acquaintance was wont to declare that the hatchet and nails were handed round whenever he went to visit [Miss Mason], as cake and wine would be handed at another house!"[17] But the peaceful life at Fairfax would end abruptly with the outbreak of civil war.

War Years

By spring 1861, Emily recognized the very real danger she and her family were in by remaining in Fairfax. Though no less than fifteen families of cousins lived in the neighborhood, they feared the developing armies. Emily resolved to save her home but without success. As she noted, "barricading, at night, windows and doors with tables, piano, and bookcases, we were alarmed by thumps upon the doors and threats to break in; and at mealtimes soldiers would enter and devour everything which was set before us."[18] Living in fright, sister Kate and her children refugeed south ten miles with one trunk and a hired carriage, leaving Emily behind. Within days, the house and contents were forcibly taken as the headquarters of Major General Phillip Kearny of New Jersey. Emily was forced to take a few clothes and leave her home, never to live there again.[19] After her departure, the greenhouse, carriage, fencing, and most of her personal effects were destroyed or stolen. This included most of her saved correspondence, explaining why much of her late antebellum record is missing. She went North, at the request of her niece (Steven's daughter) who was ill and needed nursing. Ironically, the niece, Eliza, was married to an officer on General Winfield Scott's staff of the Union Army.

Emily arrived in New Jersey to a cool welcome by the locals. Announced in the local papers as a "secesh spy", she was accused of seeking information for General P. G. T. Beauregard and coming to arouse the Catholics and Democrats of the North. She remained in New Jersey for approximately five months, but was ready to leave long before then. Due to the unfriendly atmosphere and outrageous antics such as residents stealing her mail and harassing her in the street, it was not considered safe for her to return South.[20]

Emily finally formulated a plan to return home. She went by train to Philadelphia and then took a train to Kentucky to cousins in Newport. Arriving in Kentucky about November 2, 1861, she hoped to enter Virginia and went to the Archbishop of Cincinnati for help. After several weeks of waiting, it was arranged that Emily would travel with a group of men from the Federal government carrying provisions to the Union Army in Virginia.[21] Provided with a letter to Major General William S. Rosecrans, who was an old family friend, Emily set out for a three-week trip by boat. The men were agents from Boston and assumed that Emily was going to nurse the Union wounded. After arriving in Virginia, Emily had a telegram sent to General Rosecrans requesting passage south. A flag of truce, a servant, and ambulance were sent the next morning.[22]

What happened that night while she waited for her transportation would change the course of her life. Emily recalled looking up to the cliff from the boat and noticed wagons had arrived. The teamsters set up planking to the boat deck, apparently planning to load supplies. She observed that the bundles being sent down the plank were large and heard groans. When she inquired as to what they were, she was informed that they were sick men. Emily remembered in her own words, "'An outrage upon humanity', I exclaimed, and ran down the companionway to examine the live bundles, which were coughing, groaning, and moaning. Here were men in all stages of measles, pneumonia, camp fever, and other disorders incident to camp life, sent in wagons over thirteen miles of mountain road, on a December evening, without nurses, without physician, and with no other covering than the blanket in which each man was enveloped."[23] Without food or medicine on board and with the hospital twenty miles away, Emily feared the men would die. Thirty men lay on the boat in need of care. She demanded help from the boatmen, who staunchly refused. She returned to her cabin, found a box of crackers, and stole tea from the cabin of one of her traveling companions. She fed all of the men, had them settled, and watched over them. In her words, "...this was the beginning of my ministrations amongst soldiers, which lasted to the end of the war, and which became the life of my life."[24] The life of my life. This statement seems to ring true for so many women that truly found themselves in their work during the Civil War.

The next morning the ambulance and driver arrived for Emily. They traveled through sleet and rain to a large, Union camp where she stayed at a plantation home nearby. Emily commented that the trip was wearing due to bad weather, being in "enemy" territory, and the fact that a few of the enlisted men who had been assigned to her were thieves. They stole her combs, her brushes, and even her prayer book from the wagon.[25] After another day of travel, she arrived at a Confederate camp where a physician helped her to find shelter in a local house. While there, she discovered seven soldiers from Tennessee housed in an out-building without food, water, or care. She boiled rice water for them, prayed with them, and arranged for a military doctor to come and care for them. She also promised to have them transported to Richmond for care and was as good as her word.[26]

The last leg of her journey was spent traveling to Richmond. She took a young, very sick officer with her by coach and managed to find him care along the way. She finally arrived in Richmond at night and was dropped in the street by the coach. Not knowing where to find her family, she started walking down the streets looking for a familiar home. She recognized her cousin, Mrs. Sidney Smith Lee, through a window and was reunited with family. Her family was taken aback on seeing her, thinking she had been placed in a Yankee prison, based on rumors they had heard. She rested for a few days, visited friends and family, and planned again to travel. President Jefferson Davis, being a family friend, blessed her work and provided her carte blanche for free transportation, hospital stores, and nurses.[27] Emily had found her place in the war effort.

Emily returned to the Virginia mountains, traveling with an enslaved manservant. She referred to him as, "Jim, ...her cook, nurse, maid, and sympathizer."[28] Emily set up her first hospital at Greenbriar, White Sulphur Springs, a place for water cures. A family by the name of Caldwell owned the springs and, with their support and the help of a few friends and Jim, they established a small, medical facility that treated men from Florida, Georgia, Alabama, and the Carolinas. The men were treated and sent on to city hospitals as transportation and weather allowed. Due to her connections with the Catholic Church, Emily received an offer from the Bishop of Charleston to have several of the Sisters of Mercy come and provide service at Greenbriar. The Sisters arrived on Christmas Eve of 1861. From them she learned nursing techniques, and they organized the little hospital. Emily wrote, "The men were shy of them at first, few of them having seen a Catholic, much less a 'Sister'. But very soon my pet patients hesitatingly confessed: 'You see, captain, (as I was called), they are more used to it [than] you are. They know how to handle a fellow when he is sick, and don't mind a bit how bad a wound smells.' It was not that they loved me less, but they loved the Sisters more — and I forgave them."[29] Not an official military facility and removed from more advanced care, many men died of illness at Greenbriar, and were buried in unmarked graves. Emily noted in a magazine article that she returned to the springs in 1889 and was overcome with the loss, as even she had a hard time locating the place where the makeshift cemetery had been.[30]

In the spring of 1862 Federal troops moving in forced Emily and the hospital staff to fall back to Charlottesville. When the Seven Days Battle ensued, she was sent to Lynchburg. There she cared for wounded in the Methodist College building and stayed with a local family who also provided makeshift stores for the hospital. Her sister, Kate, who had refugeed from their farm in 1861, had been nursing men since Manassas at Warrenton Springs, now with two sons in the Confederate Army. She joined Emily at Lynchburg and Charlottesville.[31]

In the summer of 1862, Emily was asked to go and act as matron of Camp Winder hospital near Richmond.[32] Camp Winder would be one of eleven hospitals opened in Richmond during the War. Organized in six divisions, the hospital could care for 4800 patients at a time and included a dairy, an icehouse, a bakery, gardens, and two canal boats for transportation. Winder would admit 76,000 patients between 1862 and 1865.[33] Emily and her sister, Kate, administered to the Georgia Division with approximately 800 men.[34]

Emily's work at Winder meant understanding the men of Georgia. She wrote letters for them, sang to them, prayed with them, and tried to make their favorite foods based on geographic preferences. One of those was sweet potato pudding.[35] As food became scarce, Emily was forced to use peas for nearly every meal. She boiled, baked, or fried them or put them in a pudding. But the steady diet of one food caused the men to break into a terrible food fight one day. Emily wrote, "...like naughty schoolboys, I found these men throwing my boiled peas at one another, pewter plates and spoons flying about, and the walls and floors covered with fragments of the offensive viand."[36] After a severe chastising, the men cleaned up the mess and apologized. In April of 1863, Emily had her own bread riot at Winder. She recounted that the meek, little steward for her division came to her pale and thoroughly frightened. The patients were convinced that the steward was holding back meat and bread provided by the quartermaster. The men had stormed the bakery, beaten the baker, and had thrown the bread about the yard. Emily wrote, "I hurried to the scene of war, to throw myself into the breach before the surgeon should arrive with the guard to arrest the offenders."[37] She found 200 excited men threatening to hang the steward because they felt he withheld rations. She declared, "And what do you say to the matron?...Do you think that she, through whose hands the bread must pass, is a party to the theft? So you accuse me, who have nursed you through months of illness, making you chicken soup when we had not seen chicken for a year, forcing an old breastbone to do duty for months...who gave you a greater variety of peas than was ever known before, and who latterly stewed your rats when the cook refused to touch them? And this is your gratitude!"[38] To Emily's surprise, the men burst into laughter and cheered "their captain." Then they actually <u>fought over</u> who would go to the guardhouse. A few days later, two patients brought her a piece of scribbled paper and a ring, purchased with funds each Georgia man had donated. "It was the ugliest little ring ever seen, but it was "pure gold" as were the hearts which sent it." The ring is now in the Museum of the Confederacy.[39]

Emily's stamina not only meant thoughtful care for the Confederate soldiers that she loved, but for others as well. She made weekly trips to Belle Isle to visit Libby Prison. There she made sure sick men received a visit from the doctor, changed bandages, and cooked delicacies for the sick. As smallpox was a dangerous problem throughout the war, its victims were separated from other patients and often received poor care. Emily recalled a tent of smallpox patients kept near Hollywood Cemetery. Knowing they received little care, she often made trips to the tent at night carrying a basket of food and salves for their sores. She considered these men some of her favorites.[40] As the War progressed, most of the male nurses were pressed into military service, leaving female nurses and volunteers to care for the ever-growing numbers of wounded. In order to maintain supplies for the hospital, Emily was forced to travel to Georgia, begging goods for her men. She remembered traveling by boxcar with the soldiers, using her carpetbag for a pillow. In between trains, she slept with the men on the station platforms. In her travels, civilians provided sheeting, food, clothing, rags, herbs, and anything they could.[41] When Emily returned to Richmond with supplies, she was told of Major General J.E.B. Stuart's death. She immediately visited the place where Stuart lay and viewed Jefferson Davis kneeling at Stuart's deathbed. Later that week, she walked in his funeral procession.[42]

In 1865, Emily witnessed the Fall of Richmond. After watching the people evacuate on foot and in wagon from the steps of the Camp Winder hospital, Emily's sister begged her to come and protect her. With typical pluck, Emily grabbed a South Carolinian soldier by the name of Sandy and asked he come as her guard. They went on foot, passing burning buildings, falling walls, and looters. She arrived safely at her sister's, but realized that Mrs. Robert E. Lee was stranded in her home just a few doors down. Buildings were burning and Mrs. Lee was wheelchair-bound. Emily and a cousin headed on foot to the capitol, now used as the military headquarters, and demanded transportation for the Lee family. Major General Godfrey Weitzel provided guards and five ambulances, allowing Emily to evacuate the Lee's, as well as the sick and very young from the immediate neighborhood.[43]

Emily's final nursing experience would be with the enemy. Once the Union Army took the city, Emily encountered an old friend, Dr. Alexander Mott, a Union surgeon. Desperate for help, he asked Emily to go the Union Officer's Hospital. There she nursed captured Confederate officers, but was soon asked to help in the Black Wards. She discovered many black soldiers who refused care from the black male nurses and white doctors. They were primarily Southern men (refugeed slaves), and had been used to being nursed when ill by their white mistress or their family. They quickly grew comfortable with Emily's southern demeanor and let her wash them and dress their wounds. Emily remained with the Union hospital well after Appomattox. As the hospital duties wound down, she left Richmond to seek out what was left of her little farm. Most of it had been burned and black refugees had taken over what was left.[44]

Post War

After visiting friends and resting briefly, Emily had already begun a new project. As the war ended, several people had approached Emily with concerns for little girls that had been orphaned during the War or had lost contact with their family. Knowing Emily's fortitude, family ties, and influence, they asked her to take in these girls and find them homes. What started as just a few young ladies would blossom into the care over thirty girls between 1865 and 1867. Many of these children came to her through refugees that had settled along the Rappahannock. Burned out of their homes, they were living a makeshift existence along the river. Emily started gathering food and clothing for these people and made weekly trips to deliver them. She would travel by steamer between Baltimore and Fredericksburg gathering supplies to disperse.[45]

In January of 1868 Emily wrote to a friend about placing children in Kentucky, North Carolina, Missouri, and other Southern states with individual families and with orders of Catholic nuns. In this letter she specifically comments on two young ladies from North Carolina by the name of Johnston. Before the war the girls had had a German governess and came from a family that owned two plantations. When the war ended, they had no family to care for them and nothing of their own. They came to Emily with an envelope containing their fortune which was a worthless Virginia Treasury note from 1862.[46]

In order to help pay for her debts due to the orphans she cared for, Emily collected original poems by Confederate authors, and arranged to publish them in Baltimore. Entitled *The Southern Poems of War*, they were published in 1867 and a revised edition was published in 1868.[47] The popular little book brought in revenue and settled her debts, making sure that she could provide for her orphans. In 1868 Emily was invited by a close friend to travel to Europe. Having settled her orphans and paid off her debts, Emily gratefully accepted. They traveled to see the historic sites and remained on the continent until 1871.[48]

On returning to America, the pilot of the tug that brought their ship into harbor informed the passengers that Robert E. Lee had died. Heartbroken at the loss of her long-time friend, Emily immediately formed the plan to write the first authorized biography of Robert E. Lee with Mrs. Lee's permission. Hardly a complete or balanced biography, the manuscript was a tribute to the life of Lee and part of the early cult development of the "Lost Cause." Mrs. Lee edited the entire manuscript and requested that large passages be removed that showed anything negative or stern in Lee's character. As Emily wrote in the preface, "Other writers will exhibit his public life, his genius... I wish to show more of his domestic character and private virtues..."[49] Mason's biography reached minor success, primarily with readers in the South.

After publication of Lee's biography, Emily continued to experience wanderlust and returned with female friends to Europe. While in Paris, she met an accomplished Frenchwoman from a private school for American girls. She asked Emily to be her vice-principal as most of the girls were daughters of Confederate ex-patriots. Emily took the position, and remained in Paris for almost fourteen years. During her summers in Europe, Emily traveled with her students, taking them to various religious sites in the Middle East. She also made several trips to Rome and to England.[50]

In 1885, Emily returned to America and purchased a small farm in Howard County, Maryland that she named "Westwood". She continued to travel extensively, summering in New York, Canada, and Europe.[51] She counted among her close associations the Lee daughters, her own niece, Kate Rowland, LaSalle Corbell Pickett, Myrta Lockett Avary, Jefferson and Varina Davis, and many other Civil War associates.

One of Emily's final public acts was for her long dead brother, Stevens, who had been buried in Marble Cemetery in New York City upon his death in 1843. But his great love had been the state of Michigan and the Detroit he helped develop. Through her efforts, Emily arranged to have Stevens exhumed and transported to Detroit where he was reintured on June 4th, 1905 on the site just below where his office as governor had been.[52] Emily spent the last few years of her life quietly; writing letters and receiving visitors and younger admirers. She remained a devout Catholic, never married, and considered her devotion to the "Lost Cause", the Church, and her extended family the most important issues in her life. She died on Feb. 16, 1909, at the age of 93 and was buried in Baltimore.

Emily is gone but her life and work are a testament to the quiet strength of American women. Over a century ago, Southern soldiers in a wartime hospital recognized that strength when they called a tall, dark-haired woman, "captain".

Endnotes

1. Mason, Emily V., *Memories of a Hospital Matron*, MD: Jeweler's Daughter, 1996.
2. "Emily V. Mason," *The National Cyclopedia of American Biography*, NY: Jason T. White & Co., 1893, p.516.
3. Tardy, Mary T., "Miss Emily Mason," *The Living Female Writers of the South*, PA: Claxton, Renisen, & Haffelfinger, 1872, Reprint MI: Gale Research, 1978, p.439.
4. Baker, Patricia, "Stevens Thomson Mason," http://www.sos.state.mi.us/history/museum/techstuf/setting/mason.html. The Michigan Historical Museum website, Accessed 06/08/00, p. 1.
5. Mason, p.viii (timeline).
6. Baker, p.1.
7. *Ibid*.
8. Hemans, Lawton T., *Life and Times of Stevens Thomson Mason*, MI: The Michigan Historical Commission, 1930, p.29.
9. Baker, p.1.
10. *Ibid*, p.2.
11. Hemans, p.49.
12. Weeks, George, *Stewards of the State: The Governors of Michigan*, MI: The Detroit News, 1987, p.20.
13. Baker, p.6.
14. Dalligan, Alice C., "Emily Virginia Mason and her Sisters", *Detroit Historical Society Bulletin*, Vol. XXVI, no.8, May-June 1970, p.7, 18.
15. Mason, p.viii.
16. Ellet, Mrs., *The Queens of American Society*, NY: Charles Scribner and Co., 1867, p.423.
17. *Ibid*, p.424.
18. Mason, p.5.
19. *Ibid*.
20. *Ibid*, pp.5-6.
21. *Ibid*, pp.8-11.
22. *Ibid*, p.12.
23. *Ibid*.
24. *Ibid*. p.13.
25. *Ibid*, pp.13-14.
26. *Ibid* pp.15-18.
27. *Ibid*, pp. 19-20.
28. *Ibid*, p.20.
29. *Ibid*, pp.21-22.
30. *Ibid*, pp.20-21.
31. *Ibid*, p.22.
32. *Ibid* p.23.
33. Current, Richard N., *Encyclopedia of the Confederacy*, NY: Simon and Schuster, 1993, Vol. 2, p. 796.
34. Mason, p.23.

35. *Ibid*, p.31.
36. *Ibid*, p.32.
37. *Ibid*, p.34.
38. *Ibid*.
39. *Ibid*, p.35.
40. *Ibid*, p.39.
41. *Ibid*, p.41.
42. *Ibid*, p.42.
43. *Ibid*, pp. 43-45.
44. *Ibid*, pp. 46-48.
45. *Ibid*, p.49.
46. Emily Mason to "Libbie", Avary Papers, 1857-1946, Correspondence, VA: Virginia Historical Society, Library, pp.1-2.

47. Tardy, pp.439-440.
48. Emily Mason to Jas. T. White & Co., Aug. 24, 1898, Avary Papers, 1857-1946, Correspondence, VA: Virginia Historical Society, Library, p.2.
49. Mason, Emily V., *Popular Life of Gen. Robert E. Lee*, MD: J. Murphy & Co., 1872, p. iii.
50. Emily Mason to Jas. T. White, & Co., Aug. 24, 1898, Avary Papers, 1857-1946, Correspondence, VA: Virginia Historical Society, Library, p.2.
51. *Ibid*.
52. Weeks, p.20.

About the Author

Karen Rae Mehaffey is an academic Library Director on faculty at Sacred Heart Major Seminary in Detroit. She has degrees in Music History, English Literature, and Library Science from the University of Michigan. Her research interests include 19th century religious movements in America, the antebellum Temperance Movement, 19th century mourning customs, and women in the American Civil War. Karen writes articles and book reviews for *Civil War Book Review, Choice,* and *Citizen's Companion.* She has published two books to date, *Victorian American Women, 1840-1880: An Annotated Bibliography* (1992) and *The After-Life: Mourning and the Mid-Victorians* (1993). She is currently completing a book manuscript on mourning and the American Civil War.

In addition to research, Karen and her husband, Colin, have been reenacting for sixteen years. She has been more active in planning lecture and activity schedules for reenactments since 1997, including the civilian activities for the Gettysburg 135th in 1998 and the Antietam 140th in 2002. She teaches adult workshops on the 19th century, topics at Greenfield Village / Henry Ford Museum, and has lectured at national and regional Civil War conferences throughout the U.S. Karen also answers reference questions on "women" and "religion" from the website of the U.S. Civil War Center at Louisiana State University. Karen resides with her husband in Dearborn, Michigan.

Ships of War—Ships of Hope:

The Women and Their Hospital Ships in the Mississippi Valley Campaigns of the Civil War

By Ronald Waddell

The day was going like any other day on the ship. The captain and the river pilot were on the bridge negotiating a particularly narrow, shallow and potentially treacherous part of the Mississippi River. Below decks, the engine crew was shoveling coal into the huge, voracious steam boilers. Five boilers provided the steam for the engines. Steam from the boilers fed to feed the two huge 28 inch wide power cylinders of the engines. The engines, in turn, produced hundreds of horsepower to the power shafts. The massive eight-foot long power shafts moved huge paddle wheels on each side of the riverboat. She was strong. Even when heavily loaded with 400 tons of cargo, weighing a total of 1200 tons, she drew only eight feet of water. Although being heavily loaded she could still make nine knots speed against the river's current. Some said she was also one of the fastest and most beautiful boats on the river. Even though there was a war being waged, there was a certain routine into which every ship falls into after awhile. Accordingly, the crew of the *Red Rover* was not concerned than that the war was going to come to them on 23 July 1863.

In the hospital ward, Sister Veronica and her staff were going about their business of tending to the needs of the sick and wounded. A batch of fresh linens was being brought up on the elevator by Sara, one of the laundry staff. The meal had just been served and dishes were being cleared. The routine was soon quickly changed as the ship shuddered under the impact of a direct hit from the Confederate shore batteries. The walls shook, glass windows blew into hundreds of destructive pieces, steam pipes were severed and the ward filled with steam and smoke. A few moments later, a second shell hit the ship, again, directly in the hospital. Splinters flew in all directions as the shell went through both walls of the ship. The noise was deafening. Chaos reigned supreme for a few minutes, but order was quickly restored. The nurses and stewards worked frantically to dress the new wounds and control the old ones which had re-opened in the scramble for safety. With full power to the engines she quickly sped out of the danger zone. The *Red Rover* was still afloat and under power and the wounded needed, more than ever, to be transported to the hospital. The staff and crew had been doing this for months and there was no reason to stop now. She berthed at the Memphis Navy Yards, discharged the patients to the Naval Hospital, and refitted for the return voyage the next day. Although not typical of the daily events on a hospital transport ship, the

Red Rover.

mission of providing care and transportation of the sick and wounded was not without its hazards. Throughout the war the actions of the women providing this care would be ones of courage, dedication, stamina, and compassion. This is their story.

All along the length of the Mississippi River and at various scenes of action on the Eastern Seaboard, the hospital ships of both armies plied the waters providing care, sustenance, and a good measure of hope to all who were brought on board. The actual beginnings of the floating hospital concept were in the harbor of Charleston, South Carolina in 1861. There the Southern forces were preparing for the coming fight to capture Fort Sumter.

The Confederate Commander, General P.G.T. Beauregard, located his heavy siege cannons in order to fire at the fort from every angle possible. One of the areas he couldn't hit was the front entrance which faced in towards the harbor. Soon two floating batteries mounting heavy cannons were built to be towed into position in the harbor to afford a clear shot at the front gate. One was built by a former U.S. naval officer, Captain John R. Hamilton, of Charleston. In reality it wasn't much more than an armored barge. It may not have looked pretty, as some observers laughed and said it looked "odd", but it worked.[1] Attached to the floating battery was another barge converted into a floating hospital. Under the charge of Dr. Columbus Vega, it was designed to provide immediate care for the wounded in the coming battle. The doctor's foresight was commendable. Never before was a hospital designed to accompany and afford care for the casualties of a naval force engaged with the enemy. Since it was a civilian enterprise, no records are available to determine how many staff members were assisting him. The small cabin that was built on the barge had room for eight to ten beds.[2] Additionally, it is not clear if this was built at the direction of the government or if it was completely Dr. Vega's idea. The floating battery did receive return fire from Ft. Sumter and one man was wounded during the siege; so, there was at least one wounded and an unknown number of sick men cared for in this floating hospital.[3] It is not known if any females were on board. It is doubtful that there were, considering the attitudes that people had in the beginning of the war about women working in battlefield hospitals. But, this is the first example of "close to the action" care during the war.

If there are any claims to being the first hospital ship designed to care for the armed forces, the prize has to go to the CSS Hospital Ship, *St. Philip*. Originally named the *Star of the West*, it was captured by Confederate raiders from the *General Rusk* ("pirates" in the Northern dispatches), on 17 April 1861, at Indianola, Texas. This was the same *Star of the West* which was chartered to re-supply Fort Sumter, South Carolina, in January 1861. Originally a steamer belonging to Morgan's Steamship Lines, it was taken from Texas to New Orleans. The *Star of the West* was a medium sized side-wheeler measuring 228 feet long and almost 33 feet wide.[4] It was decided to take her into government service and she was officially seized by Governor Moore of Louisiana on 28 April, 1861.[5] Outfitted as a Receiving/Hospital ship, the now *St. Philip* was able to accept its first patient on 18 September, 1861.[6]

Dr. Lewis Willis Minor, of Virginia, was Surgeon-in-charge. A former Assistant-Surgeon in the Federal Navy he resigned and accepted his CSA Navy commission on 10 June, 1861.[7] The *St. Philip* stayed in the Lower Mississippi River area caring for 130 patients from 18 September 1861 to 20 April 1862. The first patient cared for was Alexander Reynolds suffering from dysentery.[8]

In 1862 the Union Forces started what would be a long two year campaign to open the Mississippi River to through traffic. Numerous Confederate forts and outposts needed to be taken before supplies could flow to the various armies then in the field. One of the first operations was down the Cumberland River to open the way to Nashville and down the Tennessee River to open the way to Northern Alabama. Two of the main obstacles were Fort Henry on the Tennessee River and Fort Donaldson on the Cumberland River. Planning for the reduction of these two forts was carried out through the winter of 1861-62. Finally, on 2 February, 1862 the gunboats and troop transports left Cairo, Illinois.

Flag Officer A. H. Foote was in command of the gunboat flotilla that paved the way to Fort Henry. Brigadier General U. S. Grant and his troops followed the gunboat fleet in river boat transports. The weather had caused the roads to be almost impassible in places and travel by water was more advisable, so they disembarked only a few miles north of the fort. The plan was that Grant was supposed to attack the land side while the gunboats attacked from the river. The roads were a quagmire, the terrain was hilly and the lowlands in between the hills were flooded. Inevitably, the soldiers were delayed. Much to General Grant's chagrin the heavy barrage from the gunboats was enough to make the fort surrender on 7 February, 1862. General Grant was upset that the Navy had captured the fort! Upon accepting the surrender, Flag-Officer Foote wrote to his commander Major General Halleck, Commander of the Missouri Department, "I received the general, his staff, and 60 or 70 prisoners, a hospital ship containing 60 invalids, together with the fort and its effects."[9] This is the earliest account of anyone's hospital ship being near the action.

This un-named hospital ship was the Hospital Boat *Patton*. There were two hospital boats at anchor at the fort, the *Patton* and the *Samuel Orr*.[10] One of the two is mentioned again by a senior officer of the flotilla, *Henry Walker*. Writing about the engagement at Fort Henry in the *Century Magazine* in 1885, he states, "On the *Carondelet* not a word was spoken more than at ordinary drill, except when Matthew Arthur, captain of the starboard bow-gun, asked permission to fire at one or two of the enemy's retreating vessels, as he could not at that time bring his gun to bear on the fort. He fired one shot, which passed through the upper cabin of a hospital boat, whose flag was not seen, but injured no one."[11] The interesting phrase here is, "whose flag was not seen." What flag, and what was its design, color and/or size? Was there a regulation stating that a Hospital Boat was to fly a certain flag, or to be marked in a certain manner? This part of this story will be addressed in Appendix B.

Many of the fort's defenders left before the official surrender and retreated to Fort Donelson on the Cumberland River, ten miles to the east. The six supply transports and two hospital boats were sent away as soon as things seemed to be going against the Confederates. The *Patton* surrendered with her sixty patients. The *Samuel Orr* departed, in haste, upriver. One would hope that any patients on board would have been transferred to the *Patton* before the *Samuel Orr*'s departure because the *Samuel Orr* was now loaded with munitions! The crew tried to outrun the pursuers; but they were unsuccessful, they set it on fire to prevent its capture. The former hospital ship came to its end in a spectacular explosion.[12] There is no mention in the *Official Records* of any female attendants being on board any of these hospital boats; but, changes were going to be made in one short week with the fall of Fort Donelson on 15 February, 1862. The military was in trouble this time. With the roads a mess and no railroads to send the wounded to Northern facilities, the wounded had a place to go; but they had no way of getting there. A fleet of hospital boats would have been a nice idea, but, the North didn't have any. The various civilian relief agencies had put together a small fleet of them and they were coming to the rescue. The news of the capture of both Forts Henry and Donelson was electrifying in the North. However, the news also carried the sobering report that there were at least 3,000 Federal and Confederate wounded who needed care.

Among the first of the civilian agencies to respond was the Cincinnati Branch of the U.S. Sanitary Commission. Trying to charter a large river steamer was a difficult task as most of the large ones had been pressed into Army service to transport the troops and supplies for Grant's army. The Steamer *Allen Collier* happened to be available. It was chartered, supplied, and staffed with surgeons, nurses, and boxes of supplies. When it stopped along the way in Louisville, an additional twenty large boxes of supplies, and more volunteers were added to the relief effort. Upon their arrival at Fort Donelson the *Allen Collier* tied up next to the steamers *City of Memphis* and the *Fanny Bullitt*. The

City of Memphis already had 200 to 300 wounded on board and the *Fanny Bullitt* had just about as many.[13]

The Steamer *City of Memphis* was the first transport taken into Federal service as a hospital boat on 7 February, 1862, by order of General Grant. It was a temporary arrangement with only the most rudimentary furnishings being available at the time. The Surgeon-in-charge was W. D. Turner, 1st Illinois Light Artillery. Assisting him were his wife and a Miss Hadley of Chicago.[14] The ship had no assigned nurses prior to the battle so these ladies had to be accompanying the troops in the field and started to help wherever they could. From 7 February, 1862 to 18 February, 1862, the *City of Memphis* acted as a receiving ship, conveying a large number of sick and wounded from Fort Henry. It was estimated that over two thousand were cared for during those ten days. Bound for Paducha, Kentucky, the *City of Memphis* left Fort Henry on 18 February, 1862 with 450 on sick and wounded on board. Arriving on 19 February, 1862, Dr. Turner discharged his patients to the local General Hospitals. On 21 February, 1862, the *City of Memphis* returned to pick-up the wounded of the Fort Donelson battle. It would continue as a temporary hospital boat until 17 July, 1862 when it was taken out of service. In its six months of service it made 14 trips and carried 7,221 patients.[15]

At Fort Donelson it didn't take but a few hours until the Army and the volunteers came into conflict. Fearing a loss of control over the wounded and interference in the daily routine, the Medical Director tried to establish control over the volunteers. Clearly having no authority to do so, and also in dire need of the expertise and supplies the volunteers were willing to provide, a compromise was made and the volunteers went to work. Immediately boxes of supplies were opened and care rendered to the wounded. Unfortunately, these two steamers were totally inadequate for the task involved for they were outfitted to carry cargo, not people. They lacked sufficient amounts of proper furniture, cots, shelving, cooking facilities, etc. Due to the overcrowded conditions on the *City of Memphis* and the *Fanny Bullitt*, it was decided to transfer some of the wounded to the *Allen Collier*. Ultimately, 81 men were transferred; but not until after hours of discussion had been completed between the Medical Director and the Commission volunteers.[16]

Much was said at the time about the Army's reluctance to accept help for it was clear that the Army system was inadequate to care for the huge numbers of wounded. The Army Medical Department had changed little since the War with Mexico in 1846. Its staffing had changed with the large influx of volunteer surgeons from the various state regiments called into service. However, the 1846 era logistical network of the Medical Department was trying to cope with the ten-fold increase in demand of by the large Federal Army of 1862. It simply wasn't able to do so. Grant's forces alone were larger that than General Scott's American entire army in Mexico in 1846. Also, it must be remembered that the war was only ten months old. The requisitions from the units, the funding of the budget by Congress, the awarding of contracts, the availability of raw materials, the manufacturing of the items, and the distribution of those items all takes a lot of time. Additionally, there were very few front line surgeons who had been in combat before this time. They really did not have a concept of just how many bandages they would really use in a battle. Some of the senior officers may have been Mexican War veterans, but the military and medicine had changed considerably in the past fifteen years. It also seemed that the military didn't want civilians, particularly women, "meddling and getting in the way." This was, of course, assuming that the military knew what it was doing which it did not. Additionally, never before in the history of the United States had there been such an outpouring of support from the general public. In every other war the civilians tried to get out of the way. Now they were showing up with trained personnel and tons of supplies and they were rapidly establishing efficient transportation networks. The Army officers were mystified as to what to do with them. Some didn't want them around at all. Dr. A. H. Hoff, Surgeon in charge of the Hospital Ship *D. A. January,* derisively called them "Nightingales." A civilian contract doctor, Dr. John V. Lauderdale, who was working with Dr. Hoff on the *D. A. January*, stated in a letter to his brother that, "These three go around to the cots of the patients, and pretend to minister words of comfort & and attend to little wants. I saw one reading a Testament to a dying one. With all these kind arts, they take some liberties such as suffering the patients to complain of the attentions of the Physicians, when they are doing their best to relieve their wants. Dr. Hoff is 'down' on them and says if they don't keep their mouths closed that he will set them on shore. He doesn't appreciate their attentions at all and shows them very little respect. They appear to be of the strong minded variety of femininity."[17] These men should have remembered the stories told by their grandfathers about who were the primary medical caregivers in the Revolution. The Revolutionary War Medical Department was totally inadequate in some commands and non-existent in others. The care of the sick and wounded normally fell to the hands of the women who accompanied their men as they served in the military. Somehow this was all forgotten. Additionally, the first of the soldier assistance groups organized for the American soldier had been started during the Revolution.[18]

Common sense had to come into play here. If the civilians were frustrated with the senior officers' attitudes, the individual surgeons in the Army were not too pleased about the situation either. This battle was one of the first real tests for the Medical Department in the Western Theater of Operations. The soldiers suffered not only battle wounds, but also sickness, and in some cases severe frostbite. Some of the soldiers had fallen in muddy areas during the battle and the ground had refrozen overnight. The wounded were literally frozen into the ground. Rescuers had to use axes to chop them out before treatment could begin.[19] The doctors were on their own through all of this. They had no staff to set up a triage area, rescue patients, carry patients to and fro, or to do the paperwork. Brigade Surgeon, Dr. Thomas W. Fry, stated in his after-action report that the Medical Director was very difficult to work with, that he seemed overwhelmed by the requirements placed upon him, and that he refused to allow any of the surgeons to accompany their wounded after removal from the regimental aid stations. Fry considered the insufficient quantity of medical supplies brought on the campaign as showing sheer incompetence on someone's part. He also complained that there was no need to rush all of the wounded down river. Doing that endangered many of the wounded who needed to rest before such a trip was attempted. There were buildings in the near-by town of Dover, Tennessee, which could have been used for the care of the men. This "get them all out of here" attitude had caused the transport *Tutts* to be loaded with wounded, and quickly dispatched, without any surgeons or other medical personnel on board at all![20]

Clearly, the system was not working. This prompted the Army surgeons to look elsewhere for supplies and assistance. Word quickly spread through the Medical Department that there was assistance in the form of additional Sanitary Commission doctors and nurses. Supplies were also available and were being liberally dispensed without requisitions, justifications, or any other questions.[21] Now things were quickly being organized and care was being given in an orderly manner. There were at least two reasons for this, Mary Bickerdyke and Mary Safford. Mary Bickerdyke, or "Mother Bickerdyke" as she was called, was definitely a coarse, rough and tumble, "Lead, follow, or get out of the way!" type of a person. She was on the first boat up the Cumberland River and made four more trips in the next few weeks.[22] Having no commission or authority from any agency, Mother Bickerdyke's emphasis was to provide "creature comforts" for the patients. Wholesome food, clean clothes, and a decent place to rest were as important to Mother Bickerdyke as medications and surgery were to the doctors. In marked contrast, Mary Safford was a petite, reserved, highly cultured and very intelligent woman who spoke four languages. She would simply look at you and you would know she was right; and, there was no doubt that what she was asking of you needed to be done.[23] Mary had come up the river from her hospital at in Cairo, Illinois. Known as "The Angel of Cairo" she was in the forefront of caring for the wounded. It has been stated that she was the first of the women to start caring for the sick and wounded of the Civil War. If there was a really special favor needed, or a doctor thrown out the door, these two constituted the team to send.

The problems that occurred at Forts Henry and Donelson were not going to be fixed quickly. But something had to be done to meet the needs of the wounded. A solution to the problem was going to be the outfitting of the Hospital Ship, *Louisiana*.

The Hospital Ship *Louisiana* was chartered on 12 March, 1862 and placed in the charge of Asst. Surgeon C. Wagner. The Western Sanitary Commission liberally outfitted the ship with medical and furniture items that were not available through the Army supply system. The ship was divided into four wards, two on the lower deck and two on the upper deck, each of which had a medical officer, a wardmaster, six permanently assigned male nurses, and one female nurse. The nurses' tour of duty was six hours on, and six hours off. On the lower deck could be found the kitchen, commissary, storeroom, bakery, and ice-house. On the upper deck the captain's office was converted into the office of the Surgeon-in-charge and the barroom became the dispensary. The barbershop and the wash-room were converted into a kitchen for low and half-diet patients under the supervision of a female nurse. The bulkheads between the staterooms were removed to improve ventilation and access to the patients. Cots were also placed on the outside walkways called "the guards" as they were protected by awnings and tarpaulins in inclement weather. The main passenger's dining room, called "the Texas," was converted into rooms for the crew and staff members. The bakery on the ship could provide a thousand loaves of bread a day. The *Louisiana* could accommodate 400 patients at a time; and before she was taken out of service on 13 June, 1862, she made ten trips and carried 2,999 patients from Island No. 10, and Pittsburg Landing, Tennessee, and other points in Tennessee, to Northern hospitals.[24] It is known that two women served aboard the *Louisiana* at this time. Harriet Colfax and a Mrs. E. O. Gibson were assigned as the female staff.[25]

Additionally, another vessel was going to be made available at the next objective of the Federal Gunboat Flotilla on the Mississippi River. Preparations were made to take the Confederate fort located at Island No. 10.

The islands in the Mississippi are numbered on the navigation charts starting at the junction of the Ohio and Mississippi Rivers. The Confederates decided to fortify the place where the Mississippi makes a turn to the west from its normal southerly direction. Being a few miles east of New Madrid, Missouri, the bend in the river and its protective island would be an ideal place to put a fort and effectively halt all southbound traffic on the river.

Confederate Major General J. P. McCown, writing from New Madrid, Missouri, on 23 March, 1862 stated, "A good deal of sickness in the command. Steamers here are the *Grampus, Mohawk, Kanawha Valley*, and *Champion, Red Rover* with floating battery; small boats *Ohio Belle, Simonds, Yazoo, DeSoto, Mears*, and *Admiral*. The small boats used as watch boats, & etc: the large ones as hospitals."[26]

If the Confederates were the first proponents of the hospital ship idea, the Federal Army was not far behind with the *City of Memphis* and the *Louisiana*. The general thinking was that it would be nice to have more of them. All they needed was a suitable ship and the battle at Island No. 10 on 15 March, 1862, would provide one for them. It took weeks for the Federal forces to capture the fort, but when the smoke cleared the CS steamer *Red Rover* was in Federal hands. She was not in good shape. As the *Red Rover* had no armament, the Confederates lashed a barge along side and put cannons on the barge. This floating battery, known as the Floating Battery *New Orleans*, was formidable and attracted a lot of fire from the Federal gunboats. Known as an Accommodation Ship, the *Red Rover* was simply a barracks, hospital, and a tow boat for the Floating Battery.[27] Just before the Federal gunboats went into action, the barge was anchored and the *Red Rover* was moved behind the island for protection. After the battle, the *Red Rover* was found to be in trouble. A shell fragment pierced the deck and went out through the bottom. The damage proved to be a leak of considerable size, but not one to endanger the vessel if repaired quickly. The damage was corrected; and on 9 April, 1862, the *Red Rover* was afloat and making its way to the repair yards up-river.[28] The *Red Rover* was a prize worth salvaging. Built in 1859 at Cape Girardeau, Missouri, the 625 ton, triple decked, side wheeler was a solid, strong, and maneuverable vessel.[29] Later in the war, Commander Alden, made the following entry into the logbook of the USS *Richmond*, "At 9 a.m. the steamer *Red Rover* came down the river; she is the hospital steamer of Davis' fleet; is one of the largest and most beautiful steamers on the river, and has splendid accommodations for the sick."[30]

But, unlike the previous Confederate Hospital Ships, this one was known to have had a female on board. No mention of her was made in the reports of the gunboat officers, but she does show up in the records of the Confederate Prisoner of War Camp, Camp Douglas, Illinois. As it turned out, five women were captured at Island No. 10. Four of the women were captured with their relatives among the units inside the fort, and Amelia Davis, Stewardess of the *Red Rover*, was captured with her husband on the ship.

Colonel Joseph H. Tucker, 69th Illinois Volunteers, Commandant of Camp Douglas, wrote to Colonel William Hoffman, Commissary-General of Prisoners on 16 July, 1862, asking for instructions as to what to do with the women in his camp. His description of Amelia stated: "Amelia Davis, born in East Brandon, Vt.; is about thirty-three years of age; left Vermont at the age of 18; has lived in many parts of the Union; has been married twice. Her present husband is a sea-faring man, whom she married in Baltimore two years hence. Both husband and wife were respectively employed as cook and stewardess on the steamer *Red Rover* when taken by General Buell at Island No. 10 and both sent prisoners to Camp Douglas together with a little boy eight years of age. Does not know that she has any relatives alive."[31]

The title of "stewardess" is the most interesting of all. Just what duties would the stewardess have? One might suppose that she was a maid or housekeeper. There is also the possibility that she was a nurse for the soldiers who manned the guns on the Floating Battery *New Orleans*. This may be considered an assumption without basis of fact. However, the word "stewardess" is found in only one other place in the entire *Official Records*. That is the Stewardess of the U.S. Army Female Military Prison in Louisville, Kentucky. The term implies that she was the female counterpart of a male Hospital Steward. The fact that the prison also had a "Doctoress" in charge gives this assumption a little more credibility. The Doctress mentioned is none other than Dr. Mary Walker.[32] With no records to state definitively what Amelia's duties were, it is still a fact that she was on this hospital ship during the three week bombardment of the Confederate positions. Regardless of her official title, she would have helped with the wounded and sick. Other women in the Civil War who found themselves in the midst of battle did so, why should we suppose she wouldn't? On the opposite side of the firing line, two other women, Harriet Colfax and Mrs. Gibson, were at work on the Hospital Boat *Louisiana*.[33] Throughout the three to four week engagement the *Louisiana* was carrying the wounded of the fleet and army.

On the day that the *Red Rover* was being repaired and made ready to be taken to the repair yards, news arrived that a terrible battle had taken place near a small country church in Tennessee...a place called Shiloh.

General Grant, having secured free access to the Tennessee River, planned to go further into the interior of the state and began operations at a small river docking area called Pittsburg Landing. The battle was one of the bloodiest thus far. Fort Donelson paled in comparison. Upon hearing the news the civilian relief agencies sprang into action once again.

The *City of Memphis* was with the fleet tied up along the shore. It simply was not going to be enough. In this battle entire regiments would cease to exist. Many of the boats pressed into service were originally chartered to bring the troops and their supplies to Pittsburg Landing. They were now empty, so it was logical to start loading the wounded on them preparing to take them to hospitals at Louisville and Paducah, Kentucky, Cairo, Illinois, and St. Louis, Missouri. Among these were the steamers *Black Hawk*,[34] *Emerald*,[35] *Minnehaha*, and the *Hannibal*.[36] Once again, these were not outfitted for patient comfort. They were, just a few days before, carrying horses, cannons, troops and ammunition. Among the first of the civilian groups to react to the call was, again, the Cincinnati Branch of the Sanitary Commission. The team consisted of Dr. George Blackman, Surgeon-in-charge; Mrs. Sarah Peter noted Cincinnati philanthropist; Mrs. George Hatch, wife of the Mayor; Jenny Hatch, their daughter; Miss M. Hughes; Mrs. O'Shaughnessy; Sister Anthony O'Connell; Sister DeSales Brady; and Sister Theodosia Farn. The sisters were affiliated with the Sisters of Charity.[37] Although not being from a nursing order, these Sisters performed very well under most trying circumstances. When the male assistants of Dr. Blackwell were begging away from the surgery being done on the boat, Sister O'Connell, not one to shirk her duty, stepped into their place by the table and became Blackwell's assistant.[38]

When the Western Sanitary Commission brought its Steamer *Lancaster #4*[39] and recalled the *Louisiana* from its station on the Mississippi River, Harriet Colfax and Mrs. Gibson came with it. Mary "Mother" Bickerdyke was on the first Sanitary Commission hospital ship going up the river. She was already caring for the sick at the depot in Savannah, Tennessee, only nine miles away by river.[40] Mary Safford," Mother" Bickerdyke's hard working partner, was there also.[41] Mrs. Cordelia A. P. Harvey, wife of the Governor of Wisconsin, responded to her husband's call for nurses to help out at Shiloh. Soon after her arrival she would become a widow, as the Governor drowned in a freak boating accident at the landing on 19 April, 1862.[42] She continued caring for the wounded and sick, organizing fund raisers, and going wherever there was a need for the rest of the war. On 14 April, 1862, the Hospital Ship *D. A. January* arrived with three female nurses on board. The team was led by Mrs. Anne Eliza Peck Harlan, wife of Senator Harlan of Iowa. The other two women's names are not known.[43] Mrs. Harlan was also committed to the soldiers care for the duration of the war. Many times throughout the war she used her "official" name to assist soldiers having problems with the red tape in their pay and discharge paperwork. There were advantages of being "Mrs. Senator Harlan."[44]

Other women were already at Pittsburg Landing when the shooting started. These women were wives of officers, regimental nurses, or Sanitary Commission workers. They cared for the wounded both on the field and as they were brought on board the empty transport steamers. One of these ladies was Jerusha Small who was associated with an Iowa Regiment. She nursed her wounded husband and many others in the field and on the transports. Soon after the battle she developed a very bad case of consumption. She was returned home to Cascade, Iowa, where she died. Her body was wrapped in the flag and she was buried with full military honors.[45] Anna McMahon was also at Pittsburg Landing, although who she was affiliated with is somewhat a mystery. While there, she contracted measles and died. A coffin was made of rough boards and she was buried on the battlefield at the bank of the Tennessee River.[46] Mrs. E. C. Wetherell, a Western Sanitary Commission Nursing Supervisor from Louisville, Kentucky labored long as the Head Matron on the Hospital Ship *Empress*. Two months after Shiloh she died of a fever contracted from a patient.[47] Mrs. S. A. Martha Canfield, wife of Col. Herman Canfield, 71st Ohio Infantry, worked on the battlefield even after losing her husband. With so many of her friends and her husband's soldiers needing help immediately, there simply was not time to cry. She continued to care for "her boys" in hospitals attached to the XVI Corps. Later she would serve in hospitals in Memphis in 1863. She was also credited in with starting an orphanage in Memphis for children of freedmen.[48] Arabella McComber "Belle" Reynolds was there with her husband who was a Lieutenant in the 17th Illinois Infantry. She had arrived on the Hospital Ship *D. A. January*. While caring for the wounded being brought to the transports, she successfully defended the gangplank of the *Emerald* from a group of panicked soldiers. For her efforts she was later awarded a commission as a Major by Governor Yates of Illinois.[49] Mary A. Newcomb was there having arrived on 4 April, 1862, the day before the battle. While helping with the wounded on shore, she was assisted by a Miss Vail of Iowa and Mary E. Hood, wife of Dr. Thomas B. Hood of the 76th Ohio Infantry Regiment.[50] This threesome made repeated trips from near-by springs carrying buckets of water to the wounded on the field. Mary wrote in her book, "We tore our aprons into little squares, filled them with grass and leaves and stopped some gaping wounds that were bleeding. We made bandages from our garments and bound up shattered limbs." In another incident during the battle Mary Newcomb was caring for one young man who had been placed in a tent. She found him wounded and burning up from a fever. A few minutes later bullets tore through the tent and he was shot through the body as she was caring for him. He died ten minutes later.[51] When these accounts are read it is hard to envision the conditions under which these women labored. It would not take long for the lower portions of their skirts to become so filthy with mud, blood, and horse manure that no one would consider washing them. The burn pile would be the only course of action. The simple act of breathing was a problem. The dead men, dead horses, piles of horse manure, human waste, garbage from the ships and other materials in the water were over-powering. The atmosphere was so vile that ships re-positioned themselves up wind so as to escape the noxious odors. Unfortunately, there was no escaping the sounds made by the wounded as the agony and pain they were enduring overwhelmed them. It is to their great credit that these women volunteered to follow the Army as it moved towards the enemy. Going through something as bad as Shiloh is one thing. But, to go, knowing that those scenes will be repeated over and over again, takes a great deal of courage, dedication, and determination.

Within days, other ships were put into service because of the thousands of wounded who still needed care. Two of the largest steamers on the river, the *Empress* and the *Imperial* were added to the fleet as temporary hospital ships. The *Empress* was chartered on 10 April, 1862 and was a wise choice. Originally built for carrying cotton, it was a very wide and long riverboat; therefore, many wounded could be put on board. She made six trips to the battlefield carrying 817 on in one trip. Due to her requirement for deep water, her services were discontinued in June of 1862.[52] Although the *Empress* had the space to provide comfortable care for the soldiers, trying to get the crew to do so was another matter. The *Empress* was a cotton freighter in the pre-war days and the entire crew was very pro-South. Mary Newcomb complained about the treatment of the soldiers and the rude and vulgar words directed towards her. The problem was one of politics. The crew's pro-South feelings were exhibited by doing only the least amount necessary. They had been pressed into service and were getting little compensation. They were told to move the sick and wounded. However feeding them, setting up cots, putting out mattresses, etc. were not in those orders; so nothing would be done until they were paid for it. Mary spent her own money to buy scraps of food from the kitchen in order to give a small portion to as many as could be fed with what she was able to procure. Perhaps as a result of the nurse's complaints, the Army took over the operation of the *Empress* in the latter half of 1862. With a new crew on board, many things changed. In 1863 the crew of the *Empress* received commendations for excellent performance of duty. What happened to the previous crew is not known; and one might assume that no one cared. The *Empress* would not see the end of the war as she sank after hitting a snag on 30 October, 1864 near Island No. 34 on the Mississippi.[53] In her military service the *Empress* made six trips to the Pittsburg Landing battlefield and carried 3,375 sick and wounded to hospitals down river. The *Imperial* was chartered on 10 April, 1862 and continued moving men down river until 17 May, 1862, when she, too, started to scrape bottom on the rocky river bed. On those four trips she carried 1,781 patients[54] (another account 2,375).[55] The *Imperial* would be chartered a total of seven times between 1862 and 1865. Her career ended when she sank on 8 March, 1865, after hitting a bridge abutment near Clarksville, Tennessee.[56] Even with the help of these two large steamers the sick and wounded waited in tent field hospitals for removal down river. To assist in the movement of this overwhelming load of human cargo the Quartermaster Department also chartered the *Stephen Decatur* and the *J. S. Pringle*.[57]

After the Battle at Pittsburg Landing, the Union Army advanced further up the Tennessee River. Unfortunately, the gunboats, transports, and hospital ships could only go so far because of the shallowness of the water. Therefore, they could not be relied on for support. The support requirements were met when the Engineer Corps began restoring railroad service. The hospital boats could, and would, be replaced by hospital trains. The trains were generally able to run in all types of weather. Although steamers could go as far as Chattanooga, they were limited by the seasons in the last 140 miles from Bridgeport, Tennessee. Many times the low water levels of summer and the heavy ice in winter prevented normal river traffic. Besides, chartering a steamer was expensive. Two hundred to six hundred dollars a day was not an unusual price so the Quartermaster was not going to allow them to sit idle at the dock. That seldom happened in the central and lower portions of the Mississippi River. As the war continued, the workers in Cairo, Illinois, were not ceasing in their labors as well. A few weeks in the repair dock and the *Red Rover* was ready to go.

The *Red Rover* was repaired and outfitted for the specific purpose of providing care and transport of the wounded and sick of the Western Gunboat Flotilla. (The claim made by some that the *Red Rover* was the Army's first hospital ship is hard to prove. The *D. A. January*, as well as some ships on the Atlantic coastal areas, was also being prepared at the same time.) On 25 May, 1862 she was in the water again.[58] The first patient was received on 11 June, 1862.[59] The *Red Rover's* new Surgeon-in-charge , Dr. George H. Bixby, who was assigned to the ship in early June,[60] made preparations to get underway. Perhaps one of the best descriptions of the interior of the ship is found in a letter from the Quartermaster in charge of boat building, Captain George D. Wise. The letter was to Commodore Foote, his former boss and Commander of the Western Naval Forces:

> I wish that you could see our hospital boat, the *Red Rover*, with all her comforts for the sick and disabled seamen. She is decided to be the most complete thing of the kind that ever floated, and in every way a decided success. The Western Sanitary Association gave us, in cost of articles, $3,500. The ice box of the steamer holds 350 tons. She has bathrooms, laundry, elevators for the sick from the lower to upper deck, amputating room, nine different water closets, gauze blinds to the windows to keep the cinders and smoke from annoying the sick, two separate kitchens for sick and well, a regular corps of nurses, and two water closets on every deck.[61]

Captain Wise seemed to be impressed with everything, and typical of a soldier, especially the bathtubs and flush toilets! Additional praises came from the Commander of the Western Naval Forces, Captain C. H. Davis, in a letter to Captain Wise, dated 12 June 1862:

> Captain: I have waited until I had an opportunity to make a personal examination of the hospital boat *Red Rover* before expressing to you my great admiration for your success in this undertaking and the sincere gratitude felt to you by myself and the officers and men under my command for the judgment and humanity with which you executed this important work.
>
> No one but those who have witnessed it can comprehend the sufferings to which our sick have been exposed by the absence of proper accommodations on board the gunboats and by the necessity for frequent and sometimes hasty change of place. The wounded and the patients suffering from fever occupy, under the direction of the surgeon, those parts of the ship which are the quietest and best ventilated. When the ship is cleared for action, as of-

ten happened lying near Fort Pillow, it was necessary to take down their cots and hammocks more than quickly into out-of-way and uncomfortable places. This must always be attended with pain and distress, if not positive injury.

The arrival of the *Red Rover* will put a stop to all this, promote the efficiency of the squadron by procuring comfort and the means of restoration of the sick. All the conveniences and appliances of a hospital are fully provided, and to these are added the neatness and order essential to so large an establishment.[62]

Their first mission on 20 June, 1862 was to transport 41 patients from Memphis, Tennessee, for the General Hospitals in Saint Louis, Missouri, and Mound City, Illinois. The heart rending part of the mission was that almost half of these patients were burn victims. They were from the gunboat *Mound City* which was on the campaign up the White River near St. Charles, Arkansas. During the battle a Confederate shell penetrated the steam drum and scalded to death a large portion of the crew. Out of a crew of 175 officers and men, 133 were killed and 19 were wounded. Only 23 escaped injury.[63] The survivors were barely hanging on to their lives. Their injuries would be a challenge today for our burn specialists; it was an almost impossible one for the doctors and nurses in 1862.

In July 1862, the *Red Rover* rejoined the Gunboat Flotilla and participated in the Yazoo River Campaign north of Vicksburg, Mississippi. On 29 August, 1862 while on a return voyage from Helena, Arkansas, she caught fire. Fortunately, other boats of the fleet were near-by and crews from the gunboat *Benton* helped extinguish the flames.[64] The cause was not noted in the records, but with coal oil lanterns and sparks from the smokestacks flying around everywhere, it is a miracle it did not happen more often. But a more drastic change was in the wind. The *Red Rover* was going to be working for a new employer. On 20 September, 1862 she was sold to the Navy.

The reason for this action was a decision made by Congress on 16 July, 1862. At the beginning of the war the Navy did not have enough personnel to man the fleet of gunboats on the Mississippi River. Also they had never had a "river navy" before. Army artillerymen filled in with infantry troops being detailed from time to time. In early 1862, the Navy was leading the way to clear the Mississippi from the south as the Army was trying to do the same from the north. This caused many problems with two services trying to accomplish the same mission. The Gunboat Flotilla's officers were naval officers and many of the senior crewmen were also active duty sailors; but, the Army had overall command and control of the land and river forces. Admittedly, the Army had little expertise in this area of gunboat flotillas, and they had their hands full trying to fight the Confederate Army and hold onto the territory they had gained. The intent of the law was in essence, "If it floats, the Navy should be in charge of it."

When the *Red Rover* was transferred to the Navy in late September, she went back to Cairo, Illinois, for re-fitting as a naval vessel. There the refitting consisted of mounting a cannon on the bow of the ship![65] Firing a 32 pound projectile it gave the ship a means to fight if necessary. Today it would be inconceivable to have an armed hospital ship, but, there was no Geneva Convention agreement in effect during our Civil War.

(Author's Note: Much has been written about the women who served on the *Red Rover*. There has also been the general concept that they were the first. Yes, they were in the Navy, but, as noted in the first portion of this chapter, they were not the first of the Sanitary Commission, or the US or CS Army vessels. I highly recommend the excellent article done by Steven Louis Roca for *Civil War History*, "Presence and Precedents: The USS *Red Rover* during the American Civil War, 1861-1865," a quarterly magazine published by Kent State University Press, Volume, XLIV, No. 2, June, 1998. This article is very well researched and has remarks from the log books of the Captain, the Senior Medical Officers, and includes Muster Rolls and items about the daily routines and unusual events in the history of this vessel. Since the intent of this article is to mention, with the fullest possible accounting, all of the vessels used by the Medical Departments of both armies, the reader is deferred to the above mentioned article for an in-depth history of the *Red Rover*.)

At the same time that the *Red Rover* was being readied for service, actions were being initiated to gather the nursing staff. Sisters from the Order of the Holy Cross volunteered their services to the Navy as nurses when needed. There is a dispute as to when they officially became part of the nursing staff. After detailed analysis of the various records of the National Archives these Sisters are thought to have served in onshore facilities from late June to late December, 1862. The consensus is that, other than a one week period in late June, the Sisters worked in Mound City hospitals and had only officially reported for duty on the *Red Rover* on 24 December, 1862.[66]

It is important to state that the Sisters were not the first to be assigned as nurses to the *Red Rover*. Perhaps, "attached" would be a better word. After extensive research Mr. Roca, states in his article for *Civil War History*, "The records speak clearly. The muster rolls, surgeon's reports, and records of the General Accounting Office were recorded and filed by separate clerks from different departments. In all three sets of documents the "Rank or Rating" sections consistently identify these women as to their designation on board the *Red Rover* and within the U. S. Navy. In the sections headed "Remarks" or "Personal Description," the lines are blank for the Sisters yet relatively detailed for the African-American women, listing them variously as "contraband," "Mulatto," "Negro," often including as well their ages and physical descriptions. With such detailed record keeping, it is clear that while the Navy welcomed, accepted, and compensated the Sisters for their services in the Medical Department, they were clearly identified and recorded as non-naval personnel, retaining their titles as members of an organization outside of the U. S. Navy. These Sisters worked for the Navy as nurses, though they were not considered U. S. Navy nurses."[67]

Mr. Roca backs this statement with detailed records of the periods of service and ratings of the women serving on the *Red Rover*. But, it really does not matter when they walked up the gangplank. The Sisters cannot be given the distinction of being the first Navy nurses, as they were never considered to be part of the Navy crew, no more so than any Sanitary Commission nurse who might be on board. The Sisters certainly did not renounce their vows and join the Navy! Additionally, they cannot be considered the first Sisters to serve on a hospital ship. That special distinction falls to the Sisters of Charity of St. Joseph from the Philadelphia, Pennsylvania area. They were asked by the Pennsylvania Surgeon General, Dr. Henry H. Smith, to accompany him and other male doctors and nurses to the vicinity of Fortress Monroe. Upon their arrival at City Point, Virginia, on 19 April, 1862 they were transferred to hospital ships and the land based hospitals utilized during the Peninsular Campaign in Virginia.[68] The Sisters on the *Red Rover* however, do have the distinction of being the first Catholic Sisters to serve on a U.S. Navy ship.

The following list shows the names and job descriptions of all the women known to have served full-time, part-time, or were supernumeraries on the *Red Rover*: I have indicated in the following list the women of African-American decent (A), or mulatto or mixed race (M) as noted in the ship's records.

While part of the Western Gunboat Flotilla (Army control)

Chambermaids:	Mary Warfield, Ann Graves.
Laundresses:	Mary Bryant, Maria Cassidy, Betsy Bishop, Eliza McLothian, Mattie Perkins, Nancy Rodgers, Sarah Watson.
Attached Nurses:	Sisters Adelia and Veronica, Sisters of Charity.

While part of the Mississippi Squadron (Navy control)

Nurses:	Ellen Campbell-(M), Betsy Young-(M) Georgina Harris, Sarah Nothing-(A), Ann Stokes-(A). Ellen and Betsy were the first of the crew nurses hired. (1 September, 1863).
Laundresses:	Sarah Kinno, Alice Kennedy, Mary Dalton, Lucinda Jenkins, Sallie Bohannon, Nancy Buell, Sabra Miller, Alice McClean, Mary Ann Donald, Ann Ragan, Adelia Robertson.
Supernumeraries or part time:	
	Sisters Veronica, Adela, Calista, and St. John, Sisters of Charity. Alice Hicks-(M), Susan Hicks, Josephine Hicks. (The latter two may have been relatives of Alice.)[69]

When the Navy took control of the gunboat fleet and its support ships, the Army was still left with a mission of maintaining control of that part of the river that had been opened for traffic. There were still bands of guerrillas and regular forces of the Confederate army operating all along the river. Cotton was being transferred from Mississippi to Louisiana and beef cattle were being driven from Texas across Arkansas into Mississippi and Tennessee. It was not uncommon for a ship to receive sniper fire, or even artillery fire from these small bands of military or civilian raiders and smugglers. The *Red Rover*, *Platt Valley*, and a host of other steamers were fired upon. On one occasion the *Platte Valley* received five artillery shell hits, killing three people and wounding several others. The ship also had over 300 bullet holes in it.[70] This change-over for all ships to be controlled by the Navy was quickly amended, as there was a need for the Army to have some ships. Accordingly, the Army decided to get into the river patrol business by creating the Mississippi Marine Brigade.[71] (It was designated a "Marine" unit because its mode of transport was totally by water. It had nothing to do with the U. S. Marine Corps.) Transports were chartered to carrying the infantry, companies of cavalry and batteries of artillery. The Army was determined to wipe out these pockets of resistance and make the river and its tributaries secure for military and civilian traffic. The tactical control of the armored rams and gunboats was to be under Army control; but the over-all control was now given to a naval officer. This was a complete reversal of the previous situation. This force required supply ships and another new hospital ship — the *Woodford*. The *Woodford* was under the command of Dr. James Robarts, who was assigned on 13 June, 1862 both as Fleet Surgeon and Surgeon-in-charge of the *Woodford*. She was commissioned the later part of 1862 and continued to support the Mississippi Marine Brigade in all of their operations against the regulars and guerrillas operating along the river and its tributaries. The *Woodford* was an indispensable part of the operations; but, sadly, she was lost during the Red River campaign. On 27 March, 1864 the fleet was making its way back down the river. Near Alexandria, Louisiana, she hit a submerged wreck, tore a huge hole in her side, and sank in minutes.[72] The water was very shallow and the sinking caused no loss of life to the patients or crew. Unfortunately, all of the hospital equipment, medical supplies and food were lost.[73] Soon after the end of the Red River campaign the Mississippi Marine Brigade was disbanded. The Army never replaced the *Woodford* with another ship. The records do show that Miss Hattie Wiswall was a nurse on the Red River campaign, but it is not known if she served on the *Woodford* or not.[74]

The final major battle on the Mississippi River involved the siege of Vicksburg. Of course the *Red Rover* and *D. A. January* were there along with the gunboats and mortar boats. The *City of Memphis* and *City of Alton* were again fitted up as temporary hospital boats. Even with this additional support, it was estimated that one fourth of the transports going back up river had wounded and sick on board; and as these transports were void of staff or comforts, the mortality rate was very high.[75] Additionally, large numbers of soldiers were sick from their being camped in poorly drained bottom lands and swampy areas. Hospital boats became essential to the mission because there was not any suitable dry land to build a General Hospital or set-up a large tent hospital. Frequent trips had to be made back and forth from the Vicksburg area to Memphis and St. Louis. Rather than enter into an expensive charter, the Quartermaster Department purchased the former hospital boat *Louisiana*. Being completely remodeled into a permanent hospital ship it was renamed the *R. C. Wood*, in honor of the Army Assistant Surgeon-General. Her staterooms on the middle deck were completely removed. This resulted in one very large ward with abundant light and ventilation. This was an absolute necessity in the coming summer months. She also had bathrooms, hot and cold running water, cooking rooms, nurses' apartments, dispensary, laundry, and many other "modern" conveniences. She had room for 450 patients. From 1 April, 1863 to 11 April, 1865, she made 33 trips up and down the river. The *R. C. Wood* traveled 34,805 miles and carried 11,024 patients.[76]

But, what if all the available hospital ships were enroute to or from the hospitals up north? The US Medical Department had that problem solved with the creation of a floating hospital, called the *Nashville*.

This vessel was bought by the U.S. government and then completely gutted. From the outside it looked like a typical steamer except that it did not have any smokestacks. The main reason for that was that it had no engines. It was designed to be towed from place to place. By eliminating all of the ship's power equipment, maintenance areas, and the coal bins on the lowest deck, it could now hold a thousand patients. It had all of the facilities of a large land based General Hospital. Mary Livermore of the Western Sanitary Commission made an inspection of it; she thought very highly of the ship and the way it was operated.[77]

While all of these ships were at work, the older vessels were continuing to work along side of them. The *D. A. January* had started out at Shiloh in 1862 and continued making trips up and down the river until August of 1865. In September of 1863 it was remodeled and named the *Charles MacDougall*. No matter what her name, no other ship did more, for a longer time, than she did. She was truly the workhorse of the Medical Department during the Civil War. The records do not mention the number of the miles that she traveled; but in three years time, she made 81 trips and carried 23,738 patients.[78]

She was not one of the largest ships on the river, but the *Charles MacDougall* was a respectable 230 feet long, 35 feet wide and displaced 450 tons. This ship was built in Cincinnati in 1857. On the uppermost deck, known as the "Texas,"

Nashville.

were the Captain's and crews quarters. The Cabin Deck contained the former stateroom area. Most of the individual stateroom walls were removed and replaced with strong posts and beams. The metal folding cots for the 450 patients were located here along with stoves for heating, the nurses dining room, kitchen, two full baths with hot and cold running water, water closets (toilets), surgery room, linen rooms, steward's room, a pharmacy, and rooms for the surgeons. Next, the Middle Deck contained the nurses' quarters, nurse's bathrooms and extra space for patients. There were water faucets and drinking fountains throughout the ship. The water was supplied from river water that was used to make steam. After each power stroke of the engines, the steam would normally be released into the air. This system captured the steam, and directed it to condensing tanks for drinking, washing, and clean-up. It was essentially distilled water, generally bacteria free, and contained very little solid material. The small engines and pumps run by the main engines pumped the water to tanks on the upper deck.

Water from the tanks was pumped through a system of pipes through the ice box and out to the fountains and faucets. Hot water came from the tanks and was directed through coils of pipe in the boilers and then pumped to the bathrooms. The result was that you only had hot or cold water when the boilers were operating.

The Lower Boiler Deck, at the water line, had room for another 100 patients, wash rooms, water closets, blacksmith shop, bakery, carpenter shop, commissary room and a large kitchen area. A dumb-waiter allowed food to be brought up to all of the upper decks from the kitchen. Additionally, through the whole length of the main patient area was a steam powered system of fans. Turning at 90 revolutions a minute, these fans created a pleasant breeze even if the ship was tied up at a dock but, again, only if the boilers were producing power. As mentioned before there was always the hazard of fire on board. To counter this threat this ship had a separate steam engine which pumped water to a fire suppression system throughout the ship. Ample lengths of hose were available on all decks. (Diagram of *D.A. January* — Appendix C)[79]

Throughout the early days of the war, the *City of Alton* could be seen at all the major battlefields. She was chartered by the Western Sanitary Commission whenever there was a large influx of casualties.[80] Emily E. Parsons and Margaret Breckenridge were on this ship. Both of them served at Benton Barracks Hospital in St. Louis in addition to being part of the hospital ship service.[81] Of all of the thousands of women who served their respective causes during the war, Emily stands out as a very special person not only by what she did, but because of the limitations under which she labored. At the age of five she had an accident with a pair of scissors which resulted in the loss of vision in her right eye and impaired vision in her other eye. A few years later she contracted scarlet fever and that resulted in her having permanently damaged hearing. From this she gradually recovered, and in adult life was able to hear whatever was distinctly addressed to her but could not join freely in general conversation. At about twenty-five she severely injured her ankle, tearing some of the ligaments and tendons. There was a period of time she could not use or put weight on her foot at all. It never healed correctly and after many hours on her feet, in the wards or on the ship, she had to rest or risk being totally immobilized by the pain in her foot. And as if she did not have a heavy enough cross to bear, she contracted malaria while working the hospital boats on the river. This disease would cause her to have numerous relapses during her life.[82] Through it all, she still continued as Nursing Supervisor of the *City of Alton* and of the largest hospital in the Western Theater of Operations. *The City of Alton*, and another steamer called the *Ruth*, would team up from time to time.

At one such instance the *Ruth* had been pressed into service for an expedition up the White River in Arkansas in June of 1862. Mrs. Jane Hoge and Mrs. Henrietta Colt were on the *Ruth* as it was making its way towards St. Louis. The women were to supervise the delivery and distribution of the supplies to hospitals and hospital ships all along the river. When the ship made a stop at Memphis, the Army promptly commandeered it. Jane and Henrietta had been officially "shanghaied." The *Ruth* was primarily a troop transport; and since the fleet of transports and gunboats had no hospital ship, the women thought they might be of some use on the expedition. It was good that they did. The boxes of supplies safety secured in the hold of the *Ruth*, which they were to deliver to St. Louis, would come in very handy in the next few weeks. Their supplies were the only extra food and medical supplies available in the entire fleet. Jane Hoge described the activities on board the *Ruth*:

> The main cabin of the *Ruth* was one hundred and fifty feet in length and twenty feet in breadth. In the course of a few days after leaving Helena (Arkansas), its entire length was covered by sick soldiers, suffering with pneumonia, rheumatism, fever, and measles. The men were obliged to lie as closely as possible, leaving scarcely enough room for the sick cup or plate. There were no comfortable cots, clean sheets, or soft pillows. Providently, we had some boxes of shirts among our sanitary stores, sufficient to furnish each man who passed through the hospital. [As helpers gave the men a sponge bath the ladies set to work at getting some food for them.] We roasted apples by the barrel, stewed dried fruit by the half barrel, prepared green tea in large tin buckets, and scrambled eggs, and pickled codfish in square yard iron pans. Our detailed nurses carried the trays of nourishing food, while we followed with the tea, white sugar, condensed milk, and soft crackers.[83]

These women stayed on board throughout the expedition and later met the *City of Alton* lying in anchorage at the mouth of the White River. They transferred the sick and wounded and continued on towards St. Louis. The efforts of these two women were especially exemplary since they didn't have to go. They could have opted to stay at Memphis, to download the supplies, and to wait for another steamer to continue their journey. With all of this work, Jane and Henrietta still would not get any recognition for their service on the *Ruth*. If it were not for Jane's telling of their activities, the history books would have no mention whatsoever of their service on this expedition. This is because the *Ruth* is not mentioned in any of the expedition's official dispatches. It was involuntarily pressed into service as a last minute acquisition, and therefore was not mentioned in the "Orders of the Day" for the rest of the fleet. Officially the *Ruth* was not there, and neither were the ladies. This is just one of many examples of how difficult it is to research the day to day activities of these volunteers.

With the fall of Vicksburg, Mississippi, in July of 1863, the entire river was open for traffic and the military hospital ships had the freedom to go north or south to whatever hospital was closest. With the exception of the Red River Campaign in early 1864, the Valley of the Mississippi became relatively quiet. Occasionally the Confederates would make a raid with a large force of cavalry, but large groups of infantry were gone from the area. The war fronts moved farther to the east into Alabama and Georgia and towards the west into Texas. There simply was not a need for large numbers of support ships any longer and they were discharged as soon as possible. For all practical purposes, the war was over in the Mississippi Valley by the last few months of 1864. The Sanitary Commission ceased chartering ships as it was cheaper to pay for individual tickets and small shipments as part of the ship's cargo load, than to charter the entire ship. The nurses went back to their hospitals on land and cared for the wounded from the Eastern Tennessee and Northern Georgia battles. Others cared for refugees, both black and white. There were hospitals and camps set up for them in dozens of places. Particularly hard hit was Eastern Kansas, where thousands of women and children had fled the war torn areas of Missouri and Arkansas. These refugees suffered the most, as it was extremely difficult throughout the entire war to get relief supplies into them. The Sanitary Commission was at work well into the fall of 1865 caring for these refugees.

After the war these same women continued to work for the welfare of the soldiers, freed slaves, and the displaced. Some of the women had established Soldier's Homes for those soldiers who had difficulty caring for themselves and/or could not make a living due to battle injuries. Others established homes for orphaned children and established schools for their education.

Every memoir written by these women during, and after the war, had a story or two of their being recognized by a former patient. Whether it was at a public gathering, or on a train, or a chance meeting on the street, the gentleman might say a fervent, "Thank you, thank you, for saving my life on that miserable filthy battlefield. I was only nineteen years old, and one of the thousands of dirty, vermin infested, wounded, and feverish soldiers you cared for. You don't know me, but I will never forget you." He knew that this woman, and the hundreds of others who were to be seen on every battlefield in the war, had made a real and valuable difference. For years afterwards the ladies would complain bitterly that the national soldier's organizations would not grant them membership in their organization. But, that simple "thank you," given by one who knew how important they and their sisters were, was worth more to that woman, than some badge of membership in a men's organization. He was so grateful that that volunteer nurse had the courage to face the Angel of Death and say, "You can't have this one."

Appendix A

Medical Department Hospital Ships on the Mississippi River

The final accounting of ships chartered, or pressed into service during the Civil War by the US government alone, was tallied at 4,033 different vessels. The following list of ships which were outfitted by their respective governments to be utilized exclusively as hospital ships on the Mississippi River Theater of Operations:

D. A. January / *Charles McDougall* (US)
Louisiana / *R. C. Wood* (US)   *St. Philip* (CS)
Nashville (US)   *Red Rover* (US)
Woodford (US)   *City of Memphis* (US)

Other Medical Service Vessels

There were many boats that were chartered or pressed into service during an emergency, generally for a short period of time. Sometimes they were chartered for a week or ten days. They might be working for the Sanitary Commission; the next week for the Army; the following week they would return to carrying regular cargo; and so on. Most of the reports of a certain vessel supporting the Medical Department by carrying wounded, supplies, or medical personnel were done without mention of who was paying the bills. It is also important to realize that the majority of sailors and soldiers didn't know what that particular ship's mission was. Many officers mistakenly gave a ship the designation as a "hospital ship" simply because they saw there were some wounded on board. It was an assumption on their part as they really did not know if that was the ship's primary or secondary mission. Their men were being taken to the hospital and that is all they cared about. Due to the fact that most of these missions were on an "as needed" basis, there are few records as to what nurses served on them. A modern day comparison of this would be similar to that of the local newspaper printing the names of all of the fire companies which responded to a fire. But, there is never a listing, by name, of every member of the fire crew who showed up to put out that fire. Similarly, the records of the individual civilian ships do not reflect the presence of any of the volunteer nurses. Unlike the full-time military hospital ships, these temporary ships had no permanently assigned, paid medical staff. They were not required to maintain passenger manifests, so the Captain had no idea who they were, nor did he care.

The following is a listing of some of the other ships known to have supported the Medical Departments in some way during the campaigns on the Western Rivers:

Alice Dean: She was chartered on 23 March, 1863 by the Cincinnati Branch of the United States Sanitary Commission to carry nurses, surgeons, and 700 packages of supplies. Two months later, on 25 July, 1863, she was burned at Brandenburg, Kentucky, by John Hunt Morgan's raiders. Prior to this event, she had been holed by a CSA artillery shell while on the Mississippi River near Commerce, Missouri.[84]

Allen Collier: Her job was to transport personnel and supplies to Fort Donelson after the battle. She had 81 wounded on board for the return trip. In September 1862, she was converted into a gunboat for river security. She was burned by guerrillas near Memphis, Tennessee, in July 1864.[85]

Atlantic: She was chartered by the Albany, New York Branch of the United States Sanitary Commission to transports supplies to the armies in Tennessee and Kentucky. She was chartered six times from 1862 to 1865 for various missions and employers.[86]

Autocrat: This ship was chartered in April of 1862 to carry forty doctors, nurses, and their supplies from Frankfort, Kentucky, to the Pittsburg Landing battlefield.[87]

Baltic: Medical and Surgical History lists her as being a Hospital Ship in the Western Campaigns. No other official record of her service has been found.[88]

Black Hawk: This steamer was normally used as a Headquarters Boat or transport. She carried a load of wounded from Pittsburg Landing to Peoria, Illinois, in April, 1862.[89]

City of Alton: The Western Sanitary Commission chartered her on an "as needed" basis. She normally transported wounded and sick to Benton Barracks hospital in St. Louis, Missourio. Miss Emily. E. Parsons was nursing supervisor. Also on board were Margaret Breckenridge, Mrs. Clapp, President of the Aid Society of St. Louis, Mrs. Couzins, Mrs. Crashaw, and Mrs. Clark. She was chartered seven times from 1862 to 1865.[90]

City of Memphis: This was the first steamer to be designated a hospital ship in the Western Campaigns. She was chartered six times as a transport and outfitted as a Hospital Ship in 1864. She remained as such until the end of the war.[91]

Commercial: She left Louisville, Kentucky on the evening of 9 April, 1862 loaded with medical supplies and bound for the Pittsburg Landing battlefield.[92]

Diligent: She left Louisville, Kentucky on 10 April, 1862 bound for the Pittsburg Landing battlefield. She was chartered four times during 1862 to 1864 and sank 10 January, 1865 when she hit a snag (submerged log or tree) near Helena, Arkansas.[93]

Dunleith: She carried wounded from Pittsburg Landing, April-May, 1862. Afterwards, in 1863, the Davenport, Iowa, and Alton, Illinois, branches of the Western Sanitary Commission chartered her to carry supplies to, and wounded from, the armies in Tennessee and Kentucky. In 1863 she was used to stockpile supplies for the siege of Vicksburg and to remove the sick and wounded of the Red River Campaign in 1864.[94]

Emerald: She transported troops and supplies to Pittsburg Landing and was loaded with 250 wounded on return trip in 1862.[95]

Empress: This ship was assigned to the Mississippi Squadron in 1862, made six trips to Pittsburg Landing and carried 3,375 patients. She was chartered five times between 1862 and 1864. The ship sank on 30 October, 1864 after hitting a snag near Island No. 34. Mrs. E. C. Wetherell was assigned to this ship as the Nursing Supervisor. Mrs. Mary Newcomb also served at a later date.[96]

Emma Duncan: This vessel was used to transport sick from the Fort Donelson area to St. Louis, Missouri, in 1862. Dr. Granger was in charge with Mary A. Newcomb as the Nursing Supervisor.[97]

Fanny Bullitt: This ship was chartered for a period from March 1862 to March 1863 and carried 250 wounded from Fort Donelson area. The rest of the time she was a troop and equipment transport vessel.[98]

Ginnie Hopkins: The Medical and Surgical History lists her as having served as a Hospital Ship in the Western Campaigns. No further record of service has been found.[99]

Grampus: A CSA Transport and Hospital Ship, she was sunk to prevent capture at Island No. 10. Later she was raised and used by United States as a transport ship until she burned and sank 11 January, 1863.[100]

Grampus #2: She was formerly named the *Ion*. When the *Red Rover* was decommissioned, the last 11 patients were transferred to the *Grampus*, which was a receiving ship for the river fleet.[101]

Hannibal City: This ship was a transport chartered for the Pittsburg Landing expedition. Wounded from the army units and from the gunboat *Lexington* were placed on board for removal down river. After being chartered twice, she hit a snag and sank on 4 September, 1864. She was not on Army service at the time.[102]

Hastings: This steamer was one of a three ship convoy captured (January, 1862) by CSA forces while transporting wounded on the Cumberland River. She was chartered four times; but on her last run, she hit a snag on the Red River and sank on 23 April, 1864.[103]

Hazel Dell: This ship was chartered to transport supplies to Fort Henry and later carried wounded from Fort Donelson in March of 1862. She was chartered six times from 1862 to 1864.[104]

Henry Chouteau: This ship was part of the Red River Campaign and carried wounded down river after the *Woodford* was lost.[105]

Henry Von Pohl: From 1862-1864, she was frequently chartered as an Army transport. She had wounded on board from Milliken's Bend near Vicksburg, but there were no supplies or furnishings on board.[106]

Imperial: Starting in 1862, this ship made numerous trips transporting troops for Tennessee River operations and returned a total of 2,375 patients. She sank on 8 March, 1865 after striking a bridge at Clarksville, Tennessee.[107]

Jacob Strader: In 1863, she was said to be one of the finest and largest transports on the river. She was loaded with supplies of ice, vegetables, fruit, and clothing. Dr. Andrew was Surgeon-in-charge with a staff of 15 persons with him.[108]

J. J. Swan: In 1863, she was a troopship turned into a hospital ship. She departed from Milliken's Bend north of Vicksburg to Memphis, Tennessee. . No supplies or furnishings were supplied for comfort of the wounded on board. She was chartered seven times from 1862 to 1864.[109]

J. S. Pringle: This ship was a transport pressed into service at Pittsburg Landing and carried wounded down river to the hospitals. She was chartered six times from 1862 to 1865 and was later bought by the Quartermaster Department in April of 1865.[110]

Kanawha Valley: This ship was built in Wheeling, Virginia, in 1860. She was used as a hospital ship at Island No. 10 and was scuttled by the Confederates on 6 April, 1862 to prevent capture. She was later salvaged and chartered to carry troops and supplies from 29 March, 1865 to 6 May, 1865.[111]

Lancaster #4: She was chartered in 1862 to remove wounded from Pittsburg Landing and Savannah, Tennessee, field hospitals. She made six trips and removed over 1,500 wounded to Northern hospitals. She was chartered seven more times between 1862 and 1864 and sank on 13 November, 1864 when she hit a snag near Herman, Missouri.[112]

Laurel Hill: She was chartered by the Western Sanitary Commission in April, 1863 to carry wounded from the front and was chartered again in April, 1864 to carry more than 500 wounded from the Red River Campaign.[113]

Lewis Whiteman: She was a transport which was carrying wounded from the Battle of Baton Rouge when she collided with the Gunboat USS *Oneida*. There were 76 passengers lost, mostly wounded lying below decks.[114]

Maria Denning: She was sometimes listed as *Mary Denning* and was designated a Receiving Ship. She was based out of Cairo, Illinois from 8 November 1861 to 1 April, 1862. This type of ship received supplies and replacements for the flotilla and distributed them to the individual ships as needed. She was chartered as an Army transport from 15 December, 1862 to 6 April, 1863. Very slow and under-powered, she carried wounded and sick on many return trips from the front. Mary Livermore and her team of nurses and hospital visitors felt that she was poorly run and inadequately furnished. Mary Livermore was particularly concerned with having the refugees and wounded crowded together on lower decks along with the cargo. The *Maria Denning* was known to have taken wounded from the gunboats *Switzerland* and *Lancaster* to Memphis.[115]

Mercury: *The Medical and Surgical History* mentioned that she had service as a Hospital Ship in the Western Campaign area. Quartermaster records show that the *Mercury* was chartered seven times. There is no indication in the Quartermaster records that she was utilized especially for transporting sick and wounded.[116]

Minnehaha: She was a troopship on the Pittsburg Landing expedition and accepted wounded from the battle and moved them down river to a hospital. She was chartered for five long periods of time from 1862 to 1865. Accidentally catching on fire, she was destroyed on 15 May, 1865 while tied up to the dock in New Orleans, Louisiana.[117]

Monarch: This ship mentioned by Commander Alden of the USS *Richmond* on 6 July, 1862: "The hospital ship, *Monarch*, came alongside of us and took all of our sick and wounded on board. She proceeded at once up the river to Memphis." Throughout July of 1862 it was reported that she was "a hospital steamer", but it is not clear whether the Army, Navy or if the Sanitary Commission had fitted her up.[118]

N. W. Thomas: This vessel was part of the Pittsburg Landing transport fleet in April 1862. The Quartermaster Department purchased it on 19 September, 1863 and it saw service along the Texas coast in that month. It returned to river duty and was designated a hospital ship on the Red River Campaign in 1864.[119]

Parthenia: This was one of a three vessel convoy which was carrying wounded down the Cumberland River. It was captured by CSA forces on 13 January, 1864. Patients were moved to the *Hastings* and the ship was then burned.[120]

Pinola: This was a wooden gunboat that came to the rescue of the survivors of the collision between the steamer *Whiteman* and the USS *Oneida* on 4 August, 1862. Seventy patients were put on board and carried to the hospitals in New Orleans, Louisiana.[121]

Platt Valley: Mentioned in many reports, this transport seemed to be along on all the major campaigns. She was carrying the mail and a group of passengers when she was pressed into service to pick-up survivors of the Fort Pillow massacre on 13 April 1864. The female civilian passengers cared for the wounded on the way to the hospital at Memphis, Tennessee. The *Platt Valley* saw much service as she was chartered ten times in 1864 to 1865.[122]

Shingiss: She was a steamer chartered for government service carrying wounded from the fleet. She hit a snag on 9 July, 1862 and slowly sank seven miles above Fort Pillow, Tennessee. Wounded were then transferred to shore and later rescued by the steamer *Tycoon*, which took them to the hospital.[123]

Silver Cloud: This stern-wheel armored gunboat was dispatched to the scene of the Fort Pillow massacre in April of 1862. It transported 58 of the wounded survivors to the hospital at New Madrid, Missouri.[124]

Silver Wave: In 1862, she was a supply vessel chartered by the U.S. Sanitary Commission. Mrs. Jane Hoge, of the Chicago Branch of the U.S. Sanitary Commission, spent ten days on board dispensing food and medical supplies to the wounded. The ship received, from time to time, small groups of wounded and held them until a regular hospital ship would come to pick them up.[125]

Sioux City: This ship was primarily a transport. She was utilized as a temporary hospital ship in May of 1864 during the Red River Campaign when the *Woodford* sank. The *Sioux City* was chartered six times between 1862 and 1864.[126]

Stephen Decatur: She was a transport placed on temporary service in 1862 to carry 70 patients from Pittsburg Landing to Paducah, Kentucky, and deliver then them to the Hospital Ship *D. A. January*. She saw extensive service and was chartered ten times between 1862 and 1865.[127]

Superior: Chartered by the Cincinnati Branch of the United States Sanitary Commission in April 1862, she was bound for Pittsburg Landing towing three hospital barges with supplies. The medical team consisted of Dr. George Blackman, Mrs. Sarah Peter, and five sisters from the order of Sisters of the Poor of St. Francis of Cincinnati, Ohio.[128]

Trio: This ship was one of a three ship convoy carrying wounded on the Cumberland River when it was captured by CSA forces on 13 January, 1862. Patients were transferred to the *Hastings* and she was then set on fire and destroyed.[129]

Tuts: She was sometimes called *Tutts*. In 1862, she was an Army transport used at Fort Donelson. No supplies, personnel or furnishings were on board to assist in the care of the wounded. This ship was later captured and burned by the Confederates on 9 December, 1864.[130]

Tycoon: She was chartered by the Governor of Ohio in 1862 and was in the charge of Dr. Smith of Columbus. She was frequently used to transport supplies and wounded. This was the ship that came to the rescue of the *Shingiss* when it sank with wounded on board.[131]

Appendix B

The Use of the Yellow Flag to Signify Medical Facilities

The use of the yellow flag as a means of identifying medical facilities seems to be one whose origins go back into antiquity. In regards to its use in the Civil War, it seems to have been so common-place as not to require official regulations. The absence of any mention of the use of a yellow flag in the United States, or Confederate States, regulations implies that its use had been a long established tradition.

The first use of the yellow flag in the *Official Records of the Rebellion* occurred in October 1861. At this time the Union Navy was engaged in the capture of the port and city of Pensacola, Florida. On 9 October, 1861, Colonel Harvey Brown, the commander of Fort Pickens at the mouth of the harbor, sent a message to General Braxton Bragg, the commander of Confederate defense forces at Pensacola. He wrote, " I observe for the first time a yellow flag hoisted over a large building directly in front of my batteries. I also understand that officer's wives and children are in the adjoining buildings. I do not make war on the sick, women, or children."[132] Colonel Brown went on to state that CSA forces were seen in the area of the building and, if necessary, they would be fired upon. The General was advised to move either the troops or the non-combatants. The implication was that if the military stayed in the vicinity, fire directed towards them would also endanger the hospital and the civilians. Colonel Brown did not want to be responsible for unintentional civilian casualties.

The yellow flag he was referring to was flying over the Marine Hospital in Pensacola. The Marine hospital had nothing to do with the Marine Corps. It was a general term used for anyone who sailed the oceans, as it is also used in describing fish and other creatures of the ocean as "marine life." It had been a custom for many centuries for governments to establish and maintain hospitals for the use of all sailors in every major port, and sometimes on rivers and canals, in their country. A portion of each sailors monthly pay would be deducted and placed in a fund. This was the earliest form of medical insurance. This enabled any civilian sailor to have free medical care anywhere in the world. For example, if a sailor required medical care in a port in Portugal he would go to the building in that port that was flying the yellow flag. The cost of his care would be submitted by the Portuguese government to the American embassy. They would pay it, and then in-turn submit a request for reimbursement from the Marine Fund administrators. As stated before, Marine hospitals were already in place at major seaports, rivers, and canals in the United States. Even cities far inland, such as Richmond, Virginia, and Pittsburgh, Pennsylvania, had them for the use of the river boat and canal boat crews.

It was this "common knowledge " of that particular Marine Hospital's operation and location, which led to General Bragg's angry reply on 10 October 1861, "The building on which you had for the first time observed a yellow flag has been well known to you and all of your command, as well as the United States Navy, as the military hospital of this station, and you could not help knowing that it is now used for that purpose."[133]

The use of yellow flags on ships was also commonplace and conformed to what seems to be a code of usage.

The first method of use: Notice of plague or quarantine.

If a ship had sickness on board the yellow flag would be flown on the foremost or tallest mast of the ship. This would provide a warning to all other ships as well as the harbor master when they came into port. In 1864 part of the blockading squadron was located in Port Royal harbor in South Carolina. Yellow fever had been reported in Key West, Florida, and Rear Admiral John A. Dahlgren, the Squadron Commander, was worried that northbound ships would spread the disease to his ships. In June 1864, he issued a series of orders concerning health matters and precautionary steps to be taken to prevent the possibility of the spread of the contagion. Sanitary Orders # 44, #46, and #47 detailed the inspection of all incoming ships by the Fleet Surgeon.

Second method of use: Health Vessel.

Sanitary Order #44 dated 23 June, 1864 stated: "All vessels belonging to this squadron, or connected with it or its business, will, before entering this port, heave to near the health vessel (yellow flag at the fore) and be visited by the naval medical officer of this station." It seems that any ship continually flying the yellow flag from the forward mast, or on the mast located on the bow of the ship, would be designated a "health ship."[134] Both the *D. A. January* and the *Red Rover* flew yellow flags as shown in the images accompanying this chapter. The color is verified by Dr. Lauderdale in his letters where he included his drawing of the ship and a notation of the foremost flag as being, "Our yellow flag."

Third method of use: Wounded on board.

During the operations at Sabine Pass, Texas, in November 1862, Confederate forces fired on the Steamer *Dan* and the barge which it was towing. The after-action report of Lt. Col. Spaight states, "Captain Marsh is sure, from the fact that the decks of both vessels were crowded with men who were distinctly visible by moonlight, that the fire was deliberate, that screams and groans arose from the vessels, and that the yellow flag was displayed at half-mast for two succeeding days, that his fire did some execution."[135]

Fourth method of use: Protection of buildings.

Besides the aforementioned incident at Pensacola, another incident at Galveston, Texas shows the use of the yellow flag to designate a land based hospital. In the Galveston incident, fire from the Union fleet fell in the neighborhood of a convent that was being used as a hospital. Commodore Bell, of the U.S.S. *Brooklyn* wrote to Major General MacGruder of the Confederate forces on 20 January, 1863: "The nunnery used as a hospital, to which Surgeons Penrose and Cummings and yourself refer, has been pointed out to me by Colonel Cook and will be respected by the vessels of my command, if you will further designate it by hoisting a yellow flag over it."[136]

These are examples of the various uses of the yellow flag in naval operations. The Army restricted its use to designate large permanent or semi-permanent facilities. A red flag was used to designate a field aid station and/or ambulance depot. Since the *D. A. January* was an Army vessel, it seems that they conformed to the naval customs in variance to their own regulations.

Appendix C

D.A. January (*Medical & Surgical History*, Part 3, Volume 2, Page 977-79)

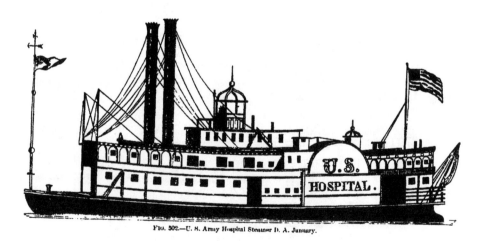

Fig. 502.—U. S. Army Hospital Steamer D. A. January.

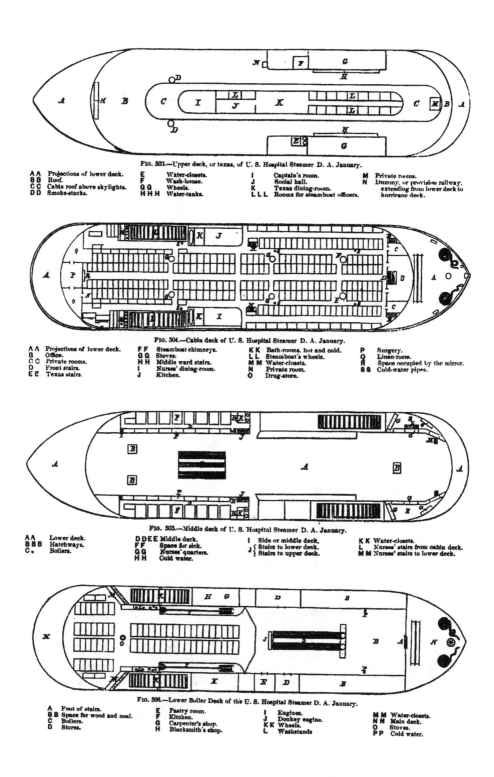

FIG. 503.—Upper deck, or texas, of U. S. Hospital Steamer D. A. January.

A A	Projections of lower deck.	E	Water-closets.	I	Captain's room.	M	Private rooms.
B B	Roof.	F	Wash-house.	J	Social hall.	N	Dummy, or provision railway,
C C	Cabin roof above skylights.	G G	Wheels.	K	Texas dining-room.		extending from lower deck to
D D	Smoke-stacks.	H H H	Water-tanks.	L L L	Rooms for steamboat officers.		hurricane deck.

FIG. 504.—Cabin deck of U. S. Hospital Steamer D. A. January.

A A	Projections of lower deck.	F F	Steamboat chimneys.	K K	Bath-rooms, hot and cold.	P	Surgery.
B	Office.	G G	Stoves.	L L	Steamboat's wheels.	Q	Linen-room.
C C	Private rooms.	H H	Middle ward stairs.	M M	Water-closets.	R	Space occupied by the mirror.
D	Front stairs.	I	Nurses' dining-room.	N	Private room.	S S	Cold-water pipes.
E E	Texas stairs.	J	Kitchen.	O	Drug-store.		

FIG. 505.—Middle deck of U. S. Hospital Steamer D. A. January.

A A	Lower deck.	D D E E	Middle deck.	I	Side or middle deck.	K K	Water-closets.
B B B	Hatchways.	F F	Space for sick.	J	Stairs to lower deck.	L	Nurses' stairs from cabin deck.
C.	Boilers.	G G	Nurses' quarters.		Stairs to upper deck.	M M	Nurses' stairs to lower deck.
		H H	Cold water.				

FIG. 506.—Lower Boiler Deck of the U. S. Hospital Steamer D. A. January.

A	Foot of stairs.	E	Pastry room.	I	Engines.	M M	Water-closets.
B B	Space for wood and coal.	F	Kitchen.	J	Donkey engine.	N N	Main deck.
C	Boilers.	G	Carpenter's shop.	K K	Wheels.	O	Stoves.
D	Stores.	H	Blacksmith's shop.	L	Washstands	P P	Cold water.

Endnotes

1. Roman, Alfred, *The Military Operations of General Beauregard*, New York: Da Capo Press, 1886, Volume 1, page 37.
2. *Ibid.*
3. *Ibid.*, page 38.
4. Gibson, Charles D., and Gibson, E. Kay, *Dictionary of Transports and Combatant Vessels, Steam and Sail, Employed by the Union Army, 1862-1868*, Ensign Press, Camden, Maine, 1995, page 300.
5. United States War Department, United States Record and Pension Office, United States War Records Office, et al. *The War of the Rebellion: a compilation of the official records of the Union and Confederate armies*. Series 2, Volume 1, pages 165 & 265. Hereafter cited as *Official Records*-Army.
6. Papers of Lewis Willis Minor, (MSS 3988), Special Collections Department, Alderman Memorial Library, University of Virginia: Register of Confederate Naval Patients in the C. S. Hospital Ship *"St. Philip"* at New Orleans, Louisiana, 1861-1862.
7. *Register of Officers of the Confederate States Navy, 1861-65*, as compiled and revised by the Office of Naval Records and Library, United States Navy Department, 1931, from all available data, originally published in Washington, D. C., 1931, reprinted in 1983 by J. M. Carroll & Company, Mattituck, New York.
8. Minor Papers, *St. Philip* Patient Register.
9. *Official Records*-Army: Series 1, Volume 7, page 123.
10. *Ibid.*, page 149.
11. Walke, Admiral Henry. "Operations of the Western Flotilla," *Century Magazine*, Volume XXIX, January 1885.
12. *Official Records*-Army: Series 1, Volume 7, page 153.
13. Letter of Dr. J. S. Newberry, *A visit to Fort Donelson, Tenn., for the relief of the wounded, Documents of the US Sanitary Commission*, Volume 1, Bulletin #42, 1866, page 3.
14. Newcomb, Mary A., *My Army Work of Four Years*, Donohue & Henneberry, Chicago, Illinois, 1893.
15. Otis, George A., & Huntingdon, D. L., *The Medical and Surgical History of the War of the Rebellion*, Government Printing Office, Washington, D. C., 1883. Part III, Volume II, page 974 (Hereafter cited *Medical and Surgical History*)
16. Newberry, Dr. J. S., *The U.S. Sanitary Commission in the Valley of the Mississippi*, Fairbanks, Benedict & Co., Cleveland, OH, 1871, page 485.
17. Josyph, Peter, ed., *The Civil War Letters of John Vance Lauderdale, M.D.*, Michigan State, University Press, East Lansing, Michigan, 1993, page 49.
18. *The Sanitary Commission of the United States Army, A Succinct Narrative of its Works and Purposes*, New York, 1864, Appendix A.
19. Newcomb, page 30.
20. *Official Records*-Army: Series 1, Volume 7, page 242.
21. Newberry Letter, *A Visit to Ft. Donelson*, page 5.
22. Livermore, Mary A., *My Story of the War*, A. D. Worthington & Co., Hartford, Conn., 1889, Page 483.
23. *Ibid.*, page 203.
24. *Medical and Surgical History*, page 975.
25. Brockett, L. P., MD, & Vaughn, Mary C., *Women's Work in the Civil War*: Ziegler, McCurdy & Co., Boston, Mass. 1868, pages 395-399.
26. *Official Records*-Army: Series 1, Volume 8, page 800.
27. *Official Records of the Confederate and Union Navies in the War of the Rebellion*: Series 2, Volume 1, page 513. (Hereafter cited *Official Records*-Navy).
28. *Official Records*-Navy: Series 1, Volume 22, Page 725.
29. Historical Sketch, Naval Historical Center, Photographic Library, Photo and caption, #49980.
30. *Official Records*-Navy: Series 1, Volume 18, page 753.
31. *Official Records*-Army: Series 2, Volume 4, page 228.
32. Massey, Mary E., *Bonnet Brigades*, Alfred A. Knopf, 1966, page 68.
33. Brockett & Vaughn, page 395.
34. Moore, Frank, *Women of the War*, S. S. Scranton, & Co., Boston, Mass., 1868, page 269
35. *Ibid.*, page 262.
36. Sword, Wiley, *Shiloh, Bloody April*, William Morrow & Co., New York, NY, 1974, page 421.
37. Letters of Sister Anthony O'Connell, Archives, Sisters of Charity, Mount Saint Joseph, Ohio.
38. *Ibid.*
39. Newberry, *Valley of the Mississippi*, page 487.
40. Livermore, page 483.
41. *Ibid.*, page 214.
42. Brockett & Vaughn, page 260.
43. Josyph, page 49. See also: Brockett & Vaughn, page 676-678.
44. Censer, Jane Turner, ed., *The Papers of Frederick Law Olmstead*, "Defending the

Union, the Civil War and the U.S. Sanitary Commission," Vol. IV, The John Hopkins University Press, Baltmore, MD, page 348.

45. Brockett & Vaughn, page 493-494.

46. Young, Agatha, *Women in the Crisis*, McDowell Oblensky, New York, page 167.

47. Larosn, Rebecca D., *White Roses, Stories of Civil War Nurses*, Thomas Publications, Gettysburg, PA. See also: Brockett & Vaughn, page 499.

48. Censer, page 568. See also: Brockett & Vaughn, page 495.

49. Moore, page 254. Mary Newcomb was also a witness to this presentation of the commission as a Major. Newcomb, *Boys in Blue*, page 49. See also: Livermore, *My Story of the War*, page 262.

50. Newcomb, page 43.

51. *Ibid.*, page 42

52. *Medical & Surgical History*, page 981.

53. Gibson & Gibson, *Dictionary*, page 105.

54. *Medical & Surgical History*, page 981.

55. Report of the Western Sanitary Commission Ending 1 June 1863, page 19.

56. Gibson & Gibson, *Dictionary*, page 105

57. *Medical and Surgical History*, page 981.

58. *Official Records*-Navy: Series 1, Volume 23, page 106.

59. Loomis, E. Kent, CPT., USN, (Ret), *History of the U. S. Navy Hospital Ship Red Rover*, Ship's History Section, Division of Naval History, Office of the Chief of Naval Operations, U. S. Navy, 1961, page 3.

60. *Official Records*-Navy: Series 1, Volume 23, page 114.

61. *Ibid.*, page 153.

62. *Ibid.*, page 207.

63. Loomis, page 3.

64. *Official Records*-Navy: Series I, Volume 23, page 674.

65. *Official Records*-Navy, Series II, Volume 1, page 189.

66. Roca, Steven Louis, "Presence and Precedents, The USS Red Rover during the Civil War," 1861-1865, *Civil War History*, Volume XLIV, No. 2, June 1998, Kent State University Press., Page 105. See also: Loomis, page 7.

67. *Ibid.* page 109.

68. *Official Records*-Army, Series 1, Volume 11, page 181.

69. Roca, page 109.

70. *Official Records*-Army, Series 1, Volume 24, page 507.

71. *Official Records*-Navy, Series 1, Volume 23, page 514.

72. Gibson, Charles Dana, & Gibson, Kay E., *Assault and Logistics, Union Army Coastal and River Operations, 1861-1865*, Volume II, page 348.

73. *Documents of the U. S. Sanitary Commission*, Volume 2, Bulletin # 22, page 692.

74. Brockett and Vaughn, page 725.

75. *Medical and Surgical History*, page 972.

76. *Ibid.*, page 976.

77. Livermore, page 303.

78. *Medical and Surgical History*, page 977.

79. *Ibid.*, page 978-979.

80. Western Sanitary Commission, 1863 Report, page 19.

81. Brockett and Vaughn, pages 188, and 274.

82. Parsons, Theophilus, *Memoir of Emily Elizabeth Parsons*, Little, Brown, and Co., Boston, Mass., 1881 pages 2 and 3.

83. Hoge, page 158.

84. *Sanitary Commission, Works and Purposes*, page 40. See also: Gibson and Gibson, page 11.

85. Newberry, *Valley of the Mississippi*, page 484. See also: *Official Records*-Army, Series 1, Volume 26, page 535. See also: Silverstone, Paul A., *Warships of the Civil War Navies*, Naval Institute Press, Annapolis, MD, 1989, page 170.

86. *Sanitary Commission, Works and Purposes*, page 40. See also: Gibson & Gibson, *Dictionary*, page 24.

87. *New York Times*, 11 April, 1862, page 3. See also: Gibson & Gibson, *Dictionary*, page 25.

88. *Medical and Surgical History*, page 981. See also: Gibson & Gibson, *Dictionary*, page 28.

89. Moore, page 269. See also: Gibson & Gibson, *Dictionary*, page 36.

90. Brockett and Vaughn, pages 188 and 274. See also: Hoge, page 170. See Also: *Medical and Surgical History*, page 981.

91. Newberry, *A Visit to Ft. Donelson*, page 3. See also: Gibson & Gibson, *Dictionary*, page 61. See also: Livermore, page 319.

92. *New York Times*, 11 April, 1862, page 3. See also: Gibson & Gibson, *Dictionary*, page 68.

93. *Ibid.*, See also: Gibson & Gibson, *Dictionary*, page 86.

94. *Sanitary Commission, Works and Purposes*, pages 140 and 203. See also: *Documents of the US Sanitary Commission*, Volume 2, Bulletin #14, page 395.

95. Gibson & Gibson, *Dictionary*, page 102. See Also: Moore, page 262.

96. Brockett and Vaughn, page 499-500. See Also: *Medical and Surgical History*, page 981. See Also: Western Sanitary Commission-1863 Report, page 19. See also: Gibson & Gibson, *Dictionary*, page 105.

97. Newcomb, page 58.

98. *Sanitary Commission, Works and Purposes*, Volume 1, Bulletin #42, page 3. See also: Gibson, *Dictionary*, page 112.

99. *Medical and Surgical History*, page 981.

100. Silverstone, page 246.

101. Loomis, page 13. See also: Silverstone, page 180.

102. Gibson & Gibson, *Dictionary*, page 143.

103. *Ibid.*, page 145.

104. *Ibid.*, page 146.

105. *U.S, Sanitary Commission Documents*, Volume 1, Bulletin #22, page 693. See also: Gibson & Gibson, *Dictionary*, page 148.

106. *Official Records*-Navy, Series 1, Volume 23, page 564. See also: *Medical and Surgical History*, page 972.

107. Gibson & Gibson, *Dictionary*, page 159. See also: Western Sanitary Commission-1863 Report, page 19. See also: *Medical and Surgical History*, page 981. See also: *US Sanitary Commission, Works and Purposes*, page 203.

108. *U.S. Sanitary Commission, Works and Purposes*, page 140. See also: Gibson, *Dictionary*, page 171.

109. *Medical and Surgical History*, page 972. See also: Gibson & Gibson, *Dictionary*, page 167.

110. *Ibid*. See also: Gibson & Gibson, *Dictionary*, page 169.

111. United States Naval Historical Center, Photograph #59024 with caption. See also: Gibson & Gibson, *Dictionary*, page 187.

112. Brockett and Vaughn, page 35. See also: Newberry, *Valley of the Mississippi*, pages 486-488. See also: Gibson & Gibson, *Dictionary*, page 195.

113. US Sanitary Commission Documents, Volume 2, Bulletin #14, page 433, and Bulletin #15, page 458. See also: *Sanitary Commission, Works and Purposes*, page 209.

114. *Official Records*-Army, Series 1 Volume 15. See also: Gibson & Gibson, *Dictionary*, page 199.

115. *Official Records*-Army, Series 1, Volume 22, pages xvi and 428. See also: Livermore, pages 341-345. See also: Silverstone, page 180. See also: Gibson & Gibson, *Dictionary*, page 213.

116. *Medical and Surgical History*, page 981. See also: Gibson & Gibson, *Dictionary*, page 224.

117. Gibson & Gibson, *Dictionary*, page 226.

118. *Official Records*-Navy, Series 1, Volume 18, page 752. See also: Gibson & Gibson, *Dictionary*, page 228.

119. US Sanitary Commission Documents, Volume 1, Bulletin #22, page 693. See also: Gibson & Gibson, *Dictionary*, page 233.

120. Gibson & Gibson, *Dictionary*, page 250.

121. *Official Records*-Navy, Series 1, Volume 19, page 720 and Series 2, Volume 1, page 179.

122. *Official Records*-Navy, Series 1, Volume 26, page 224. See also: *Official Records*-Army, Series 1, Volume 24, page 507. See also: Gibson & Gibson, *Dictionary*, page 258.

123. *Official Records*-Navy, Series 1, Volume 23, page 255.

124. *Official Records*-Navy, Series 1, Volume 26, page 224. See also: Gibson & Gibson, *Dictionary*, page 293.

125. Moore, page 358. See also: Hoge, page 226. See also: Gibson & Gibson, *Dictionary*, page 294.

126. U.S. Sanitary Commission Documents, Volume 1, Bulletin #22, page 692. See also: Gibson & Gibson, *Dictionary*, page 295

127. Censer, page 89. See also: *Medical and Surgical History*, page 972. See also: Gibson & Gibson, *Dictionary*, page 302.

128. Maher, Sister Mary Denis, "To Do With Honor," *The Roman Catholic Sister Nurse in the United States Civil War*, Thesis, Case Western Reserve University, 1988, page 158. See also: Gibson & Gibson, *Dictionary*, page 306.

129. Gibson & Gibson, *Dictionary*, page 318

130. *Official Records*-Army, Series 1, Volume 7, page 242. See also Gibson & Gibson, *Dictionary*, page 313.

131. Newberry, *Valley of the Mississippi*, page 490. See also: *Official Records*-Navy, Series 1, Volume 23, page 255. See also: Gibson, *Dictionary*, page 319.

132. *Official Records*-Army, Series 1, Volume 6, page 670.

133. *Ibid*.

134. *Official Records*-Navy, Series 1, Volume 15, pages 546-548.

135. *Official Records*-Navy, Series 1, Volume 19, page 804.

136. *Official Records*-Navy, Series 1, Volume 19, page 546.

About the Author

Ronald Waddell has been active in recreating history since 1975. He has published 45 articles on the subject of colonial history of the Central Pennsylvania region. In 1986 he joined J.E.B. Stuart's Staff and Escort as the regimental surgeon, Dr. John B. Fontaine, and participates in their living history that concentrates on the life and duties of various staff officers with General Stuart.

He has given over 350 programs from Canada to South Carolina to civic groups, schools, universities, and conventions on a variety of subjects; the Revolutionary War soldier, colonial women, Civil War medicine, women of the Civil War, women of Gettysburg, and the country and people of Vietnam.

Mr. Waddell is President of the Hygeia Foundation, a nonprofit organization, formed to commemorate the activities of the women of the Civil War. One of the foundation's projects is to build a monument in Gettysburg to the women who served there in 1863.

He served in the United States Army in Germany and Vietnam and is retired from the Pennsylvania National Guard. As a Senior Army Aviator, he has nearly 2400 flight hours, of which 956 are combat hours that include almost 1500 combat missions. He was awarded the Bronze Star Medal, the Air Medal for Valor and an additional 31 oak leaf clusters, the Meritorious and Presidential Unit Citations, the Vietnam Cross of Gallantry with Palm, the Medal for Humanitarian Service from the Secretary of Defense for six air-sea rescues during Hurricane Eloise, two Good Conduct Medals, and ten other campaign and service medals.

Mr. Waddell lives in Lebanon, Pennsylvania, with his wife, Beverly, and has two daughters, Heather and Rebekah.

THE LIFE AND TIMES OF FANNY HARALSON GORDON
CONFEDERATE HEROINE

By Tommie Phillips LaCavera

Frances Rebecca "Fanny" Haralson was born September 18, 1837, in LaGrange, Georgia, the third daughter of General Hugh Anderson Haralson and Caroline Matilda Lewis.[1]

Fanny's war activities are well documented by letters and the book, *Reminiscences of the Civil War*, written by her husband, Major General John B. Gordon. Noted author Allen P. Tankersley wrote several articles on the life of Fanny, one for the United Daughters of the Confederacy Magazine in 1952 and a brochure in 1955 for the Georgia Division United Daughters of the Confederacy's Annual essay contest for the school children of Georgia entitled "Mrs. John B. Gordon, Heroine of the Confederacy." Tankersley's articles contained a mistake that has been perpetuated in other writings that needs to be corrected. Tankersley wrote that "She (Fanny) is one of the founders of the United Daughters of the Confederacy (UDC)."[2] This is not correct, Anna Davenport Raines of Georgia and Caroline Meriwether Goodlett of Tennessee were the Founders of the National Daughters of the Confederacy in 1894.[3] At the Annual Convention held in 1895 in Atlanta the organization's named was changed to the United Daughters of the Confederacy and the Georgia Division of the UDC was organized.[4] Fanny is not listed as a charter member and a thorough search of the minutes of both the Georgia and the national organization of the UDC contain no mention of Fanny either as a member or attending meetings. Although no application papers could be found that she ever joined the organization, it also cannot be stated for certain that she was not a member. It is possible she was an honorary member in which case no application papers would be needed.

Fanny did attend the Confederate reunions and meetings of the United Confederate Veterans (UCV)[5] and later the Sons of Confederate Veterans (SCV) with her husband. The United Confederate Veterans Association was formed in 1889 and General Gordon was made its first Commander-in-Chief, a position he held until his death in 1904. Fanny was much loved by the veterans who considered her one of their rank.[6]

My interest in Fanny came in a round-about-way. While searching for information in the late 1980's, on what I considered some of Georgia's "unknown" or "forgotten" women," I came across the papers of Caroline Haralson and her family in the Hargrett Rare Book and Manuscript Library, at the University of Georgia Libraries.[7]

Fanny between two of her sisters, circa 1853.

Courtesy Hargrett Rare Book and Manuscripts Library, University of Georgia.

Fanny Haralson Gordon, circa 1865.

Courtesy Hargrett Rare Book and Manuscripts Library, University of Georgia.

The Haralson letters that Fanny and her sisters and mother wrote her father during his years in Washington contain a wealth of information on every aspect of the day-to-day family life and give a thorough and fascinating description of life in the ante-bellum South. The letters also give us the background that prepared Fanny for the life she would face in the future.[8] Though this article concerns Fanny's life during the war, I feel it would not be complete without including her childhood and her mother who provided her daughters with a role model that was to serve them well in the future — and she deserves to be remembered.

There are no books written about Fanny's mother and the only reference to her, in the county where she lived for 30 years, is that she was the wife of Hugh Anderson Haralson.[9] Caroline, regrettably, is known only through her letters. But these letters add to our knowledge of Fanny's growing up years. The family plot where Caroline is buried beside her husband contains a grand monument to him and a memorial marker with the names of four children they lost in infancy. Her name is not even inscribed on her grave maker.[10] As was the case with the majority of women in that period — she is an "invisible" woman.

But Caroline was an energetic, vibrant woman, devoted to her husband and children. Of necessity, she became an adept businesswoman, managing not only the family home in town, but also the plantation with its overseer and slaves during the long months Haralson was away. She was a strong woman, coping with the ordinary day-to-day problems and those that arose in times of illness and death.

Hugh Haralson graduated from Franklin College, now the University of Georgia, in 1825 and before he was twenty-one he was admitted to the bar by a special act of the Georgia Legislature. In 1828 he married Caroline Matilda Lewis of Greene County and they moved to Monroe, Georgia, where he began practicing law. Not long afterwards, the family moved to LaGrange, where they would reside the rest of their lives, and Haralson entered politics.[11]

In 1831 and 1832, Haralson was elected to the Georgia legislature. Fond of military life, he and his brother Kinchen organized two companies of LaGrange volunteers during the Seminole War in 1836. For his services, Haralson was given the rank of Major General in the State Militia.[12]

At one time a staunch Whig, until a disagreement over the National Bank and tariffs, Haralson separated from the party in 1841 and became a Democrat. He was elected to the United States Congress in 1842, and re-elected in 1844 and 1846. During the Mexican War he served as Chairman of the Committee on Military Affairs, a crucial position.[13]

By the time Haralson was elected to Congress, he and Caroline had a family of four daughters and one son: Elizabeth (Lizzy), Clara Caroline (Carrie or Carry), Frances Rebecca (Fanny), Leonora (Nora), and "Buddy."[14] As was often the case in this period of time, women generally gave birth every year or two and Caroline was no exception. There was always a baby in the house and due to the fact that each boy child was always called "Buddy" or "the man," it was difficult to know the names of the different sons who were born and who died young. Only one son lived to adulthood, Hugh A. Haralson, Jr.

Although Caroline's life was very busy during the years that Haralson was in Washington, her letters reveal that she missed him desperately. Mail was extremely important to the entire family and every letter mentioned either receiving or not receiving a letter. Caroline wrote her husband:

> I have suffered because I didn't get a letter from you for three weeks, but I saw your name among the ayes and nays. I saw a notice in the UNION of January 19 taken from the NEW YORK GLOBE, it said that you were winning for yourself fresh laurels this winter.[15]

Not a day went by that either or Caroline or one of the girls didn't write to Haralson, but he did not respond as frequently. Fanny wrote her father, "We've had no letters for days. Perhaps it is the fashion of the mails, unless you have failed writing."[16] When she was ill she wrote:

> I will write you everyday I am sick to keep you from being uneasy. If I get worse I will put Sussex on one of the carriage horses and send him down to Columbus and send you word by the telegraph. Ma got three papers from you this morning, but no letters."[17]

Caroline's responsibilities were at times a burden, but more than these were her frequent worries about the illnesses of the children and her frequent pregnancies. Caroline's problem with her pregnancies were not unusual for that period of time. Because of lack of effective birth control there was a high birth rate and infant mortality was common. Caroline never complained about her frequent pregnancies, but in 1850, at the age of 43 she wrote her husband:

> You must excuse the feelings that showed in my letter, but thank kind providence, since yesterday morning, I have reason to hope it is not so. Now don't you rejoice with me? I know you do. I have been having children regularly for twenty years and I think that is long enough. My mind is relieved of a load.[18]

Illness was frequent among the family and among the servants. In the winter colds, chills and sore throats abounded and in the summer worms, fevers, and bowel trouble appeared. Calomel was prescribed for a variety of the illnesses, and also paragoric (sic) and Dovers (sic) powders.[19] For colds and sore throats, the remedy was often a dose of onion syrup along with greasing the throat and feet and wrapping them with flannel.[20]

The children became accustomed to having worms. Fanny wrote her father in 1849:

> I am sick as a dog today — the worms are galloping all inside me like race horses. Dr. Hill has just sent me some terrible medicine to make them gallop out. It's something like that Dead Shot that he sent out to the plantation to them wormy children. I have to take it three times a day. It has a little bit of everything in it — oil, turpentine, molasses, Jerusalem oak, and a great deal many other things. I am a sick chicken all over. My lips look like someone has taken a pin knife and slit it downward all over and they are so sore that I can hardly laugh.[21]

Dental problems arose too and the doctor's advice generally was to pull the teeth or take calomel. Cholera and fever were the most dreaded diseases. Fanny wrote her father, "You must write us about the cholera, whether it has reached Washington or not, if it has you must keep clear of it if you can."[22]

The babies worried Caroline the most. She frequently mentioned little Walter's health for a year or so, then he is never mentioned again.[23] Possibly he died, for in a later letter Lizzy mentioned, "Buddy has on one of dear little Walter's dresses."[24]

In all her letters, Caroline always revealed her deep concern that Haralson was away from the children too much. One of the most poignant letters concerning the children was the one Caroline wrote on behalf of her baby son:

> Oh Pa! I do wish you would make haste and come home. I don't know much about you, but I do hear my Ma and sisters talk so much about you and wish for you so often. Ma calls me "Pa's little boy" almost every time she takes me. I know I will love you too when I come to know you a little better. I see gentlemen very seldom, when I do I look at them just like I would any other strange animal. I am still fond of my jumper and have a great deal of pleasure jumping. My Ma has kept me at home very close all of my life for fear of the whooping cough, but as she don't hear of any new cases now she is beginning to let me go out a little. She let me go to church on the 4th of July, but she put a great big head of garlic in my bosom as big as my fist. It didn't smell very sweet, but as my dear Ma put it there, I will wear it, for I know she loves me and no mistake — goodby my dear Pa. I have no name to sign, but I am your own little boy.[25]

The loneliness of a wife and mother, and fear for her child were unmistakable in the letter. The Haralson's were slow to name their infant sons and the letters never revealed exactly what the problem was. Lizzy wrote in July 1848: "Oh Pa. That boy of yours, he gets sweeter and sweeter everyday. What say you to the name Wilford for him? Ma likes Wilford Carroll."[26]

Six months later she wrote about a name again: "Little Buddy is just learning whittling. Do think of a name for him. John, Frederick Alexander, Charles Carroll — or what? Ma is obstinately silent on the subject and you had better do it before he is dubbed Bud Haralson."[27]

Willie is one of the names on the memorial marker in the cemetery in LaGrange and it is possible that the child was named Wilford and called Willie.

Several years later Fanny wrote, "Bud is the same, fattens everyday and is the finest looking little fellow about town. He gets furious if we call him anything but Frederick Lewis."[28] It is unknown if this was actually the child's name. There was no Frederick Lewis on the cemetery marker, although there is a Hugh, and a Hugh is mentioned in one letter, "Little Hugh is better, but still unwell."[29] It was not unusual to name a child the same name as one who had died earlier. In a later letter, Caroline mentioned "that boy Fanny calls Frederick."[30]

The Haralson plantation required much work though an overseer was in charge. Caroline wrote of visiting the plantation often so that they (overseer and slaves) would know that she was aware of what was happening, and to make sure everything was running smoothly.[31] She advised her husband on all matters pertaining to the plantation. It is interesting to note that as the years went by, Caroline made decisions and then told him that she did the best she could. Although she always wished his approval, she began to gain confidence in her own judgement and did not require his approval as she did when he first went to Washington.[32]

In 1847, she inquired if he ever heard of any cotton news in Washington:

> I heard the other day it was eleven cents and that's a pretty good price. I've been making some calculations recently (don't laugh for I am serious) and I think your remaining cotton, at present prices will just about pay your Castleberry debt. Am I far wrong? Then you can save a good little lump of your Congress salary, and soon I hope you will be able to walk perfectly erect, anywhere, and say 'I owe no man anything.[33]

A year later she reported she was compelled to have a new thrasher. She was having one built and made an agreement to pay for it in corn at a dollar and three-quarters a barrel: "That's all you can get for corn now, and the men say soon you won't be able to get that. This was the best arrangement I could make. I had no cash to pay out, not even to have the old thrasher mended.[34] In another letter she asked: "Do you want anything done with the cotton before you return? Let me know (as I am a great businessman or rather woman?). I'll have it sent to Columbus and follow on — nothing but the highest market price would satisfy me.[35]

Pork, along with corn and cotton provided a good income for the family.[36] The amount of pork packed away impressed Fanny and she wrote:

> Mr. Combs killed the rest of the hogs, packed them away nicest of anything you ever saw. It would do you good to go in the smoke house and look around and see meat all piled up most as high as your head. Ma says she's the richest woman in town. Mrs. Poythress not excepted.[37]

A major concern was the changes in the weather which could cause pork to spoil even though it was salted down. References to various neighbors who lost theirs because the weather turned warm appeared frequently in the letters.[38]

In addition to selling pork, cotton was sold and also used in exchange of other goods. Caroline wrote:

> I sent to the factory and got a bale of cloth, 505 yards. Sent the remaining cotton and exchanged it for thread, got 13 bunches . . . sold 10 bags of your cotton at 4.33 1/3 cents, brought $213.41. $164.44 applied to your account and balance $48.97 handed to me. Dixon sent one bag of old cotton for which he could only get 1 cent offered, think we'd do better to save such at home for mattresses. Tom Mitchell says the mattress maker will make a mattress and keep the cotton for pay.[39]

In addition to the responsibilities associated with crops and animals, Caroline was also responsible for clothing the slaves.   It is unlikely she did the actual sewing, but she mentioned at one time she had, "Bought 2 pieces of Negro woolen cloth — 20 and 25 yards at cost of $10.00. All hands now have an entire suit except for the youngsters. I have yet to clothe them and the children," and later, "I have to send for some more cloth to finish the little Negroes winter clothes. I hope I am now done with that troublesome work."[40]

Sickness affected the overseer and slaves just as it did the family and Caroline was responsible for their care and well being. They received the same remedies and medicines as the family, and occasionally it was necessary for the doctor to prescribe the medicine for them.[41]

There were frequent mentions of the Negroes holding prayer meetings in the kitchens in the evenings, and the girls mentioned the praying and singing they heard as they sat, read their books, did their homework, and wrote their father.[42]

Caroline's life was not always sad and painful and Haralson did not always neglect the family. He did write the family regularly, even though he did not write as often as they did. (This is supported by the many references in their letters to him where they answered questions he asked in his letters). The family also referred to visits to Washington. Lizzy did go and stay with him for a period of time, as shown by Caroline's letters to her during that period.

Even though Haralson was away from home for long periods of time, he was quick to respond to Caroline's needs and wishes. In 1846, she thanked him for the new horses he had gotten her and said, "I go where I please and feel quite independent." Several years later she wrote that a new carriage was desperately needed, and she was delighted when he sent her notice that he had purchased a barouche, "especially since you said it has four seats independent of the driver's seat."[43] Fanny wrote, "We are all tired of hearing that old rattle box roll about town, but is was the best old carriage I ever saw, I almost became attached to it. Sussex is tickled at having a new carriage and fine pair of horses to drive."[44]

It was obvious that each son was spoiled. Perhaps this was because each lived such a short time. Fanny praised her baby brother in 1849:

> Buddy is as sweet as ever, when he can get out of Sarah's arms (his nurse). He runs about the yard — takes a stick — beats the flowers, pulls them up, throws them down. He can do all sorts of smart and sweet things.[45]

In a later letter she continues her praise:

> Buddy is getting to be such a bad boy that his Ma or nobody else can do anything with him. If he sees anything he wants he will have it or look like he would turn everything upside down — and hollows (sic) and screams like he would have fits — but he is mighty sweet anyhow and has more sense than anything you ever saw for his age. He can call his Ma and smack the cat.[46]

The Haralson's were obviously well off financially, but their income was derived mainly from the plantation, and this meant that there were periods of no income until the crops and animals were harvested and sold.

In 1848, when the doctor told Caroline that a bathhouse would be good for her health she had one built. The children loved it. Lizzy wrote:

> We will go to the bath-house as soon as Ma returns. She was there all morning with Sussex, cleaning and chinking. We take the life preserver

down every day. I think if it was a little longer and deeper I could learn to swim. Fanny comes nearer to swimming than any of us. She would learn to swim if she had someone to show her.[47]

Nora later wrote:

It is a cool morning and Carrie and Fanny are disappointed because Ma said it was too cool to bath (sic). We have got the bath fixed so it gets right full and runs out at the top. I can go in with the other children when I am well.[48]

At the end of the summer, Lizzy wrote they had never been in better health, and no doubt much of their health and fine spirits could be attributed to the bath. "We take it almost every evening and Ma says she wonders where she has been all her life that she has never taken it before," Lizzy wrote her father. Before long many family members and friends visited regularly to "take the bath."[49]

Local and state politics drew Caroline's attention in June. Her feelings of disillusionment and the sacrifices demanded of the family by her husband's career in Democratic politics emerged in these letters:

You can't conceive my dear husband of how glad I would be if you never suffer yourself nominated again. Oh how I dread the approaching contest this summer — particularly if you are a candidate. It is so disagreeable to live in a community where the Whigs have the majority.[50]

Haralson left Georgia the first part of December 1847, and by the summer of 1848 was still unable to make a trip home to see his family. Writing in June, Caroline mentioned a mass meeting (Democrat) scheduled at Stone Mountain in August:

It's to be hoped you will be at home long before that time. If you go, I want to go with you. Home is a mighty sweet place I know, but I feel now like a little jaunt — it would do me good.[51]

School played an important role in the life of Fanny and her sisters, and provided not only learning, but literary programs, lectures and concerts. The girls attended the LaGrange Female Seminary, a Baptist institution chartered in 1843 by Rev. Milton Bacon. Situated on fifteen acres, the main building was a three storied structure. It had apartments for boarding students, study rooms, lecture halls, a chemical laboratory, and an auditorium. In 1849, ten professors and teachers directed an average of 100 students. Tuition was between $165.00 and $200.00 per year.[52]

At the beginning of school in January 1847, Lizzy wrote the school had 50 or 60 students, and she would study[53] "Logic, chemistry and continued arithmetic, and I will take one or two more, one of which would be astronomy.[54] A later letter in 1847 mentioned that she went to Mr. Bacon's to receive assistance she needed and usually stayed an hour each day. Lizzy was sixteen at the time and it is not known if she attended regular classes or if the daily meeting with Mr. Bacon was the extent of her schooling. Towards the end of the term she wrote, "Nora is beginning to spell — in two letters, and she is fond of her books. I only require two lessons a day of her."[55]

At the beginning of 1848, Fanny wrote her father there were a great many new scholars, "some very pretty ones and some horrid ugly ones." Two weeks later she wrote the school had grown from 40 students to 80. By May, Fanny was complaining that Lizzie wrote to him all the time, but, "I never had so much studying to do. In the day I never have a moment to lose and at night I have to get two lessons, but I will take time out to write you anyway."[56]

In a letter to Lizzy in May, Haralson wrote:

> I don't hear of you reading any books . . . while I would not have you devote too much time to books, I hope you will not neglect them altogether. You might read aloud to your Ma and then let her read to you. It would be a source of pleasure to both of you.[57]

Lizzy soon responded, "I will commence my reading again. The gentle reproof in you last letter I richly deserve."[58] That summer she wrote that everyone was busy ready, Fanny was deeply interested in *Elizabeth: The Exile Of Liberia*, Carry was reading Bancroft's *History Of The United States*, and she was reading Milton's *Paradise Lost*. She said she liked it better than any political book she had ever read except Pollock's *Course Of Time*.[59]

Caroline wrote her husband that the children were all reading and that "Fanny is the best reader in the family except for you and me. She reads rapidly and correctly."[60]

Nora was only seven years old when Lizzy wrote a letter to her father for her:

> I am always asking Lizzy or Fanny to write a letter for me, but they are always too busy. I wish I could write as I am too little to work or go to school. Lizzy taught me to write my name and when she finishes this letter I'll sign my name with my own hand — and no one to hold it either. I can spell almost any word. (This letter was signed Nora.)[61]

Lizzy wrote her father in December she had indulged herself with a novel, *Jane Eyre,* a new work by an unknown author, and that she was very pleased with it.[62] A week later Fanny wrote that Lizzy was reading the novel *Rob-Roy*, and that she and Carry were reading *Youth's Cabinet* which had a great deal of information. She went on to say, "Ma reads a good deal to us and explains what we don't understand."[63]

Novels and history books were not the family's only reading. In addition to the many newspapers Haralson sent from Washington, Caroline occasionally asked him to send books, such as "the account of the Dead Sea Scrolls expedition as soon as it's published. It will be very interesting for the children as well as for myself."[64]

In January 1850, an excited nine year old Nora wrote her father that she was very happy that he wrote she must go to school, but, "Ma says I have to wait until the weather is better and she fixes me up better."[65]

Weather was a big problem with the children attending school. If it was too cold or raining too bad, they did not attend school. However, often when the weather cleared or warmed up later in the day, the children were sent to school in the evening. It is not known if evening included the late afternoon or the night, but shopping and going to the post office or to the doctor in the evening was also frequently mentioned.[66]

In January 1850, Caroline wrote Lizzy, who was in Washington visiting her father, about problems in school:

> Carry is much in earnest about improving herself and takes her books to school to read at recess. Fanny had a good cry last night because Mr. Bacon put some of the class in Armistead's Philosophy class and kept her back, when in reality she was a better scholar than those he advanced, although they were older. It puts me in a bad position, I don't want to see her mortified, but I don't want to question Bacon's judgement.[67]

In less than a month Caroline wrote her husband about a more serious problem: "Mr. Bacon does not have much patience with Fanny in her arithmetic and threatened to whip her. This he shall not do, at least if I can prevent it and I hope he won't attempt it."[68]

A totally fascinated Fanny wrote her father in 1850 of a lecture she had attended at Mr. Montgomery's school on electricity and magnetism and of a magic lantern that showed:

> ...many pretty pictures, among them the children of Israel crossing the Red Sea and Pharaoh's army after them — all drowning in the water, the blowing up of a ship, a burning mountain, two enemy vessels meeting and one setting the other on fire — death on a pale horse — but the prettiest thing he showed was a cupid in a moss rose. When he first showed it, it was on a bud, BUT WE COULD SEE IT GROW — very slowly until it was a full grown rose. Then all at once it gave a sudden jerk and we saw the little cupid sitting in the rose pointing his arrow at the crowd. You must not think we went by ourselves for Ma went with us and we got there early and got a good seat in front.[69]

She went on to describe the heads that were read among the crowd. One she said was "Mr. Kiner, and a very good account of him was given and it was very correct. He said Mr. Kiner was fond of the ladies and very fond of music."

If the caliber of the school the girls attended is to be judged by the penmanship, vocabulary and articulation of its students, the LaGrange Female Seminary must be judged an excellent school, for Fanny and Lizzy excelled in all three areas.

The summer of 1850 found Caroline and the children at White Sulfur Springs, Virginia. Apparently, while visiting in Washington with their father, there was an outbreak of cholera in the city. Haralson took them to White Sulfur Springs, then he returned to Washington.

In July, Lizzy wrote they were all well but, "We fear for your health — do be careful for our sakes. Don't expose yourself to either the sun or night air. We have gulped as much of the water as we could because everyone told us it would increase our appetite." The biggest problem however was the lack of reading material and she asked her father to send her *Georgia Scenes* and a novel by Miss Frederica Bremer called *The Neighbors*. She thanked him for the newspapers he sent them.[70]

A letter from Fanny in August said they were "well and anxious to see you and to know when we can go home. Though we are afraid for you to come through Harper's Ferry. We have heard no further news on cholera today."[71]

The final letter of the collection is January 1851. With this last letter one was left with a sense of loss, for there were many unanswered questions needed to complete a more thorough portrait of the Haralson family. With the exception of the two letters written by Haralson, and one by his niece, the rest are written by Caroline, Lizzy, Fannie and Nora (Nora's are all written by her mother or sisters). It is strange that Carry did not write any of the letters, although there are numerous references to her in the letters of her mother and sisters. Most refer to her as a "blessed little creature."

Of necessity, only a few of the areas covered in the letters are contained here. Missing are accounts of the church and its role in the lives of the women and in the community; frequency and mode of travel, the close bonds of friendship many women felt with other women in similar circumstances, and the various organizations in which the community participated, such as the Sons of Temperance. Of special interest was the account of the runaway marriage of Alfred H. Colquitt, who later became a famous general in the War Between the States, Governor of Georgia and a United States senator.[72]

The letters also serve another purpose, they put to rest the myth of the Southern woman as pampered, weak, and spoiled. In many respects many of them were as strong. or stronger than many women of today. Because they shared many of the same experiences and common concerns, they supported and gained strength in each other.

Haralson was not a candidate for renomination in 1850 and when his term of office was up he returned to LaGrange and resumed his law practice. Not much is known about the family for the years 1850-1853.

In June 1854, Lizzy married an Atlanta attorney, Basil Hallman Overby,[73] and moved to that city where Overby had formed a partnership with two other men, Logan E. Bleckley and John Brown Gordon. During a visit to her sister after her marriage, Fanny met John Brown Gordon and it was love at first sight. Soon after her return to LaGrange, Gordon followed to press his claim for her hand in marriage. Haralson willingly gave his consent to the marriage of his daughter, who was too young to contract on her own account.[74]

The wedding was set for September 18th, Fanny's seventeenth birthday. Gordon was to go back to his law office, continue to build up his practice, and wait for the 'day of days' when he would come back to claim his bride. After the wedding they were to live in Atlanta. But fate had other plans.

Soon after Gordon returned to Atlanta, General Haralson became seriously ill. Fearing he would not live, he wrote his last will and testament and named his prospective son-in-law as one of the executors of his will and specified, "I give and bequeath unto John B. Gordon in Trust and for the sole use, benefit and enjoyment of my daughter Fanny R. Gordon another lot of like value (slaves) and to be selected by the same men at the same time, said property not subject to debts of said John B. Gordon or any future husband she may have."[75]

Fanny, grieving over her father's illness, wanted to postpone the wedding, but he would not hear of it. Plans for a church wedding were canceled. There would be just a quiet ceremony at home. On September 18, Gordon, his partner Basil Overby and his wife, Lizzy (Fanny's sister), came down from Atlanta.

When they arrived, they found that Haralson was too ill to sit up. The wedding was transferred from the parlor to his bedside with only family members and a few close friends present. Overby, who was an ordained Methodist minister as well as a lawyer, performed the ceremony. When asked, "Who giveth this woman to be married to this man?', Haralson mustered enough strength to say softly, but firmly, "I do."[76]

Pressed flowers were found in a Token Album in the Haralson Family File: dried rosebuds— "Rosebuds given me by my husband on our first acquaintance in 1853. FHG" and a dried gardenia, "The only ornament worn in my hair the night of my marriage by my father's bedside, September 18, 1854. FHG"[77]

According to the Southern custom of the day, the wedding party remained at the home of the bride for several days, but without the usual festivity and merriment, for Haralson grew steadily worse. Exactly one week later, on September 25, 1854, he died. Haralson County, Georgia, was created by a Legislative Act, January 26, 1856, from Polk County and Carroll County and named in his honor.[78]

Efforts to find the date Caroline Haralson died have been unsuccessful. She is not listed on the 1860 Census so it must be assumed that she died prior to that year. In death, as in life, she was an "invisible woman" and her death remains unrecorded.

In 1857, Caroline "Carry" married Logan E. Bleckley,[79] the third member of Gordon's law firm. Thus, the mutual devotion which had already bound the three men together was strengthened by ties of marriage. Nora married James M. Pace,[80] who was also a lawyer, of Covington, Georgia.

Because his law practice was slow, Gordon decided to give up his law practice and to become a newspaper reporter. In November 1855, he and Fanny and baby boy, Hugh Haralson, left Atlanta and moved to Milledgeville, where he began his new profession. In March, 1856, Gordon returned to the mountains of North Georgia and aided his father in developing coal mines discovered on his father's plantation. In 1859, the family moved to Jackson County, Alabama. So near to three state lines did he live that his home was in Alabama, his mines in Georgia, and his post office in Tennessee.[81] When the War came in 1861, Gordon immediately raised a company of volunteers and on May 14, 1861, was commissioned major of the "The Racoon Roughs." This name was chosen because of the coonskin caps the men wore instead of the standard army issue.

As the time approached for the newly organized company to leave, Fanny boldly announced that she would go to the front with her husband and leave their two sons, Frank and Hugh, with their Grandmother Gordon. General Gordon wrote, "We had two children, both boys. The struggle between devotion to my family on one hand and duty to my country on the other was most trying to my sensibilities. . . what was I to do with the girl-wife and the two little boys? The wife and mother was no less taxed in her effort to settle this momentous question. But finally yielding to the prompting of her own heart and to her unerring sense of duty, she ended doubt as to what disposition was to be made of her by announcing that she intended to accompany me to the war, leaving her children with my mother and faithful 'Mammy Mary.'

I rejoiced at her decision then, and had still greater reasons for rejoicing at it afterwards, when I felt through every fiery ordeal the inspiration of her near presence, and had, at need, the infinite comfort of her tender nursing.[82]

For the next four years Fanny endured the hardships of army life and lived so close to the fighting men that they considered her one of their number. Sometimes she was a volunteer nurse for the men in the ranks, and even after Gordon had become a Major General, many privates of his command received her personal care.

When the army was in winter quarters, "Mammy Mary" an old servant of Fanny's mother. would bring the Gordon's two little boys to visit their parents. Though Fanny and the General spent as much time as possible together at the front, when separated by even a few miles they wrote each other daily.[83]

Regarding the mental strain and anxiety under which Mrs. Gordon labored during that trying time, General Gordon later wrote about Fanny's uncle Major John Sutherland Lewis, "As he was without a family of his own, and was devoted to his niece, he naturally watched over her with the tender solicitude of a father, when it was possible for him to be near her during the war. He died in very old age some years after the close of hostilities, but he left behind him touching tributes to his cherished niece, with whose remarkable adventures he was familiar, and whose fortitude had amazed and thrilled him. Major Lewis wrote, 'The battle (Seven Pines) in which Mrs. Gordon's husband was engaged was raging near Richmond with great fury. The cannonade was rolling around the horizon like some vast earthquake on huge, crashing wheels. Whether the threads of wedded sympathy were twisted more closely as the tremendous perils gathered around him, it was evident that her anxiety became more intense with each passing moment. She asked me to accompany her to a hill a short distance away. There she listened in silence. Pale and quiet, with clasped hands, she sat statue like with her face toward the field of battle. Her self control was wonderful; only the quick drawn sigh from the bottom of her heart revealed the depth of emotion that was struggling there. The news of her husband's safety afterwards and the joy of meeting him later produced the inevitable reaction. The intensity of mental strain she had been subjected to had over tasked her strength, and when the excessive tension was relaxed she was well neigh prostrated; but a brief repose enabled her to bear up with a sublime fortitude through the protracted and trying experiences which followed the seven days battle around Richmond.'"[84]

When General Gordon fell almost mortally wounded at Antietam, (five bullets, one in the face) Fanny rushed to him. General Gordon later wrote, "The doctors were doubtful about the propriety of admitting her to my room, but I told them to let her come. I was more apprehensive of the effect of the meeting upon her nerves than upon mine. My face was black and shapeless — so swollen that one eye was entirely hidden and the other nearly so. My right leg and left arm and shoulder were bandaged and propped with pillows. I knew she would be greatly shocked. As she reached the door and looked, I saw at once I must reassure. Summoning all my strength, I said: 'Here's your handsome (?) husband; been to an Irish wedding."[85]

For seven months the General's life hung in the balance, his doctor and friends had little hope of his recovery. Many years later Gordon recalled, "The doctor told Mrs. Gordon to paint my arm above the wound three to four times a day with iodine. She obeyed the doctors by painting it, I think, three or four hundred times a day. Under God's providence, I owe my life to her incessant watchfulness night and day, and to her tender nursing through weary weeks and anxious months."[86]

Many interesting incidents, some of them combining elements both amusing and pathetic, marked the experiences of the soldier and his wife during those tumultuous years. In his book, Gordon referred to the gloomy Christmas of 1864. Fanny on leaving home had brought with her some excellent coffee, which she kept for special occasions. On Christmas Eve he asked her what she had in store that was suitable for a Christmas meal. She answered, "Some of that coffee I brought from home." Never he declared, did he hear more welcome words and the novelty of enjoying once more a good cup of coffee made Christmas cheer indeed for them and those who shared that meal.[87]

Her personal bravery was hardly excelled by that of her husband. In September 1864, the battle of Winchester began. Fanny had stopped at the home of her friend Mrs. Hugh Lee. As she saw the Confederates retreating she stood on the verandah urging them to return to battle. Many did turn back, but not all. As the men went by she called out to them to find their command. When she heard the answer "We are Gordon's men," it was too much for her. With shells from Sheridan's batteries flying all around, seemingly unconscious of danger, she rushed into the streets and urged the retreating Confederates to turn back and meet the enemy. She and her six year old son Frank who was with her at the time barely escaped with their own lives.[88]

General Early had long before stated an opposition to wives following their soldier-husbands, and once even muttered, "I wish the Yankees would capture Mrs. Gordon and hold her til the war is over." Fanny learned of his remark and teased him about it at a dinner. Embarrassed, Early replied, "Mrs. Gordon, General Gordon is a better soldier when you are close by him than when you are away, and so hereafter, when I issue orders that officers wives must go to the rear, you may know that you are excepted." When Early learned that Fannie had managed to catch up to the Army at Winchester, he exclaimed, "Well, I'll be! If my men would keep up as well as she does, I'd never issue another order against straggling."[89]

When the General received orders to evacuate Petersburg on April 2, he did so with "a personal woe" for Fanny was ill. She was left in the home of James Pinckney Williams with the hope that "some chivalric soldier of the Union army would learn of her presence and guard her home against intruders."[90]

On April 12, 1865, General Lee surrendered at Appomattox Courthouse. As soon as the formalities were over the General Gordon started for Petersburg to join his wife and new son. As he approached Williamson's home he was stopped by a guard of Union soldiers stationed there to protect Fanny from intruders. The men demanded his mission and when the General explained that he was "only the husband" of the sick woman, the soldiers cheerfully admitted him.[91]

Although Fanny was rapidly recovering she was not able to begin the long trip to Georgia. While waiting for her to recover, the General learned of the assassination of President Lincoln and sold his horse "General Shaler" for $300 to make the trip home. When Fanny was able to travel, she and the General, accompanied by Captain and Mrs. James M. Pace (Fanny's sister Nora) began the long journey home.[92]

After the war, Fanny shared the hardships and poverty of Reconstruction with the same fortitude that she had experienced the perils of the battlefield.

The General's first visit upon reaching Georgia was to his parent's home. Afterwards the family went to live with Fanny's sister Lizzy Overby. Lizzy's husband had died in 1859 and to support herself and her children she ran a boarding house.[93] Later that year, the family moved to Glynn County, Georgia, where the General began a lumber business and purchased a rice plantation which Fanny helped him manage. Labor problems connected with the Reconstruction Acts were so discouraging that the family moved back to Atlanta in 1867.[94]

Fanny was a charter member of the Atlanta Ladies Memorial Association which was organized April 15, 1866. Mrs. Joseph H. Morgan, the first president of the association, was forced to resign her position when her husband's job necessitated a move to Augusta, Georgia, and the association was inactive for almost a year.[95]

On May 7, 1868, a large group of women in Atlanta met for the purpose of forming a permanent organization and electing new officers and Fanny was elected President. After completing the organizational work, a notice was sent to the newspapers inviting the various fraternal organizations and the citizens to unite with the Memorial Association in observing a Memorial service on May 10th. At this time the city was still under occupation by the Union, but General Meade and many of the army attended the exercises.

The good work of the first association was continued during Fanny's administration. An appeal to the state legislature for an appropriation to remove the bodies of those soldiers who had fallen in battle and were buried in trenches around the city, and to re-interr them in Oakland Cemetery was denied, but the ladies were not discouraged. A committee of ladies from each of the churches was appointed to solicit subscriptions of twenty-five cents for the cemetery fund. In addition, entertainments and Memorial concerts were given until the required amount of $6,000.00 was raised to provide boxes (coffins) and remove the bodies. Fanny and Mrs. J. M. Gordon, vice president of the association, personally superintended removing the dead for ten miles around and throughout the city. For three years the women of Atlanta had done nothing at the memorial exercises held but pray, exercising their rights under the United States Constitution which guaranteed religious freedom. May 10, 1869, was different for the first Memorial Address was delivered. It was a joyous day for all in attendance.[96]

During Fanny's administration a movement was initiated to erect a monument to "Our Confederate Dead, which would be an eternal testimonial of their patriotism and valor." The ladies worked diligently and enthusiastically in their labor of love. As money for the monument accumulated, a difference of opinion arose as to its location, some members desiring that it should placed in the center of the business district; others wished it to located at Oakland Cemetery. The question was finally settled at a meeting called for the purpose. The most prominent people of the city assembled at the city hall and voted by ballot to place the monument at Oakland Cemetery.

Following this action, Fanny immediately resigned her office as President of the Ladies Memorial Association. Obviously Fanny was in favor of placing the monument in the center of town. Or she may have resigned due to the fact that the General entered politics in 1868 and she was busy helping him. She read the newspapers for him, marked or clipped items she thought he ought to see, assisted in his campaigns, and accompanied him on speaking tours.[97]

By the fall of 1870, enough money had been collected to defray the cost of laying the cornerstone of the monument and placing the coping around the base. On October 15, 1870, General John B. Gordon was the orator for the ceremony of the laying of the cornerstone.[98]

In 1886, the General traveled to Montgomery to accompany President Jefferson Davis and his daughter Winnie to Atlanta where Davis was to speak at the unveiling of a statue to the late Senator Benjamin Harvey Hill. At West Point, Georgia, Davis was too weak to speak and asked the General to speak for him. It was there, from the platform on the back of the train that the General introduced Winnie: "My countrymen, I want to introduce you to the daughter of the Confederacy. This is the war baby of our old chieftain, Miss Winnie Davis." This was the first time Winnie had ever been called "The Daughter of the Confederacy," a name she was to carry for the rest of her life.[99]

On a visit to LaGrange by Jefferson Davis before his death in 1889, he paid tribute to Fanny when he said: "I love it (LaGrange) also because it was the home of Hugh Haralson, who took me up when I first entered Congress. It was also the birthplace of the heroic wife of the heroic man, General John B. Gordon. She was one of the noble women who sat up all night to make white badges for the arms of our men who went in the night charge at Petersburg, which was led by her chivalric husband. Young ladies and gentlemen, I thank you from the bottom of my heart, and now I wish to present to you the lady to whom I referred as a native of LaGrange, Mrs. Gordon."[100]

Through the years, good and bad, through the trying times of the war and Reconstruction, as wife of a three-term United States Senator and two-term Governor of Georgia, Fanny was always at the General's side. In 1897, the General did not stand for reelection in the Senate and after his retirement he devoted the rest of his life to trying to help heal the scars of the war. Tankersley wrote that in none of the General's speeches or public utterances was plea for reconciliation more evident than in his *Reminiscences of the Civil War* published in 1903.

At the Atlanta reunion of the United Confederate Veterans in 1898, the General had requested to have a reception at his home but due to time constraints his request was denied. In addressing the group he said, "I have a big house, big grounds, and a bigger heart. You would not have had much to see in me, but you would have seen the most beautiful woman in the whole world. It was she who followed me from the earliest sound of the cannon in 1861 to the last dying murmurs in 1865, and without her knowledge or consent I am going to present her to you." As he led Fanny to the front of the stage, "The entire audience rose en masse, and the old building echoed with the ringing cheers of the veterans. It was a magnificent ovation they gave Mrs. Gordon."[101]

It was at this reunion that Winnie Davis, the Daughter of the Confederacy, made her last public appearance. A sudden summer shower arose and before the top of the carriage could be raised, Winnie was drenched and took a severe chill. Instead of retiring to her hotel, she insisted on a full review of the Confederate veterans, most of whom she knew by name or face. That night she attended the grand ball and the next day traveled back to Narragansett Pier, Rhode Island, feeling desperately ill. She died September 16, 1898.[102]

Fanny was also recognized at the reunions in South Carolina in 1899 and in Kentucky in 1900 where she shared honors with Mrs. Jefferson Davis and Mrs. Stonewall Jackson.[103]

A few weeks after the publication of his book, the General went to spend the Christmas season at his winter home near Miami, Florida. While there he became sick on January 5th and never recovered. He died January 9, 1904.[104]

Following the General's death the Ladies' Memorial Association of Atlanta wired Fanny:

> The Ladies Memorial Association of Atlanta begs Mrs. Gordon for the privilege of giving to General Gordon and herself a lasting resting place in the Confederate Memorial Grounds at Oakland Cemetery. Fanny thanked the Association for the offer it made, and accepted for her husband a resting place among his beloved comrades of the memorable struggle of 1861-1865.[105]

Fanny later wrote the Association:

> My Dear Mrs. Ellis: I wish to assure you and the ladies of the Memorial Association of my appreciation of the tribute paid General Gordon in your desire to have his body rest among his old comrades. No more appropriate spot could be found for his last resting place than among the martyrs of the cause he loved so well. Please express to the ladies my heartfelt thanks for the beautiful floral offering. Very sincerely and cordially, Fanny H. Gordon.[106]

For the first time in almost fifty years Fanny was alone. She had spent most of her time being a good wife and mother, and as long as Gordon lived he was romantically in love with the woman whom he had married on her seventeenth birthday.

During her last years Fanny was interested in the activities of patriotic organizations. On April 25, 1908, the Fannie Gordon Chapter, United Daughters of the Confederacy was chartered in Eastman, Georgia.[107]

Fannie survived her husband by more than 27 years and died at the age of ninety-three, on April 28, 1931. She was laid to rest beside her beloved General in Oakland Cemetery, Atlanta.[108]

The esteem with which she was held by the Confederate veterans is strikingly revealed in their resolution, published shortly after her death:

The recent passing of Mrs. John B. Gordon, the widow of one of the South's most outstanding and beloved leaders, at the advanced age of ninety-three years, almost last survivor of the dignity, beauty and culture of the ante-bellum period, closes a page of history incomparable in our American civilization. Gifted with rare charm and dignity, she was a polished cornerstone in the temple of idealism of the Old South. When her gallant husband heard the call to arms, she made ready as quickly as he to answer the summons. She was found ever near behind the lines, ready to minister to every call that came. Unused to hardships, she faced privations and danger undaunted and in closing the eyes of the dying, with a prayer on her lips for the surviving mothers far away. When the horrors of war ceased and her gallant husband answered the call of his State, she, as the First Lady of Georgia, was the queenly, gracious hostess to stand beside him; and when later the honor of United States Senator called her husband to the capitol of the nation, again she stood beside him, giving honor to her State by her gracious, queenly dignity and beauty; and when in her hour of Desolation she stood alone in her sorrow, the heart of the South grieved with her and now rejoices in the reunion around the great white throne. "Requiescat in Pace" (May she rest in peace); until the dawning of the morning when the mists have rolled away.[109]

A number of obituaries were published when Fanny died:

Mrs. Fanny Haralson Gordon, widow of Confederate veteran, former United States Senator, and former governor, John B. Gordon, died at the home of her daughter, Mrs. Frances Gordon-Smith, Augusta, with whom she spent her winters yesterday. She is survived by another daughter, Mrs. Orton Bishop Brown of Berlin, New Hampshire and a son, Hugh Gordon, of Athens.

The funeral will be at North Avenue Presbyterian Church, April 30, at 11:00 A. M. Rev. Orme Flinn will officiate. Interment will be at Oakland Cemetery beside John B. Gordon.

She was a member of the United Daughters of the Confederacy, and former president of the Georgia Confederate Memorial Association. She was also a member of The Colonial Dames of America and the Presbyterian Church.[110]

Mrs. Fanny Haralson Gordon, the devoted and heroic wife of the gallant John B. Gordon, died at the home of her daughter in Augusta, Georgia, on April 28, in her ninety-fourth year. The last survivor of the dignity, beauty and culture of the ante-bellum period, closes a page of history incomparable in our American civilization.

Mrs. Gordon was the first president of the Memorial, which she served with the loyalty characteristic of her life. Every patriotic organization of Augusta was represented in the procession that accompanied her remains to the depot for the journey to Atlanta, where the final obsequies were held.[111]

Years later, the Gordon's grandson, Hugh Haralson Gordon, Jr., wrote of his grandparents:

I was very close to my Grandfather, he was my 'beau ideal' . . . one of the clearest memories that comes to me is the unruffled happiness that marked the relationship between Grandfather and 'Feedama' (as Fanny was called). Rarely have I seen such devotion as existed between them. He was always a Chesterfield in his dealings with her. She was the object of his devoted attention, and his unfailing attention toward her was a constant example to all of us in the home. He saw to it that none of us was delinquent in holding her in the first place of the family.

He also wrote of Sarah and Jim — servants of his grandparents:

One of the wedding presents given Fanny by her father was her Negro maid, Sarah. John B. Gordon's Negro servant Jim married Sarah. Preparations for Fannie and Sarah's wedding were made at the same time, and Fanny saw that Sarah had an appropriate trousseau. Later during the War Between the States, Jim was John B. Gordon's body servant during the entire war, and Sarah stayed with Fanny as her maid as near the battle lines as possible so as to be near Gordon. The loyalty of these servants continued for years and years after the war was over. In later years, Sarah was just one of the household and had no duties of any consequences. She looked after the children's clothes, watched that buttons were sewed on, stockings darned and wardrobes kept in order. Gordon had a small house built for them in the rear of his property and they lived there for years. When their children were grown and moved to California, Sarah and Jim went to live there.[112]

Such were the life and times of Fanny Haralson Gordon. Outspoken, adventuresome, and a tomboy as a girl, Fanny grew into a remarkable woman filled with patriotic fever. One of the many Confederate women to brave the dangers of the battlefield to give aid and comfort to the fighting men, Fanny Gordon was truly one of the "Heroines of the Confederacy."

Endnotes

1. Tankersley, Allen P., *John B. Gordon: A Study in Gallantry*, Atlanta, GA, The Whitehall Press, 1955.
2. In all of Tankersley's writings on General and Mrs. Gordon he states this information.
3. United Daughters of the Confederacy, *The History of the United Daughters of the Confederacy, 1894-1929*, Vol. I, Raleigh, NC, Edwards and Boughton Company.
4. LaCavera, Tommie Phillips, *The History of the Georgia Division, United Daughters of the Confederacy*, Vol. I, Atlanta, GA, Georgia Division of the United Daughters of the Confederacy, July, 1995.
5. *Confederate Veteran*, 1897, 1898, 1899, 1900.
6. Tankersley, *John B. Gordon: A Study in Gallantry*.
7. MSS 1637, Haralson Family File, Hargrett Rare Books and Manuscripts Library.
8. *Ibid.*
9. Hugh A. Haralson will, Troup County Court House, LaGrange, Georgia.
10. Hill View Cemetery, LaGrange, Georgia.
11. Tankersley, *John B. Gordon: A Study in Gallantry*.
12. Northern, William J., *Men of Mark in Georgia*, Atlanta, GA, 1910-1912.
13. United States Government, Biographical Dictionary of the U.S. Congress, 1774-1989, Bicentennial Edition, Washington, DC, United States Printing Office, 1989.
14. Tankersley, *John B. Gordon: A Study in Gallantry*.
15. Haralson Family File, Letter, January 26, 1847.
16. *Ibid.*, Letter, February 5, 1848.
17. *Ibid.*, Letter, December 7, 1844.
18. *Ibid.*, Letter, January 3, 1850.
19. *Ibid.*, Letter, January 21, 1851
20. *Ibid.*, Letters, June 21, 1848, January 23, 1850, and November 29, 1850.

21. *Ibid.*, Letters, February 17, 1849 and January 9, 1851.
22. *Ibid.*, Letter, January 9, 1849.
23. *Ibid.*, Letters, December 7 and 20, 1846, and January 1 and 26, 1847.
24. *Ibid.*, Letter, May 13, 1848.
25. *Ibid.*, Letter, July 7, 1848.
26. *Ibid.*, Letter, July 5, 1848.
27. *Ibid.*, Letter, December 20, 1848.
28. *Ibid.*, Letter, January 13, 1851.
29. *Ibid.*, Letter, January 8, 1847; Hill View Cemetery.
30. *Ibid.*, Letter, February 10, 1850.
31. *Ibid.*, Letters, December 22, 1846 and December 11, 1848.
32. *Ibid.*, Letter, December 26, 1844.
33. *Ibid.*, Letter, January 1, 1847.
34. *Ibid.*, Letter, Myrtle Hill, 1848.
35. *Ibid.*, Letter, January 7, 1848.
36. *Ibid.*, Letters, December 20, 1846, December 22, 1849, and January 3, 1850.
37. *Ibid.*, Letter, May 22, 1848.
38. *Ibid.*, Letter, April, 1848.
39. *Ibid.*, Letters, December 7, 1844 and May 22, 1848.
40. *Ibid.*, Letters, December 19, 1849, and January 3, 1850.
41. *Ibid.*, Letter, June 9, 1848.
42. *Ibid.*, Letter, December 20, 1846.
43. *Ibid.*, Letters, December 20, 1846, February 10, 1848, and February 14, 1849.
44. *Ibid.*, Letter, February 14, 1849.
45. *Ibid.*, Letter, January 9, 1849.
46. *Ibid.*, Letter, February 23, 1849.
47. *Ibid.*, Letter, July 12, 1848.
48. *Ibid.*, Letter, August 1, 1848.
49. *Ibid.*, Letters, June 27, 1848 and August 5, 1848.
50. *Ibid.*, Letter, June 9, 1848.
51. *Ibid.*, Letter, June 28, 1848.
52. Johnson, Forrest Clark III, *A History of LaGrange, Georgia, 1828-1900 and Genealogical and Historical Register of Troup County, Georgia*, LaGrange, GA, Family Tree Publishers, 1987.
53. Haralson Family File
54. *Ibid.*, Letters July 10, 1841, December 7, 1844, and January 29, 1847.
55. *Ibid.*, Letter, January 17, 1849.
56. *Ibid.*, Letters, January 19, 1848, January 24, 1848, and May 26, 1848.
57. *Ibid.*, Letter, May 31, 1848.
58. *Ibid.*, Letter, June 8, 1848.
59. *Ibid.*, Letter, July 5, 1848.
60. *Ibid.*, Letter, undated, 1848.
61. *Ibid.*, Letter, July 15, 1848.
61. *Ibid.*, Letter, July 15, 1848.
62. *Ibid.*, Letter, December 8, 1848.
63. *Ibid.*, Letter, January 14, 1849.
64. *Ibid.*
65. *Ibid.*, Letter, January 15, 1850.
66. *Ibid.*, Letter, June 3, 1848.
67. *Ibid.*, Letter, January 10, 1850.
68. *Ibid.*, Letter, February 12, 1850.
69. *Ibid.*, Letter, undated, 1850.
70. *Ibid.*, Letter, July, 1850.
71. *Ibid.*, Letter, August 15, 1850.
72. *Ibid.*, Letters, May 18, 1848, June 11, 1848, and July 25, 1848.
73. Marriage License, Troup County Courthouse, LaGrange, GA.
74. Tankersley, *John B. Gordon: A Study in Gallantry.*
75. Hugh A. Haralson will.
76. Knight, Lucien Lamar, *Georgia's Landmarks, Memorials, and Legends*, Vol. I and II, Atlanta, GA, Byrd Printing Company, 1913.
77. Haralson Family File.
78. Knight.
79. Tombstone, Oakland Cemetery, Atlanta, GA, and obituary.
80. *Ibid.*
81. Tankersley, Allen P., *John Brown Gordon: Soldier and Statesman*, Historical Essay Contest Brochure, Georgia Division United Daughters of the Confederacy for the Schools of the State of Georgia, Athens, GA, Speering Printing Company, February, 1949.
82. Gordon, John B., *Reminiscences of the Civil War*, New York, Charles Scribner & Sons, 1903.
83. Tankersley, *John B. Gordon: A Study in Gallantry.*
84. Gordon.
85. *Ibid.*
86. *Ibid.*
87. *Ibid.*
88. *Ibid.*
89. *Ibid.*
90. *Ibid.*
91. *Ibid.*
92. *Ibid.*
93. Tankersley, *John B. Gordon: A Study in Gallantry.*
94. *Ibid.*
95. Malone, Alberta, *History of the Atlanta Ladies Memorial Association, 1866-1946, Markers and Monuments*, Atlanta, GA, unpublished minutes, 1946.
96. *Ibid.*
97. *Ibid.*
98. *Ibid.*
99. LaCavera, Tommie Phillips, *Varina Anne "Winnie" Davis: The Daughter of the Confederacy*, Athens, GA, Southern Trace Publishers, 1994.

100. *Confederate Veteran*, 1902.
101. *Ibid.*, 1898.
102. LaCavera, *Varina Anne "Winnie" Davis: The Daughter of the Confederacy*.
103. *Confederate Veteran*, 1899.
104. Tankersley, *John B. Gordon: A Study in Gallantry*.
105. Malone.
106. *Ibid.*

107. LaCavera, *The History of the Georgia Division, United Daughters of the Confederacy*.
108. *Ibid.*, Obituary, Tombstone.
109. *Atlanta Constitution*, April 29, 1931.
110. *Ibid.*
111. *Confederate Veteran*, June 1931 and January 1932.
112. Gordon, Hugh H. Jr., *A Letter to My Sons About their Forebears*, privately printed, 1954.

About the Author

Tommie Phillips LaCavera is a free lance writer and independent researcher. An avid genealogist, she began researching women of the South about twenty years ago when she discovered the lack of published material concerning them. As a native Georgian, her main focus has been on the women of Georgia. She has contributed to numerous historical and genealogical publications, as well as magazines and newspapers. Her publications include: *A Georgia Patriot: Sexta Eavenson Strickland*, Life of the authoress of the Pledge of Allegiance to the Georgia Flag and the Georgia Creed; *Anna Mitchell Davenport Raines*: Co-founder of the United Daughters of the Confederacy; *Varina Anne "Winnie" Davis: The Daughter of the Confederacy; The History of the Georgia Division United Daughters of the Confederacy 1985- 1995*, Vol. I and II. Her current projects include books on the Davis Women (Varina, Winnie, and Maggie) and Georgia Women 1861-1865. She is called upon frequently to speak on women during the War Between the States.

Tommie has served as President General of the United Daughters of the Confederacy and two terms as Historian General. She attended the University of Georgia on a UDC scholarship for women over thirty where she received an AB in History in 1990. She was the second women at the university to receive a Certificate in Women's Studies when at the time there was no degree available.

WHEN THE PEN BECOMES THE SWORD:
THE PROPAGANDA OF ANNA ELLA CARROLL AND AUGUSTA JANE EVANS

By Sara Bartlett

The weapon of propaganda was not new to the 1860s. For centuries, generals and politicians have been trying to find ways to sway public opinion. Although it was considered a male occupation, two women, one from eastern Maryland and one from Alabama, elevated their version of propaganda to a truly effective art form during the Civil War. Anna Ella Carroll centered her efforts on keeping the Union together while Augusta Jane Evans communicated her trust in the Southern cause. Both women were quite successful in their efforts but both also suffered lasting consequences from placing themselves on the very visible stage of public opinion.

The two women differed wildly in their patriotic viewpoints but had remarkably similar backgrounds. Both were the first-born children of wealthy families. Anna Carroll's ancestor, Charles Carroll, was a signer of the Declaration of Independence. Charles' grandfather was a founding father of the state of Maryland. Augusta Evans was born in Columbus, Georgia, to Matthew and Sarah Evans, who had inherited wealth from Sarah's family.[1] Both girls' lives of privilege were drastically altered by the Panic of 1837; as each of their fathers, whom they adored, failed to keep their families from the pain of financial loss and recovery. This was also the lot of Louisa May Alcott and Susan B. Anthony, whose adored, intellectually strong fathers, were flawed in their abilities to manage the family fortunes.

Anna's father and Augusta's mother were major influences in the girls' education. Both were parents that valued a good education for both boys and girls. Anna's father was a lawyer and encouraged his daughter to read the books in his enormous library along with her regular subjects. Augusta was often ill as a child and so was taught by her mother, who stressed the need for a good grounding in classic literature, Latin, Greek and other studies that usually were taught only to boys. These educational advantages proved their worth when the great crisis of the war arrived. They may not have known it then, but these daughters were primed at an early age to join, in adulthood, a larger, public community than most women of the day seldom dreamed of.

Family crises often force great responsibilities upon first-born children. In Anna Carroll's case, she had already learned a great deal from her father's legal and political career and was prepared to shoulder burdens that many 22-year-old women from a plantation upbringing could not possibly handle. The

Jane Augusta Evans.

Anna Ella Carroll.
Special Collections (Miscellaneous Map and Photograph
Collection), Maryland State Archives.

Carrolls of Somerset County, Maryland, were a border state family, who treasured the union of states but utilized the system of slavery that the original Carrolls had established in their lives. To prevent her father from selling all of the slaves to pay off debts, Anna secretly purchased some of the slaves herself. As she became more and more influenced by the writings and speeches of abolitionists such as William Lloyd Garrison, she eventually freed the remaining slaves that she had purchased. But this was several years later, after her family had endured near financial ruin for quite some time.

Through all of this, Anna did not view marrying into security as the answer to her family's difficulties. Perhaps she felt that this could be handled better by her sisters. Instead she cultivated relationships with her father's friends who became her mentors. Some were powerful men like Major General Winfield Scott and Maryland Governor Thomas Hicks. Anna also began to help her father write his legal documents when he was Judge of the Orphans Court and later his political speeches as he ran successfully for Governor of Maryland. Anna's education was also "rounded out" with a year at Miss Margaret Mercer's Boarding School,[2] but she was ready for a public, political life, something that Miss Mercer never dared think about.

For Augusta Evans, the disruptions of her family's financial downfall were lost in the haze of early childhood. When Augusta was two, Matthew Evans had moved his family to San Antonio, Texas, to try for a new start. He found work and the family did well for a time. However, living in the wilds of 1830s and 40s Texas was very hard on the family, and they eventually moved back east to Mobile, Alabama. Fifteen-year-old Augusta wrote about her years in Texas and Mexico in her first novel, *Inez*. It was published but did not sell many copies. She had impressed her publisher, though. He encouraged Augusta to write more and she did.

Both women were writing on their own by the antebellum years of the 1850s. It was the time of the hot voices of Southern Fire Eaters, the Know-Nothings, abolitionists, and Protestant Reformationists — all propagandists ruling the newspapers and pulpits of the country. These people already had discovered the power of oratory and the written word. Anna and Augusta saw its usefulness as well and plunged into the fray.

Augusta had written her second novel, *Beulah*, which hinted at her growing patriotic support of the Southern cause that would be featured so prominently in future writings. *Beulah* was a much bigger success than *Inez* and made her quite a famous young woman. It also brought financial security back to her family. She was even able to purchase the house that her family had been renting.[3] With a bolder confidence in her writing abilities, she submitted a series of articles to the *Mobile Daily Advertiser* in 1859 that broadened the scope of her propaganda career. Staying within the genre of literature, she laid down, chapter and verse, the differences between the Northern and Southern culture and literature:

> We believe that no attentive reader of the various mediums through which our Northern literature finds its way to the public, can fail to see its decided tendency to evil. The golden era of English literature — and by this we mean

literature as exemplified by the English language — is passed, or if not passed, we certainly have no indications of its continued existence in the productions of northern writers . . . the literature, if it may be dignified by that term, which daily floats over the country from northern sources, is a disgrace to its authors and insulting to the intelligence of the American people.[4] . . . the North believes no good can come out of Southern latitudes, and will not read anything to which a Southern odor attaches.[5]

Subtlety was not in Augusta's lexicon. Neither was it a part of Anna's. They had axes to grind and they ground them into dust. These writers' opinions were blunt and defiant. Their novels and pamphlets possessed a directness that was characteristic of the masculine writing of the day and earned them a respect that eluded other female writers of that time. This positioned them to be looked to as voices of propaganda for their beloved causes.

The Dictionary of American History[6] defines propaganda as "any form of controlled communication for the purpose of influencing the opinions, emotions, attitudes, or behavior of an intended audience. . . . Any person or group with a message, an audience to receive the message, and a communications carrier may become an advocate or sponsor of propaganda." Anna and Augusta had both found their "communications carriers" (newspapers, pamphlets, books), and both of them entered the public world unashamed and confident. There seemed to be no easing into these beliefs and attitudes, nor did they choose to hide behind the alias of a man's name. Despite the mores of the day, they both received a great deal of positive reinforcement for their efforts.

In the late 1850s, Anna became a supporter of the American or Know-Nothing Party that began in the Baltimore area and was at the peak of its short-lived political clout when Anna lived in that city. The party began as a secret political movement called the Order of the Star Spangled Banner at a time when secret societies and orders were quite popular.[7] Anna fully supported the Know-Nothings, writing and giving speeches for the party and its candidates. Despite her Catholic family roots, by the time she became involved with the Know-Nothings, she was a firm supporter of the party's pledge to resist Roman Catholicism and non-Anglo Saxon immigrants.

Anna was taken with the politics of former president, Millard Fillmore,[8] and wrote a pamphlet in support of his 1856 second presidential campaign against James Buchanan. (There are reports that Buchanan was an escort of Anna's at certain political events[9] but that she secretly did not care for him and believed him to be involved in a governmental fraud. Whether this is true or not, Mr. Buchanan does not appear in the best of light in Anna's pamphlet, *Which? Fillmore or Buchanan!*):

> There is one other act, in the public history of Mr. Buchanan, which betrays a moral turpitude, a practiced hypocrisy, which sickens the very heart of every honest man. It is the treachery he displayed towards Henry Clay, which three times kept him from the Presidential office.[10]

In later months, she further berated Buchanan for his slow reaction to the taking of Fort Sumter in her reply to a July 16, 1861, speech of J.C. Breckinridge, when she reminded now President Buchanan that he swore to "preserve, protect and defend the Constitution of the United States," and that, "He needs, therefore no statue law to enable him, in the absence of Congress, to defend the assault on the nation's life. . . . The express grant of the war conducting power conferred upon the President carries with it the implied power to use every belligerent right known to the law of war."[11] Anna expanded on this topic in her Civil War pamphlet, *The War Powers of the General Government*, a definitive description of what the presidential wartime powers were. Besides these definitions, she believed her clarifications would quell the accusations that Lincoln had become a dictator by detailing the history of past uses of these policies and Lincoln's legal implementation of them.[12]

There is no subtle symbolism in Anna's writing. Mr. Buchanan got thoroughly thrashed while Mr. Fillmore took his place upon Miss Carroll's exalted pedestal:

> My countrymen, God has looked graciously and pitied our condition, and by his providence, the American party comes as the break-water of liberty, against which the waves, and torrents of discord and disunion will beat in vain. And now, when mind is in close and sharp contact with mind, and division of opinion makes men impatient for decision, Millard Fillmore is seen as the rainbow on the storm![13]

Anna also published a book at that time called *The Great American Battle*. Despite its title, it was written before the Civil War with the Know-Nothing Party as its central subject. The author played with various styles of metaphoric writing, including a chapter called "The Tea-Party of the Know Nothings."[14] In it she created a "family" which gathered for tea "around the luxurious table of America." The Mother then announced, ". . . to us 'Know-Nothings,' who could afford to be sincere, we recognize the highest rights of personal freedom, and love in all things to trust and revere the social conventions of our fathers, who made *worth* the only fig leaf which can make American men and women useful, graceful, or formidable."[15] The "children/citizens" eagerly assembled in their idyllic home to be taught by the Mother, who's "presence is frankincense and flowers."[16] She told them:

> All the qualities, my children, ascribed to kings, every true American appropriates to himself. For you the laws exist, the land was discovered, the blow struck which decided liberty. . . . An American feels, and knows that he is greater than all geography and all the governments of the world. And with might and main we can sit here at home and hold it if we will, as an anchor, a cable, or a fence, which defies the bullying of despots and theological autocrats. American nationality demands that we stamp our own portrait upon all our statutes. And the dear American Party or the "Know-Nothings," insist that we shall see and introduce not only what was there and then when it sprang into existence more than seventy-nine years ago, but what is here and now! The Know-Nothings, my children, show us ourselves. It is the man not the work which speaks his nationality. It is not the Romish Catholic Church, its crosses, its music, its processions, its image-worship, but it is the clear vision that these causes are working effects which

are to soak our soil in blood, and create an other inquisition to butcher American citizens! The very faculties, my children, of an American point to the world he is to inhabit.[17]

With this one bucolic scene, Anna drove home to the reader the isolationist and anti-Catholic planks of the Know-Nothing Party platform. Although dated and as far from politically correct by today's standards as it can be, this pamphlet, along with Anna's other writings, were very popular and proved to be an effective way to spread the word at that time.

By the time of the Civil War, Augusta had become a political star and was part of a circle of influential statesmen. She traveled to Montgomery and Richmond to observe the activities of the new Confederate government. A friendship grew between her and J.L.M. Curry, a Confederate Congressman, who sought her advice in writing some of his political speeches. In her letters to Curry,[18] she talked of her fears for the passage of the Exemption Bill[19] and the status of the defense capabilities for the city of Mobile. In contrast to most young women letter writers of the day, Augusta spent little or no time writing of the weather or the blooms of the flower garden. Rather she was eager to educate herself in the politics and opinions of the day and to introduce herself to as many prominent figures as she could. Robert Toombs, the Confederate Secretary of State, was also a correspondent and supporter of Augusta. He had been a family friend, and the Evanses hid him in their home during the closing days of the Civil War.

Augusta was developing her own style of propaganda with each new article she wrote and in her subsequent novels. In the *Gulf City Home Journal* of Mobile, she submitted an article called "The Mutilation of the Hermae,"[20] an account of the destruction in 415 B.C. of all marble images of Hermes just before the Athenian war against Sicily — one of history's unsolved mysteries. In her new style, the author floridly and poetically unfolded the story and left the sting of its propagandistic messages for the very end. Augusta's solution to the ancient mystery was a fiery comparison of the statues' vandalism with the "destruction" of the U.S. Constitution by the "Northern Black Republicans." Future writings kept to this formula, reserving the political harangues for the end paragraphs or last chapters.

As the war progressed, Augusta threw herself, with immense patriotic zeal, into sewing and gathering supplies for the Confederate soldiers. She helped raise $1,500 to send to the women of Richmond for re-interment in Hollywood Cemetery of their fallen loved ones.[21] She also located an available private home in Mobile and had it converted into a hospital, christening it "Camp Beulah" after her novel.[22] It was here that she began writing her most famous novel on scraps of brown wrapping paper as she sat with patients. *Macaria: or Altars of Sacrifice* would be Augusta's masterpiece.

Augusta's nursing endeavors caught the attention of Confederate General P.G.T. Beauregard and he began a correspondence with the young authoress. Some of the surviving letters between the two show Augusta's mastery of the details of military strategy and how impressed the general was with his young friend. One of the general's letters began:

I thank you most kindly, my dear Miss Evans, for your letter of the 23rd. . . . It is indeed most gratifying to me, to find so many strong friends among persons known to me only by name and reputation. . . . I am most happy to hear of our successes in Virginia and Kentucky, but although having great confidence in our troops and their able commanders, I cannot suppress the presentiment that our triumphs there will not be of long duration. This is probably due to our total want of "Armies of Reserve" with which to fill up the gaps made by disease and the Enemy's balls. We must however hope for the best, putting our trust in a kind Providence, the justices of our cause, and the Patriotism of our people.[23]

A month prior, Beauregard had written:

I fear the Tombigbee [River in Alabama], like the River Lethe[24] of old, deprives of the memory of the past, whoever travels on its torrid waters — or is it that the attractions of "Evansville" are such that whenever any one enters within its enchanting precincts, absentees are entirely forgotten? . . . Permit me now to thank you for your article to the Hon. Sothrop Motley, Minister to Austria, who will no doubt find it difficult, if not impossible, to explain, notwithstanding his Yankee shrewdness, why he condemns in the Southern Confederates of 1860s what he extolled so highly in the Netherland Rebels of 1560.[25]

In one letter, Augusta requested information about the general's campaign at First Manassas.[26] He responded with a copy of his official report of the battle, which she used in the later chapters of *Macaria*. The general also gave Augusta a gift of the pen that he had used to sign some of his important documents. Their correspondence continued throughout the war and after. It was indeed a close relationship.

When the Know-Nothings' day had come and gone, Anna moved her already powerful support to an Illinois lawyer of the new Republican Party. Being the all-or-nothing lobbyist that she was, she and her father's circle of friends would later boast of nearly single-handedly holding Maryland, the most important border state, for Abraham Lincoln.

Lincoln was well aware of this, and he asked to meet Anna in the very early days of his first term. The new president had not known many women of Anna's caliber and intellect. Lincoln said that independent, intellectual women in his own life reminded him of children with gingerbread crying that nobody likes gingerbread more than they do, and nobody gets less of it.[27] It pleased him even more to learn that Anna was acquainted with powerful Maryland secessionists before the war, and thus had useful knowledge of the plans of both sides. She was also an unofficial Washington representative of Governor Hicks, and she kept her eyes and ears open always. She continued her writing which now supported the Republicans and the Union cause. Prominent politicians called on her for advice, as some had done for many years, but now these politicians were in the highest offices of the land. Anna Carroll had, by this time in her life, accumulated an impressive list of politicians that she could count on and defer to, and these contacts drew her further in to the highest echelons. In fact, a new "Unofficial Cabinet" developed in the early days of the Civil War that included Thomas Scott, Assistant Secretary of War; Salmon Chase, Secretary of the Treasury; Attorney General Edward C. Bates and Anna. Senator Henry Wilson, Benjamin Wade, and Texas Judge Lemeul Evans were also part of her powerful circle of friendships and advisors. Judge Evans had even been officially appointed Anna's military advisor as part of his Secret Service duties.

General Winfield Scott had been one of Anna's earlier, favorite mentors. She loved visiting the ailing general whose body was failing him but whose military mind was operating as efficiently as if it were the height of the Mexican War. Scott taught her, amongst many things, how to analyze military maps. He also told her that usually "pure geography" can win or lose a war. One needed to know the terrain and its extensions. Anna proved to be a good student, and when Lincoln ordered an expedition to St. Louis to oversea the construction of gunboats for the Union Army, Anna went along. She also wanted to be part of the expedition in order to do some research in the St. Louis Mercantile Library on the new pamphlet that she was writing for the president.

Lincoln believed that the Mississippi River must be controlled by the North as soon as practicable. He saw it as the key to starving the South of resources and moving the war along to as early a conclusion as possible. The "Unofficial Cabinet" had been studying the maps and various possible solutions for this issue, and now it was time to examine things in person. Anna joined the expedition formed to examine the construction of gunboats in St. Louis, Missouri.

Anna was apprehensive at first to be a woman traveling alone for such a great distance, but she soon discovered that in wartime social rules could be quite different. Widows, wives and daughters were spilling into trains and wagons in search of sons and husbands who had left home to join the army. They all traveled together.

Anna stayed with her uncle, Cecil Carroll, a staunch secessionist, and again she opened her ears for all of the gossip and information that was the propaganda of the border state of Missouri. She caught a stroke of luck when she learned that the librarian of the St. Louis Mercantile Library was the brother of Confederate General Sydney Johnston.[28] She had several conversations with him, both of them aware of the other's political leanings. At some point, the subject of their heated discussions turned to control of the Mississippi River. Unnerved by the indisputable truth of his claim that the river was firmly in Confederate hands, Anna set out to find another way.

She studied the railway maps that she had brought with her from her work in the railway offices of Baltimore. She poured over them, trying to remember all that General Scott had taught her. Slowly she pieced together a new idea as she looked away from the Mississippi and turned instead to the advantages of the Tennessee and Cumberland Rivers. They flowed another way, and if they were held by the North, river traffic could conceivably be open for the Federals all the way to Alabama, dividing the South nearly in half. Anna had been introduced to the wife of river pilot, Charles Scott, and after speaking with her, Anna knew that she must meet Captain Scott herself. The information he gave her was of tremendous value. He gave her in-depth information about the Tennessee River, navigation information for each season and other important data. She had struck gold.

With the help of Judge Evans, who had been a friend and companion for some years, Anna wrote her report for the president. The Judge had come to St. Louis to visit her and was immediately sold on her idea. This was Anna's masterpiece. It was to be for what she was best known and what would cause a rift between her and her government in the years to come. Her river plan was propaganda aimed at the smallest audience — the president and his generals, but the influence stakes were as high as they could be. The war was nearly a year old, and the South was winning it at that point. Anna's plan was a rethinking of the importance of river traffic control, and she had to convince Lincoln of that as soon as possible.

There are few written accounts of the president's reaction to Anna's plan presented to him on November 30, 1861. When Judge Evans told the story, even as late as 1872, however, he said that, after reading Anna's proposal, the president lost his famous poker face and was at a loss, for once, for one of his famous stories. His face took on a form of excitement that Evans had never seen before.

There was surprise in some corners that no one had thought of this idea before, and there were, of course, other corners that refused to believe that it was a woman who had come up with the idea. The latter proved to be loud corners, and it was agreed that, for the time being, Anna's civilian authorship of the plan should remain a secret. Anna agreed feeling that the most important thing at that point was the implementation of a campaign that would effectively incorporate her river plan and speed the end of the war.

Her plan culminated in the [Forts] Henry and Donelson Campaign in February of 1862. It was the first major victory for the Union and for General Ulysses Grant, who took Fort Donelson with his famous declaration of "unconditional surrender." There was great rejoicing in Washington over the victory, and as a result, Anna's influence was even more sought out by those who knew of her involvement in the campaign. She had finished her pamphlet, *The War Powers of the General Government*, and presented it to Lincoln. It defended many of the policies that Lincoln had already implemented, such as a validation for the suspending of the writ of Habeas Corpus, and others that he would implement later on in the war. He was pleased enough with it to have copies of it given to many top officers as required reading.

On one occasion, Lincoln verbally complimented Anna in a cabinet meeting when she was not in attendance. Attorney General Bates wrote her later of how Lincoln said he appreciated her views and her "general usefulness to her country." Other presidential associates put their opinions on record of Anna's value to the country. Congressman William B. Mitchell said that when all was said and done that Anna would stand taller historically than Charles Carroll, her famous ancestor. But others mentioned that Lincoln had admonished them that Miss Carroll's authorship of the Tennessee River Plan must be kept a secret so that the generals would not find out that such a brilliant campaign had been authored by a civilian.

These were exciting days for Anna — exciting but not financially reward-ing. Because she was an "Unofficial Cabinet" member at best, she was not given a regular salary. She had been given a stipend for the printing and cir-culation of some of her pamphlets, but that amount was not enough for such a large circulation. She had used her own money to supplement it, and now that was slipping away fast.

Augusta's finances, however, were better than most Confederates could boast because of the success of her novel, *Beulah*. She had found a publisher in New York before the war and was able to receive royalties from him regard-less of the difficulty of communications with the publisher through enemy lines. Augusta had also finished the novel that was her gift to the soldiers of the Confederacy. *Macaria*[29] was her most mature novel and the one that de-livered all the passion of her patriotic love of the South. Her hope was that "Yankee readers," after experiencing the story of these brave and accomplished characters, would realize the error of their abolitionist and pro-union beliefs.[30]

Augusta was already an extremely popular novelist and she wrote *Macaria* using the same formula from her previous novels. The characters were writ-ten to derive the most identity and sympathy before they each experienced the horrors of the Civil War. A poor accountant with an ailing mother becomes a noble Confederate colonel. The woman he loves is a nurse caring for wounded soldiers in a hospital. The Colonel has an orphaned cousin who marries a man she loves less than another. There is also a Northern character[31] who is won over to the Southern cause. As in earlier fiction, Augusta kept the beginning chapters of her saga in her familiar storytelling style. Toward the end of the novel, she wrote of the battles in detail with which General Beauregard had helped her. Augusta gave them a retelling that most of the generals from ei-ther side would not recognize:

> "McClellan has evacuated Malvern Hill and is in full retreat toward his gunboats,"[32] answered the doctor. "Then there will be no more fighting. My shattered regiment will rest for a season. Poor fellows! They did their duty nobly yesterday. Tell my men for me that I am inexpressibly proud of their bravery and their daring, and that, though my heart clings fondly to my gal-lant regiment, I glory in the death I die — knowing that my soldiers will avenge me. Give my love to one and all, and tell them, when next they go into battle, to remember him who led their last charge. I should like to have seen the end of the struggle — but Thy will, oh, my God! Not mine." He lifted his eyes toward heaven, and for some moments his lips moved inau-dibly in prayer. Gradually a tranquil expression settled on his features, and his eyes closed again.[33]

In the last one hundred twenty pages of *Macaria*, Augusta used her research of General Beauregard's battle reports and the height of her patriotic passions to bring the story to a close:

> In July, 1861, when the North, blinded by avarice and hate, with the cry of "On to Richmond," our Confederate Army of the Potomac was divided between Manassas and Winchester, watching at both points the glittering

coils of the Union boa-constrictor, which writhed in its efforts to crush the last sanctuary of freedom.[34]

Macaria includes the story of how a member of Rose Greenhow's Confederate spy ring[35] brought coded messages of troop movements and numbers, hidden in her voluminous hair, to General Beauregard before the onset of the Battle of First Manassas:

> Carthaginian women gave their black locks to string their country's bows and furnish cordage for its shipping; and the glossy tresses of an American woman veiled a few mystic ciphers more potent in General Beauregard's hands than Talmudish Shemhamphorash.[36] Her mission accomplished, the dauntless courier turned her horse's head and, doubtless, with an exulting, thankful heart returned in triumph to Washington. When our national jewels are made up, will not a grateful and admiring country set her name between those of Beauregard and Johnston in the revolutionary diadem, and let the three blaze through coming ages, baffling the mists of time — the Constellation of Manassas? The artillery duel of the 18th of July ended disastrously for the advance guard of the Federals.[37]

The author also made known her feelings about the anti-slavery movement:

> Abolitionism, so long adroitly cloaked, was triumphantly clad in robes of state — shameless now, and hideous; and while the North looked upon [its] loathsome face, . . . the South prepared for resistance.[38]

Augusta devotedly incorporated the details of General Beauregard's military reports that he had sent to her:

> Like incarnations of Victory, Beauregard and Johnston swept to the front, where the conflict was most deadly; everywhere, at sight of them, our thin ranks dashed forward, and were mowed down by the fire of Rickett's[39] and Griffin's[40] batteries, which crowned the position they were so eager to regain. At half-past two o'clock the awful contest was at its height; the rattle of musketry, the ceaseless whistle of rifle-balls, the deafening boom of artillery, the hurtling hail of shot, and explosion of shell, dense volumes of smoke shrouding the combatants, and clouds of dust boiling up on all sides, lent unutterable horror to a scene which, to cold, dispassionate observers, might have seemed sublime. As the vastly superior numbers of the Federals forced our stubborn bands to give back slowly, an order came from General Beauregard for the right of his line, except the reserves, to advance and recover the long and desperately-disputed plateau. With a shout, the shattered lines sprang upon the foe and forced them temporarily back.[41]

The novel culminated in the death of most of the main characters, except the heroine, and an admonition to all surviving women everywhere:

> The rays of the setting sun gilded her mourning-dress, gleamed in the white roses that breathed their perfume in her rippling hair, and lingered like a benediction on the placid, pure face of the lonely woman who had survived every earthly hope; and who, calmly fronting her Altars of Sacrifice, here dedicated herself anew to the hallowed work of promoting the happiness and

gladdening the paths of all who journeyed with her down the chequered aisles of Time.

> "Rise, woman, rise! To thy peculiar and best altitudes
> Of doing good and of enduring ill,
> Of comforting for ill, and teaching good,
> And reconciling all that ill and good
> Unto the patience of a constant hope.
> . . . Henceforward, rise, aspire,
> To all the calms and magnanimities,
> The lofty uses and the noble ends.
> The sanctified devotion and full work,
> To which thou art elect for evermore!"[42]

The style of this novel was very popular in its day, and *Macaria* became Augusta's most successful work. She was honored by Southern reviewers and readers but reviled by the North. Some Union officers banned *Macaria* while others had copies of it burned. Sales of that book, along with her other novels, helped Augusta and her family worry less about money than most Southern families during the war.

Both Anna and Augusta received praise and admiration for their work that was unique for that or any time. They were both well known throughout the North and the South during the 1860s and 70s. Why, then, is a woman like Anna Ella Carroll, with her role as presidential advisor, political lobbyist, and author brushed aside into history's back channels? Why is August Jane Evans hardly known outside of Alabaman historical and literary circles today? They were two of the most well known women of the 1860s. Is it just the usual problem of history textbooks written with an accent on the accomplishments of the presidents and the generals, or is it something else?

Both women, whether they were aware of it or not, walked a tightrope of propriety in their dealings with men, and with the unusual amount of male attention and acceptance that both received, it would be very easy to forget that there was a line that women, no matter who they were, must not overstep.

It can be seen that Anna's first step on the road to historical invisibility came as her financial situation worsened. She slowly realized that her secret role in the military strategies of the Union was going to remain so. She may have come to the realization, looking at her emptying purse, that being an unofficial advisor and a secret strategist was not a blessing. She made several verbal requests for compensation, and when these did not bring results, she submitted a Claim Before Congress on January 14, 1863. In that Claim, she revealed her part in the Tennessee River Campaign and asked for the balance due, since 1862, for work she had done for the War Department and the payment for two pamphlets — a total of $6,250. She stated in the *Affidavit of Memorialist* that:

> [She had discovered that] by moving the army along that line [of the Tennessee River], a position could be readily gained in the center of the rebellion to the destruction of the rebel Power. [She noted all of the obstacles and advantages and reported them to Assistant Secretary of War, Thomas A.

Scott.] He manifested the utmost gratification, and fully concurred . . . [that it] . . . was the first solution of the problem he had seen.[43]

She assumed from Scott's acceptance that, "it was the first suggestion for this campaign that was ever made to the government."[44] The document indicated that no less than President "Lincoln, Secretary Stanton, Attorney General Bates, . . . Rev. Dr. Breckinridge [a longtime friend of Anna's and her family], Edward Everett,[45] and [Maryland] Governor Hicks "severally bore testimony to the ability of her publications and their usefulness to the cause of the Union."[46]

One would have hoped that, by the time of the writing of President Grant's memoirs just prior to his death, that he would have been informed of Anna Carroll's role in his great Tennessee victory. However, there is no naming of Miss Carroll in his book, even though he did write, "The distance from Fort Henry to Donelson is but eleven miles. The two positions were so important to the enemy, *as he saw his interest,* that it was natural to suppose that reinforcements would come from every quarter from which they could be got. Prompt action on our part was imperative."[47] She continued with further quests for money until the amount had grown to $50,000.

Grant and others also referred to the information that they had gleaned from Grant's own river pilots that reiterated Anna's findings. It seems to boil down simply to who got there first and wrote about it, which is still a very hazy thing.

In desperation, Anna wrote a letter to President Lincoln. It was perhaps the single most obvious indicator of how her abrasiveness added to her downfall:

> I am just informed, that at a public dinner table in a Washington hotel, a gentleman, whose name I do not know, stated that the president had said "a lady demanded $50,000, for writing a document" i.e.; meaning myself. I forbear to write, as I desire to forget, the very disparaging manner in which it was represented by the gentleman, as coming from you. I saw, Mr. President, that you did not comprehend me, and I said so at the time of my interview. But you insisted that you did . . . [b]ut the fact, that you have given a partial publicity, to that interview, to my prejudice, proves conclusively, that you wholly misconceived its object.[48]

There is no time when it is a good idea to chastise the leader of the country, nor to presume to educate him on any matter: Nevertheless, Anna chose to do both:

> Mr. President, government is something more than a machine, which requires simply the presence of a skillful engineer. It is an institution, which for the successful accomplishment of its ends, depends at last not so much, upon the skills of the functionaries, as upon the temper and spirit of the people.[49]

The final crushing blow for the beautiful Anna probably was Mr. Lincoln's jealous wife, Mary. She had taken an immediate dislike to Anna and particularly to her unique access to the president. When the First Lady had her husband's private attention, she no doubt filled his ear with her utter dislike and suspicions of the "Unofficial Cabinet" member.[50]

It also does no good to anger the president or his family. Anna learned in 1885 that Robert Lincoln, the president's eldest son, had ordered all of Anna's remaining memos and papers removed from the office of the War Department except those which had already been printed in the *Miscellaneous Documents* of the United States House and Senate.[51]

Although other politicians from her heyday wrote in her defense over the years,[52] these documents were not largely made known to the general public, and certain of her accomplishments were forgotten. Mary Livermore, in her *My Story of the War*, put it quite simply when she described Anna's two "formidable obstacles" which were "first, the unfavorable attitude of the military mind towards what emanates from outside circles; and secondly, the fact that the claimant is a woman — a fact for which she is not responsible — has operated against her through all these years in a powerful manner."[53]

Anna kept up her requests for reparations and was awarded the money, but not until fourteen years after she had begun her requests. These repetitive appearances, asking for money, no doubt put her in a bad social light in many peoples' eyes, and the gossip and negative reputation took off from there. It is reminiscent, in some ways, of the unrelenting efforts of Dr. Mary Walker, who made many congressional appearances requesting compensations for her work as an "unofficial" member of the Union Army medical corps.

Augusta's fame suffered primarily from simply being on the losing side of the war. Her novels, written in an outdated and over-romantic style, had served their propaganda purpose during the war and were no longer needed. Today she is barely heard of at all in the North.

Another possible reason for their disappearance into the mists of time is that neither Augusta nor Anna participated in the women's suffrage movements after the war, which gave notoriety to others such as Elizabeth Cady Stanton, Susan B. Anthony and Lucretia Mott. These women had paid their dues toiling in many spheres of the war while waiting for the vote to be granted to the freed slaves first. Now they were visibly escalating their demands for the female voting franchise.

Augusta had been opposed to the suffragists nearly her whole life saying, "I believe that the day which endows women with elective franchise will be the blackest in the annals of this country, and will ring the death-knell of modern civilization, national prosperity, social morality and domestic happiness. Every exciting political election will then . . . mournfully attest how terrible is the female nature when perverted."[54] As the granting of the female vote got closer, Augusta became more out of step and was buried with the memories of the war.

Anna and Augusta both witnessed the end of the war, Reconstruction, and beyond. Augusta's wealth had dwindled considerably toward the end of the war and as *Macaria* had a New York publisher, she had not expected to see any royalties from them with a book that was so pro-Confederacy in its nature. However, on a postwar trip to New York City with her brother, Howard, who went for treatment of his war wound, she visited Mr. J.C. Derby, who had published *Beaulah* and was a long time friend of her's. Derby had saved the royalties for Augusta that he could not deliver to her during the war. This was a life saving surprise for her and her family. Augusta was unaware that Mr. Derby had fought with the Lippincott publisher of *Macaria*, who had wanted to strip her of any income from a book that so supported the Southern enemy. Derby prevailed and personally saw to the supervision of the income from *Macaria* which was a fair amount of money. The book was read in the North and South and was one of the best known books of the 1860s.

In December of 1868, Augusta married her neighbor and family friend, Lorenzo Madison Wilson, who was a bank officer, the director of the Mobile and Montgomery Railroad and co-owner of the Spring Hill Streetcar Line. The couple moved into Wilson's home, Ashland, where they lived happily until his death in 1891. Augusta then moved to Mobile to live near her relatives.

In her later years, Augusta continued to have "a weekly reception day, when all accredited persons were received with a grace and charm that made a lasting impression."[55] She continued writing novels, publishing *A Speckled Bird* in 1902 and *Devota* in 1907. On the day after her 74th birthday, May 9, 1909, she passed away in her Mobile home. She is buried in Magnolia Cemetery in Mobile.

Anna Carroll's unpaid, secret government roles took a serious toll on her personal finances. She had struggled for many years to keep her family home from being sold and had finally been forced to free the family's remaining slaves in order to hang onto her Maryland home. By 1865 she had also depleted most of her savings. She continued writing for the government after the war and had at least one meeting with President Lincoln where they discussed his plans for Reconstruction.

Anna also kept up her official pleas for recognition and compensation for her role in the wartime government. A public announcement of her authorship of her river plan was scheduled to happen in April of 1865. The president was to be there as well as others who had worked with her in the "Unofficial Cabinet," but Lincoln was assassinated before it could happen and the veil of anonymity fell even more soundly upon Anna's accomplishments. Although she never fully received the financial compensation that she had requested, she received late recognition from such important players as Secretary Stanton who remarked that her sacrifice was that she performed work that made others famous.[56]

In the 1880s Anna formed a correspondence friendship with James Garfield that began before he became president. He became a strong supporter of her and promised to do what he could for her in official channels. One of Anna's compensation requests was before Congress during President Garfield's term of office. But tragedy struck again. Garfield was assassinated in 1881. Anna's bill did not pass and she suffered a paralyzing stroke the following September.

Anna never married and went to live with her sister, Mary, in Washington while she slowly made a partial recovery from the stroke. Mary found a job with the help of President Cleveland's sister but it did not bring in much money for them. Then Mary became ill and lost her job. The sisters became quite destitute and their health declined even more as they could not afford medical care. They could not count on help from their family as Anna had alienated the Catholic members with her writing and the secessionist members with her role in the Union government. In 1893 Anna suffered another stroke and a bout of pneumonia. Never completely recovering from those, she died on February 19, 1894. She is buried in the Old Trinity Church yard near her father's grave in Dorchester County, Maryland.

Today there are still fighters for Anna's cause. A website on the internet contains a petition to Senator Tom Daschle that states that the undersigned, "desire that Anna receive her proper place in history, that she is taught to our children and our children's children as a matter of course in our schools. And to this purpose we beseech you to recognize Anna Ella Carroll as a national hero in the halls of Congress and Senate, and not the least of which, Presidential recognition. We ask this for Anna who was denied this in her time and for the Nation and its children who have been denied Anna as a role model and hero."[57]

Even if it is true that both of these women, in their services to their country, overstepped both reason and propriety, whether they were abrasive or misguided, the time is long overdue to forgive them and rediscover their many talents and sacrifices to the causes in which they so firmly believed.

Endnotes

1. *Mobile Register*, May 10, 1909□. Fidler, William Perry, *Augusta Evans Wilson, 1835-1909: a Biography*, University of Alabama Press, Montgomery, AL, 1951

2. Coryell, Janet L., *Neither Heroine Nor Fool*, Kent State University Press, Kent, OH, 1990

3. Fidler, William Perry, *Augusta Evans Wilson, 1835-1909: a Biography*, University of Alabama Press, Montgomery, AL, 1951

4. *Mobile Daily Advertiser*, October 11, 1859 (Vol. XVII, No. 165)

5. *Mobile Daily Advertiser*, October 30, 1859 (Vol. XVII, No. 182)

6. National Urban League — Quasi-Judicial Agencies, *Dictionary of American History*, Vol. V, Charles Scribner's Sons, New York, NY 1976

7. Carroll, Anna Ella, *The Great American Battle*, Edwin Mellen Press, Lewiston, NY, 1996

8. Millard Fillmore was a Whig Party member in his first term as president. When he decided to run again, he chose to run as a candidate for the Know-Nothing Party.

9. Greenbie, Marjorie Barstow, *My Dear Lady: The Story of Anna Ella Carroll, the "Great Unrecognized Member of Lincoln's Cabinet,"* Whittlesey House, New York, NY, 1940

10. Carroll, Anna Ella, *Which: Fillmore or Buchanan!* James French and Company, Boston, MA, 1856

11. Carroll, Anna Ella, *Reply* [To the Honorable

J.C. Breckinridge], Henry Polkinhorn, Washington, D.C. 1861

12. Wise, Winifred Esther, *Lincoln's Secret Weapon*, Chilton Company, Philadelphia, PA, 1961

13. *Ibid.*

14. Carroll, Anna Ella, *The Great American Battle*.

15. *Ibid.*

16. *Ibid.*

17. *Ibid.*

18. Curry, J.L.M. Papers, Library of Congress, Washington, D.C.

19. The Confederate Exemption Bill would allow some Southern men to avoid army service dependent on the size of their farm or plantation.

20. Curry, J.L.M. Papers, Library of Congress, Washington, D.C.

21. Owen, Thomas McAdory, LL.D., *History of Alabama and Dictionary of Alabama Biography*, Vol. IV, S.J. Clarke Publishing Company, Chicago, IL, 1921

22. Fidler, William Perry, "Augusta Evans Wilson As Confederate Propagandist," *Alabama Review, A Quarterly Journal of Alabama History*, Vol. II, No. 1, University of Alabama Press in Cooperation with the Alabama Historical Association, Montgomery, AL, 1949

23. Letter from General Beauregard to Augusta Evans dated September 28, 1862, P.G.T. Beauregard Papers, Library of Congress, Washington, D.C.

24. The River Lethe was the "river in the lower world, from which the shades drank, and thus obtained forgetfulness of the past," according to the *Smaller Classical Dictionary*, Sir William Smith, Editor, E.P. Dutton & Co. Inc., New York, 1958.

25. Letter from General Beauregard to Augusta Evans dated August 22, 1862, P.G.T. Beauregard Papers, Library of Congress, Washington, D.C.

26. Jones, Katharine M., *Heroines of Dixie: Confederate Women Tell Their Story of the War*, Bobbs-Merrill Company, Inc., New York, NY, 1955

27. Greenbie.

28. Wise, Winifred Esther, *Lincoln's Secret Weapon*, Chilton Company, Philadelphia, PA, 1961

29. Macaria was a Greek woman who offered to sacrifice herself on the alter of the gods to save the threatened city of Athens.

30. Sterkx, H.E., *Some Notable Alabama Women During the Civil War*, Alabama Civil War Centennial Commission, 1962

31. Riepma, Anna Sophia Roelina, *Fire and Fiction: Augusta Jane Evans in Context*, Atlanta, GA, 2000

32. James McPherson, in *Battle Cry of Freedom*, Oxford University Press, New York, NY, 1988, reminds us that by the time of the close of the Battle of Malvern Hill, Lee had lost nearly a quarter of his army (twice the number of Union losses) and would probably not have been able to mount a successful attack if the retreating Federals had instead attacked. Lee's general, D.H. Hill, later wrote that Malvern Hill "was not war — it was murder." Hence, it was not the out and out Confederate victory that Miss Evans would have it seem to the reader.

33. Evans, Augusta Jane, *Macaria: or Altars of Sacrifice*, West & Johnson, Richmond, VA, 1864

34. *Ibid.*

35. The lady's name was Betty Duvall. For more information on Mrs. Greenhow's spy ring, read *My Imprisonment and the First Year of Abolition Rule at Washington* by Rose Greenhow, Richard Bentley, Publisher, London, England, 1863; and *Rebel Rose* by Ishbel Ross, Mockingbird Books, St. Simons Island, Georgia, 1954.

36. Talmudish Shemhamphorash is defined as "the Ineffable Divine Name" from the teachings of the Jewish Talmud, LaMeD Academy of Malchi-Zedek, "Glossary," St. Charles, MO, 2002

37. Evans, Augusta Jane, *Macaria: or Altars of Sacrifice*.

38. *Ibid.*

39. Union Captain James B. Ricketts commanded the artillery on Henry Hill during the Battle of First Manassas.

40. Union Captain Charles Griffin added his 10-pound Parrott guns to Captain Ricketts' artillery on Henry Hill at First Manassas.

41. Evans, Augusta Jane, *Macaria: or Altars of Sacrifice*.

42. *Ibid.*

43. Carroll, Anna Ella, *Affidavit of Memorialist* [Claim Before Congress, January 14, 1863], Library of Congress, Rare Books, Washington, D.C.

44. *Ibid.*

45. Edward Everett was a noted orator of the day and featured speaker at the dedication of the Union Cemetery at Gettysburg in November of 1863 along with President Lincoln, who also delivered a few words that day.

46. Carroll, Anna Ella, *Affidavit of Memorialist* [Claim Before Congress, January 14, 1863], Library of Congress, Rare Books, Washington, D.C.

47. Grant, U.S.S., *Personal Memoir of U.S. Grant*, Da Capo Press, New York, 1952. Many critics have pointed out Grant's notorious habit of puffing up his favorites and his unfair ignoring of credit where credit was due.

48. Letter to President Abraham Lincoln, August 14, 186__, Papers of Anna Ella Carroll, Maryland Historical Society, Annapolis, Maryland

49. *Ibid.*

50. Greenbie.

51. *Ibid.*

52. In 1869, upon his retirement from the Ohio Senate, Benjamin Wade wrote a letter to Anna, in which he told her, "I cannot take leave of public life without expressing my deep sense of your services to the country during the whole period of our national troubles. Although a citizen of a state almost unanimously disloyal and deeply sympathizing with secession, especially the wealthy and aristocratic class of her people, to which you belonged, yet, in the midst of such surroundings, you emancipated your own slaves at a great sacrifice of personal interest, and with your powerful pen defended the cause of the Union and loyalty as ably and effectively as it had ever yet been defended."

53. Livermore, Mary, *My Story of the War: A Woman's Narrative of Four Years Personal Experience as Nurse in the Union Army*, Da Capo Press, New York, 1995

54. *Mobile Register*, May 10, 1999.

55. *Ibid.*

56. Greenbie.

57. www.usd.edu/~acjones/petition.html.

About the Author

Sara Bartlett is nationally known as an actor, historian, speaker and musician. Her latest voice and music work can be heard on the audio book of Rose Greenhow's *Excerpts from My Imprisonment and the First Year of Abolition Rule in Washington*, edited by Eileen Conklin. She has written a documentary entitled *First Word Home: Clara Barton and the Office of Missing Soldiers* and is a featured speaker at Civil War Round Tables and women's history events. Ms. Bartlett's career includes over twenty years of theatrical roles in numerous theaters, films, and hundreds of radio and TV commercials. She can be seen in the upcoming film, *Fredericksburg*, and has an article appearing in the 2002 summer issue of *The Minerva Quarterly Report* on "Women in the Military."

WHO DID WHAT:
WOMEN'S ROLES IN THE CIVIL WAR

By Juanita Leisch

This article is a survey — an introduction — to women's roles in the Civil War. It addresses the scope and significance of those roles, but it, like any work of this length, offers a mere sampling of the breadth and depth of the topic.

Katherine Wormeley was one of a number of women who published accounts of their war-time experiences in the decades after the Civil War. Wormeley prefaced her book on one woman's roles in the war by noting a trend in books on the Civil War:

> Most of the writings relating to the War of the Rebellion have been confined to accounts of battles, or to adventures so closely connected with battles as to seem an essential part of the conflict itself. The book here given to the public...touches on matters almost entirely outside the noise and smoke, the glory and pomp of military operations.[1]

As the generation of participants in the Civil War died off, the trend Wormeley described continued and intensified, with writings on battles and leaders, and arms and equipment, and hundreds of thousands of pages examining almost every political and military aspect of the Civil War. Recent years have brought a renewed interest in women's roles of the Civil War. But perhaps inevitably, many recent works address the priorities and interests of the current generation more than those of the people who lived through the Civil War. This article attempts to reflect the scope and significance of women's roles in the Civil War from the perspective and priorities of those who were there.

Imagine for a moment that all the people who have spent time since 1865 studying the Civil War were gathered together in a massive, indoor, sports arena. Mounted on a platform at the center is an enormous and minutely detailed painting depicting major and minor events of the war. The audience, all those people who have who ever studied or written about the Civil War, have been seated on the tiers of bleachers in the order they arrived at the arena. Those who lived through the War and were there when the picture was painted occupy the floor and first rows. On each subsequent tier of seats is a subsequent generation of historians. Thus the historians of our current and most recent generations are the most distant from the painting. We have technologically advanced telephoto lenses and equipment for doing microscopic color analyses. We have a superior vantage point for seeing the "big picture." Still, for all the time we spend, we might yet miss an entire line of analysis, of things that were perfectly obvious to anyone who was around while the painting was being produced. We may not have the opportunity to look at the canvas on which the picture was painted. Yet anyone in the room when the picture was made, even the most casual observer, would remember the canvas. The people in the first rows may have watched — and exclaimed — mainly over the picture taking form, but they would remember the canvas and the effort expended in stretching and preparing it. The earlier audience would be far more likely than we recent arrivals to recognize the importance and significance of that canvas. They might even stand alone in recognizing and acknowledging that without the support of the canvas, the picture could not have taken form, certainly not in the way that it did.

In searching for women's roles in the Civil War, we will study the surface of the above mentioned painting for the major and minor events involving women. We will find, on the vast and detailed pictorial, unmistakable instances of women procuring and presenting flags and banners to the troops. We will find them on the periphery of the fields of battle assisting the wounded and dying and even burying the dead. And yes! Unmistakably and undeniably, we find them serving as spies, scouts, smugglers, and soldiers.

But even with the most generous estimates of the numbers of these women depicted on the surface, we do not find that they represent any sort of a significant portion of the population of women. We are hard-pressed to find evidence that their actions, however brave or gallant, affected significant portions of the war efforts. The problem with our analysis — and with others taken from this distance — is in the view. To find women's roles in the war, we must find a way to go "behind the scenes."

For like the canvas of the painting, women's roles in the Civil War are integral and important, but easily overlooked, particularly if your view is only from a distance. The author of this article is sitting in one of the rows of bleachers that is more than a century distant from the painting. She has been able get a view of the canvas very simply: by listening to the people sitting in the front rows.

So what was the scope of women's roles in the Civil War? The answer, in a nutshell, is that women's roles are found at every point where the ability of a woman or group of women intersected with the need of a soldier or group of soldiers. The scope of their roles lies not in what women did, but in what soldiers needed. The significance of their roles lies not in whether it made a difference to the women (or our opinions of them), but in whether it made a difference to the soldiers.

Enthusiasm/Encouragement

What do soldiers need? They need the impetus to become soldiers in the first place and, by all accounts, women had a hand in creating an atmosphere of enthusiasm and patriotism. One regimental history described that a young lady, swept up in the emotion of a recruiting rally "...became more expressive and enthusiastic than ever. At last she spoke right out in meeting as follows: 'John, if you do not enlist, I'll never let you kiss me again as long as I live!'" The success of her proposition is not recorded, but the reaction of her parents and others at the meeting is.[2]

Women provided encouragement, too, to men they barely knew and to complete strangers.

> They were soon going to "whip the rebels." They looked so gay and fine in their new uniforms, with their knapsacks strapped on their backs and the shining muskets glinting in the sun. Tears which I could not repress would stream down my face as I watched them and realize that many would never return, for I had given my best and dearest and my heart went out to the boys and the women who were left behind and had to "labor and wait." But we gave the marching men a word and smile of friendly cheer as they passed by and for which they always seemed pleased and grateful, and we served them the "cup of cold water" in His name.[3]

But these actions would have had little significance if the soldiers had not noticed them. We know from the comments of the soldiers themselves that they did notice. Spencer Glasgow Welch, a Confederate surgeon, mentioned this sort of enthusiastic support in a letter to his wife: "The ladies wave their handkerchiefs from every little farmhouse we pass and cheer us onward. Such sights are enough to make anyone feel enthusiastic."[4] There are also accounts of young ladies who festooned their clothing with patriotic symbols such as cockades, military buttons, and even flags.

Waving a handkerchief and cheering troops as they go off to war is easy enough. Perhaps more significantly, women continued to encourage the soldiers even in difficult times, as when women encouraged a sickly son and only remaining male in the family to return to war with his company leaving his family behind enemy lines. Mary Gay recalled the scene as her brother and his comrades took their leave: "Instead of yielding to grief, we repressed every evidence of it, and spoke only words of encouragement to these noble men who had never shirked a duty."[5]

Was it significant? Did the soldiers notice and remember? Did the incidents have any effect on them? Indeed they did. Twenty years after the Civil War, when Sam R. Watkins wrote Company Aytch, he still remembered the encouragement of two young ladies:

> When we got back to Knoxville we were the lousiest, dirtiest, raggedest looking Rebels you ever saw. I had been shot through the hat and cartridge-box at Perryville, and had both on, and the clothing I then had on was all that I had in the world. William A. Hughes and I were walking up the street looking at the stores, etc., when we met two of the prettiest girls I ever saw. They ran forward with smiling faces, and seemed very glad to see us. I thought they were old acquaintances of Hughes, and Hughes thought they were old acquaintances of mine. We were soon laughing and talking as if we had been old friends, when one of he young ladies spoke up and said, "Gentlemen, there is a supper for the soldiers at the Ladies' Association rooms, and we are sent out to bring in all the soldiers we can find." We spoke up quickly and said, "Thank you, thank you, young ladies," and I picked out the prettiest one and said, "Please take my arm," which she did, and Hughes did the same with the other one, and we went in that style down the street. I imagine we were a funny looking sight, I know one thing. I felt good all

over, and as proud as a boy with his first pants, and when we got to that supper room and those young ladies waited on us, and we felt as grand as kings. To you, ladies, I say, God bless you![6]

Clothing

As historians study the painting, they identify the soldiers and officers who participated in the war. The uniforms of these men assist in their identifications, and thus merit a great deal of study. But the fact that the men even had uniforms is part of the story of women's roles in the Civil War.

At the outset of the war, women helped to manufacture the uniforms that communities provided for "their" soldiers. Throughout the war, when supplies and the mails permitted, women sent replacements to "their" soldiers. They did this individually and in efforts organized by local, state, and national organizations. And finally, throughout the war tens of thousands of women labored day after day stitching the uniforms and being paid on a piece-work basis, often at rates that amounted to starvation wages.

It is this last group of women who produced the most clothes, and who are the most forgotten of the lot. They worked for the depots or for contractors. Some were the wives and families of soldiers left destitute when their sole support was away at war or died in the war. Most were illiterate.[7] A further examination of the pay records may yet reveal the output of individual women, but the little available evidence indicates that their labors left them little time to keep diaries or write letters, even had they been able to do so.

Cyrena Bailey Stone, a unionist living in Atlanta during the Civil War, provided in her diary one of the few anecdotes about the depot women, reported a girl, aged sixteen, who walked daily the two miles back and forth to Atlanta to get sewing work: "This girl is intelligent and refined in her feelings, and she often cries when she tells me of the insults she receives from the men who deal out the work. She was worn out by carrying the heavy goods, and had been working months to save enough to buy a pair of shoes.[8]

The plight of women working for depots and contractors was a subject of concern to many. Some, like Katherine Wormeley, turned their concern for these women into a plan of action. Before and after the months in which she worked in the hospital transport service, Wormeley obtained government contracts to produce shirts for soldiers and arranged the finances of the contract so that she might pay the seamstresses better-than-average wages for their work.

> I received...a contract for the making of flannel army-shirts, given me by Deputy Quartermaster-General D. H. Vinton, U.S.A., for the purpose of giving employment to the families of volunteers and other poor women. During the winter of 1861-62 we made over seventy thousand. The Department paid me fourteen cents a shirt, and furnished the flannel and the buttons. I paid the women eleven cents a shirt (they could easily make four a day, without a machine), and the remaining three cents just covered the cost of linen-thread, transportation to and from New York, office and workroom expenses. The ladies of Newport helped me to cut the shirts.[9]

The distribution of labor for making men's clothing was fairly universal. In the case of shirts and drawers, women cut the fabric and sewed the garments. In the case of coats, jackets, and pants, men drafted the patterns and cut the fabric. Kits were assembled and issued to women to sew the garments together. But in this, as in all things, there were exceptions. A Mrs. Blackburn who worked at the Staunton, Virginia, depot seems to have been a prodigious cutter.[10] But for this woman and others who may have been her peers, we have, only the official pay record; no diaries, letters, or journals.

In contrast to the lack of accounts from the women who earned their living making uniforms, there are numerous accounts by women who voluntarily made uniforms on an occasional or part time basis. Many of these women worked as individuals, supplying goods for soldiers they knew. Others worked with organized groups. And their efforts began at the very outset of the war as militia units and community companies were still forming. One of the first tasks that faced the officers of new recruits was finding uniforms for their men. Mother C. S. Branch wrote to her son:

June 17, 1861

...I must try and do all I can for the soldiers among us.... We met at Mrs. Bartows on Saturday to answer to a call from her in the newspapers, the business before us was to see who would make clothes [&] uniforms for the OLI [Oglethorpe Light Infantry]. There was a very large meeting all appeared to be anxious to do what they could   I shall make four suits, one a piece for each of you, one for a young man by he name of Carolin whom I am interested in and the other is for a man I don't know, a stranger Francis Lunts...you know these 2 men have no friends and so some body must make for them— ... I have been so busy all morning attending to the uniform that I can't write more now.
    — Mother CS Branch to her "Dear Child"[11]

Katherine Wormeley put into words the general experience "As the men mustered for the battle-field, so the women mustered in churches, schoolhouses, and parlors, working before they well knew at what to work, and clinging everywhere for instructions...Little circles and associations of women were multiplying, like rings in the water, over the face of the whole country...[12]

Throughout the country, individual women and groups of women procured, produced and presented flags and colors for "their" troops. Some of these colors saw service; others were used only for ceremonial purposes. Some were presented back to the women for safe keeping during or after the war. In the newspaper coverage of the flag presentations ceremonies, women received some of the rare public notoriety of their involvement in the Civil War.

The Woolsey family arguably gave as much in support of the war as any family. The family consisted of widow Jane Woolsey, her seven daughters, one son, and their respective spouses and in-laws. The entire family took an active interest in the war and not only spent the war years finding roles for themselves, but also suffered to have their wartime correspondence compiled and published by two of the sisters. The resultant book *My Heart Toward Home: Letters of a*

Family During the Civil War offers examples of women's roles for those who stayed at home and those who volunteered full-time. As the excerpt below indicates, the Woolsey's jumped in to volunteer from the first months of the war.

> Do find out from Joe's Dr. Crandall what style of garments he things best for hospital wear, as we are constantly cutting them out, and may as well make them with reference to his wants. Should the night-shirts be of unbleached or canton flannel, and drawers ditto? Should the shirts be long or short? And are extra flannel shirts necessary for hospital wear? I am going to the Cooper Union today to try and get some simple patterns for calico gowns. They advertise to supply paper patterns of garments to ladies, and their published circular, a copy of which I have seen, is far more particular and satisfactory in its directions that the one we have had.
>
> — Abby Howland Woolsey to Eliza Woolsey Howland letter of May 17, 1861[13]

In the South, especially, women contended with providing goods for soldiers even when materials became scarce. Catherine Ann Devereaux came from a prominent family used to living with every luxury. In her extensive journal of life during the Civil War, she expressed a common experience of Southern women.

> The wants of the Army lie very near my heart. The thought of what I can do for them occupies me constantly. I can, by using my table covers, scraps of flannel, etc., manage to piece out six flannel shirts. Patrick will give cotton cloth from the plantation supplies for six pr of drawers & woolen cloth for six pr of pantaloons & six pr of shoes, even if the old women who never go out but sit by the fire & burn wood all the winter go without. I can I think spare 2 blankets more & will take my chintz coverlids & make four comfortables. So together we will fit out six soldiers.
>
> — Catherine Ann Devereaux's journal entry for December [14?] 1862[14]

In addition to sewing, women also knitted. The diaries, journals and letters written by the literate observers and participants in the war provide thousands of references to women sewing and knitting for their soldiers. As Mary Gay reported in her memoirs:

> Many of us who had never learned to sew became expert handlers of the needle, and vied with each other in producing well-made garments, and I became a veritable knitting machine. Besides the discharge of many duties incident to the times... I knitted a sock a day, long and large, and not coarse, many days in succession...When the Knitting of a dozen pairs of socks was completed, they were washed, irons and neatly folded... Each pair formed a distinct package. Usually a pretty necktie, a pair of gloves, a handkerchief and letter, deposited in one of the socks, enlarged the package. When all was ready, card bearing the name of the giver and a request to "inquire within," was tacked on to each package. And then these twelve packages were formed into a bundle, and addressed to an officer in command of some company chosen to be the recipient of the contents.[15]

Fannie Beers, who traveled through a number of southern states during the war, reported:

In the wide halls within the plantation houses stood tables piled with newly-dyed cloth and hanks of woolen or cotton yarns. The knitting of socks went on in the performance of household or plantation duties, sock in hand, "casting on," "heeling," "turning off." By the light of pine knots the elders still knitted far into the night...[16]

By war time the technology existed to make socks with commercial knitting machines and there were some commercial establishments that manufactured socks. However, there is little evidence that the commercial knitting establishments of the time could have produced sufficient quantities of socks to meet the soldiers' demands. It was widely believed and promoted at the time that hand-knit socks lasted three times as long as machine-knit ones.

Soldiers did not, as a rule, wash their socks with great frequency. This generally reduces the lifespan of any sock. Armies issued socks in about the same quantities that they issued shoes. It is virtually certain that without the supplemental supplies of socks sent by women, men would have been marching in shoes or boots without socks. Did it make difference that women knit socks for soldiers?

This woman may be knitting socks. When knitting, using three or four needles enables you to knit a tube as for a sock.
Author's collection

Take a break from studying the painting. Put on leather shoes or boots, wearing no socks. Walk a mile or two. As you limp home to nurse your blisters — or worse — reflect that soldiers did more than walk a mile in those shoes; they marched and counter-marched over entire states, and much of the continent. Could they have done even a fraction of that marching — executed even a single campaign — without the socks the women knit? It is perhaps in wielding the knitting needles that women played one of heir most important roles of the war.

Delivering the Goods

Individual women concerned about individual soldiers endeavored to anticipate and meet their every need. Throughout the war, members of the Woolsey family spent time investigating needs and seeking to meet them, from sending simple boxes like the one described below, to buying and sending "air beds,"[17] rocking chairs, newspapers, or whatever else Mrs. Woolsey's daughters reported to her was needed either for the soldiers in the hospitals or for soldiers who were friends and acquaintances.

> This morning Mother has been putting up a tin box of stores for Mr. Davies — sardines, potted meats, arrow root, chocolate, guava and the like, with a box of cologne, a jar of prunes and a morocco case with knife, fork and spoon, fine steel and double plated, "just out" for army use.... The box, a square cracker box, holds as much in its way as the trunk.
> — Abby Howland Woolsey to Eliza Newton Woolsey Howland[18]

Mrs. Woolsey could well afford to put up boxes of stores but thousands of others who were less well situated also sent boxes to the soldiers. Phoebe Yates Pember was a matron of a hospital in Richmond, Virginia. She reported on the boxes that arrived for troops in the hospital:

> There was indescribable pathos lurking at times at the bottom of these heterogenous home boxes, put up by anxious wives, mothers and sisters; a sad and mute history shadowed forth by the sight of rude, coarse homespun pillow-cases or pocket handkerchiefs, adorned even amid the turmoil of war and poverty with an attempt at a little embroidery... The silent tears dropped over these tokens will never be sung in song or told in story. The little loving expedients to conceal the want of means which each woman resorted to, thinking that if her loved one failed to benefit by the result, other mothers might reap the advantage, is a history in itself.[19]

While some women worked as individuals, others joined sewing societies and Ladies Aid Societies and worked in concert with each other. Many such sewing societies had existed before the war, and were an important venue for social interaction in some communities. Some of these organizations were quite formal with elected officer, constitutions, and even minute-books.[20] These societies were already accustomed to gathering and distributing clothing for the poor, and it required only a small change in mission to instead supply goods to soldiers.

The means by which women and groups of women delivered their gifts of food and clothing to the troops were an object of concern. The women's efforts could not meet needs if the goods didn't reach the soldiers. With armies commandeering all available trains to move troops, or military supplies, and other armies blowing up bridges or destroying tracks, the wonder is that private boxes ever got to the troops for whom they were intended.

The visions of depots of misdirected boxes with food spoiling as they sat on platforms may have been one of the impetuses behind the creation of the U.S. Sanitary Commission. The U.S. Sanitary Commission is a prime example of an organization in which women played key and integral roles and in which some women even aspired to leadership roles as the heads of various committees. It was, however, organized in a traditional nineteenth century manner with men prominently seated at the top. This quasi-governmental organization served a number of important functions for the North.

The U.S. Sanitary Commission helped to coordinate the distribution of supplies to those most in need. At times, the Sanitary Commission would get supplies to the sites of major battles before the Army wagons arrived. It collected donated goods from individuals and organizations throughout the country, packed or purchased needed goods, and sent them in consolidated shipments wherever they were most needed. While these consolidated, general efforts were arguably the most economical way to operate, the Sanitary Commission also worked with organizations that designated their assistance for the troops of certain states.

The Sanitary Commission tried to ensure that services, (as well as supplies) were available when and where they were needed. The Commission operated hospitals in many locations until U.S. Army hospitals were established in the locations or the need was no longer felt for a hospital in a given location. Partially as an outgrowth of these activities, agents of the Sanitary Commission maintained up-to-date rosters for each of their hospitals and, eventually, for many other hospitals, on soldiers and their status. Families could write to the Sanitary Commission with hope of finding out the location and status of an individual who had been reported sick or wounded. Agents of the Sanitary Commission inspected camps and promoted practices that improved the health of soldiers, such as ensuring uncontaminated supplies of water. For these activities alone, the Commission claimed to have reduced deaths in camp from disease by a third.

The U.S. Sanitary Commission needed funds in order to conduct all these activities, and it may be for its innovative and enormously successful fundraising efforts that the U.S. Sanitary Commission is most remembered. During the course of the war, it is estimated that the value of funds raised and goods distributed totaled in excess of $15,000,000. In some active communities, a single fair would raise the equivalent of nearly $2 for every man, woman and child in the area.

Various communities held "Sanitary Fairs", which were large bazaars held to raise funds. These fairs were so large that blocks of land were secured, buildings built, and sectioned off for various theme exhibits and areas. Many of the theme areas raised funds by selling products or services. At one of the fairs in Brooklyn, girls running one booth wore exaggerated Alsatian costumes and made pancakes from batter delivered to them by Delmonico's Restaurant. Other booths included handiworks that were sold, such as dolls, floral displays, beaded pillows, and so on. Many commercial establishments and artists donated items for sale at the fairs. Florence Nightingale autographed copies of her books on nursing in the Crimean War. Abraham Lincoln provided signed copies of his Emancipation Proclamation for at least one of the fairs.

Antiquarians have credited the "New England Kitchen" displays at the Sanitary Fairs as being the founding of modern antique collecting. They are credited as being among the first instances of domestic antiques being displayed and promoted simply because they were antiques. Some have credited them with launching the trade in domestic antiques in America.

The fairs also included events, such as performances, tableaux, auctions and "voting booths" where attendees could vote for their favorite military general in a spirited competition. One the most unique and most successful booths of the Sanitary Fairs were the post offices. Attractive young ladies ran these post offices, at which young people could exchange flirtatious letters. Stationary was sold, as were envelopes and special stamps. Letters were posted and cancelled at the Fair post office. Presumably letters posted at a Fair had to be picked up from the post office at the Fair, but in truth, the U.S. Sanitary Commission and its agents were so well connected with the U.S. government that in many cases letters posted at a USSC post office and stamped with USSC stamps were actually delivered by the U.S. Postal Service.

The connections between the U.S. Sanitary Commission and the U.S. Postal Service extended beyond the Sanitary Fairs. Agents of the Sanitary Commission were instrumental in effecting changes that ensured that letters to and from soldiers in the field received special treatment. Troops often moved from the location to which the letters were addressed and one change implemented during the war established that no additional postage was required when a letter had to be forwarded. Many of these negotiations were undoubtedly conducted by men but it probably did not hurt their efforts that one of the Postmistresses of the Sanitary Fair in Philadelphia was Mrs. E. D. Gillespie, granddaughter of Benjamin Franklin, first Postmaster General.

Katherine Wormeley paid a tribute to the organization and its efforts:

> ...the Sanitary Commission...show[ed] that by a great united effort their work was a fundamental good to the whole army; that lives were to be saved, the vital force protected; and that women, guided by the wisdom of men, were to bear no small part in helping to maintain the efficiency of the troops, and thus to share upon the field itself the work of husbands and brothers.[21]

Only one other organization rivaled the U.S. Sanitary Commission. It was the U.S. Christian Commission, organized to minister to the spiritual as well as physical needs of the soldiers. The United States Christian Commission published and distributed, quite literally, millions of religious tracts during the war.

At times, individual agents of the two organizations cooperated with each other. At other times, they seem to have been in competition and even in conflict. The U.S. Christian Commission, like the U.S. Sanitary Commission, was disbanded after the war. At the final meeting of the Christian Commission, Trustees voted to permit the sale of a book on incidents of the war to be sold for "the spiritual and temporal benefit of those who are, have been, or may be, soldiers or sailors in the service of the United States."[22] Typically, the book does not relate successes of the organization itself but rather incidents of individual soldiers being saved. And the authors are careful not to credit the organization itself for the good that occurred.

> This Volume has its origin in the...forces of Christianity developed and exemplified amid the carnage of battle and the more perilous tests of hospital and camp.
> These religious forces were not begotten of the Christian Commission; they came with the army fro the Christian homes of its citizen soldiery. The Commission was, rather, born of them.[23]

Like the Sanitary Commission, the Christian Commission was managed by men, but supported (and, in some cases, staffed) by thousands of women. From the perspective of the participants, working under the leadership of men in no way diminished the value of the women's roles and participation. As Miss Wormeley noted, "We of the "staff" are specially subordinate to Mr. Olmsted; and though we are not his right hand — Mr. Knapp and Dr. Ware are that — we are the fingers of it, and help to carry out his ideas.[24]

Ammunition

Civilian organizations may have provided for many needs of the solders but there are tools of the soldier's trade that are nearly always provided by his government. Among these are weapons, ammunition, and the accoutrements to hold that ammunition.

When Southern civilians learned their government was short of funds to produce additional gunboats, they organized fundraising drives to help raise money. Women's roles in these organizations were recognized in that they were often called "Ladies Gunboat Societies." The "lady directors" of the local Soldiers' Aid Society were reported in a local newspaper as having raised nearly $2000, which they forwarded to a shipbuilder in an undisclosed location.[25]

Accoutrements, too, were generally provided by the government but were made by contractors. Some women owned or ran firms or establishments that manufactured accoutrements for the armies. For example, when Mrs. (Laura) Baker's husband died part-way through the war, she took over his company and his contracts, changed the name of his firm to "L.S. Baker & Company," and continued to produce leather accoutrements for military contracts and to win contracts on her own.

These female contractors were few in numbers; far more significant numbers of women worked in ammunition factories during the war. Indeed, it has been estimated that 90% of the workers in ammunition factories during the war were women (and children). These women risked their lives working in an environment in which explosions were not rare. One such explosion at Brown's Island in the River near Richmond, Virginia, resulted in the death of dozens of women. This particular incident also resulted in an order that may have been one of the few Occupational Safety and Health orders of the Confederacy, declaring that henceforth ammunition would not be stored in the same room where it was being manufactured and assembled. It further ordered that workers in these establishments should wear "fireproof" garments.

Was it significant? Imagine the shortage of ammunition that would have resulted from removing the vast majority of the workers who produced ammunition during the war. By the numbers alone, the answer must be "yes."

Shelter

In some cases, women helped to meet a basic human necessity like shelter. Women, (voluntarily or not) opened their houses and barns to soldiers. At times, civilians found that providing shelter for soldiers could be detrimental. As a Confederate surgeon reported to his wife; speaking of his observations during the Battle of Gettysburg:

> There were a good many dwellings in our path, to which the Yankees would also resort for protection, and they would shoot from the doors and windows. As soon as our troops would drive them out, they would rush in, turn out the families, and set the houses on fire. I think this was wrong, because the families could not prevent the Yankees seeking shelter in their houses. I saw some of the poor women who had been thus treated. They were greatly distressed, and it excited my sympathy very much.
>
> — Spencer Glasgow Welch, Camp near Orange Court House, VA 8/2/63[26]

Food

Great truth lies in the quote sometimes credited to Napoleon Bonaparte that "An army marches on its stomach." When large portions of the adult, male population, of an agrarian society is occupied with war, an interruption in the food supply is all but assured. Large portions of the South were agrarian. When distribution of food is dependent on rail service that the war systematically and repeatedly destroys, an interruption in food distribution is all but assured. When military strategies include the purposeful devastation of important food-producing areas, food shortages are all but assured. When all three of these things take place, as they did in the South during the Civil War, the mystery is that things weren't worse. The men and women left at home worked hard to keep the farms going and the crops growing while the ordinary workforce was otherwise occupied. In some parts of the country, this was made even more difficult as draft animals were confiscated for military use. Yet civilians persisted in producing food crops during the war, and in sharing those crops with soldiers. Kate Stone's family relocated several times during the war, which required planting crops in each new location. Of their final relocation, Kate commented, "We have an excellent garden, though our neighbors said Warren [a slave] was not doing the right thing in it. We can send salad to the hospital every day and soon other vegetables.[27]

Fannie Beers reported on efforts just like these, but from the perspective of the hospital recipients:

> As the summer waned, our commissary stores began to fail. Rations, always plain, became scant. Our foragers met with little success. But for the patriotic devotion of the families whose farms and plantations lay for miles around Ringgold, ...even our sickest men would have been deprived of suitable food. As it was, the supply was by no means sufficient.[28]

Such efforts would not, could not, provide enough. Especially in the South, civilians and soldiers ate less and had less variety in their diets than many were accustomed to prior to the war. Southerners showed great creativity in finding substitutes and prided themselves on their "ersatz" oysters, coffee, and treats. Women's diaries and journals of the period are filled with descriptions and reviews of various substitutes.

But the difficulty is not always in having enough food, but rather it is in getting food to locations where the soldiers need it. In the North and the South, it was through the efforts of thousands of women that food was available for tens of thousands of soldiers arriving at railroad depots in large cities. As Fannie Beers related, "I do not believe that a squad of sick soldiers arrived in Richmond, at least during the first year of the war, who were not discovered and bountifully fed shortly after their arrival."[29]

In Philadelphia, a boathouse and a cooper shop were transformed into the "Union Volunteer" and "Cooper Union" refreshment saloons for the soldiers. Shortly after the war, F. B. Goodrich enumerated some of the ways in which civilians assisted the war efforts. In his massive tome, *The Tribute Book*, he described how these institutions met the needs of soldiers:

> "We were speaking," wrote a gentleman in a letter to...one of the officers of the Union Saloon, "of the demoralizing influences of camp life, and a friend remarked that while at East New York, his regiment...had become sadly demoralized. The camp was surrounded by grog-shops, and the rations were of the poorest...the men had become dispirited and disgusted...orders came for the regiment to march, and the men went on board the steamer much as if they were going to the gallows. We reached Philadelphia, and marched to the Union Volunteer Refreshment Saloon, and warm welcome, the hearty shake of the hand, and the ample and delicious fare served for us, put a new spirit into the men. They had landed in a mood fit for mutiny or desertion; they left Philadelphia, feeling that they were the cherished soldiers of the nation...[30]

The men who visited the refreshment saloon, and the hospital associated with the Cooper Saloon recognized and appreciated the efforts of women volunteers. After the war, veterans in the Philadelphia area named their Grand Army of the Republic (GAR) post after Anna Ross, one of the Cooper's most stalwart and dedicated volunteers. The soldiers who daily drew refreshment at the Cooper Refreshment Saloon may not have been dying for the food, but they certainly found it refreshing and convenient as it revived their bodies and spirits.

One way that women contributed to feeding the soldiers was not merely convenient, but actually lifesaving. It is in providing food and drink to soldiers too sick or wounded to get it for themselves. Early in the war, the U.S. military began using hospital transport boats to ship soldiers from the sites of major conflicts to the sites of major hospitals. Women were employed to work on these ships as both cooks and nurses. In fact, the *Red Rover* was notable for training and employing African American woman as nurses, rather than relegating to them the title of "cook" more usually given to African American women in similar situations.[31] While the government supplied most of the boats, private individuals sometimes supplied the bedding, food, and medicines with which the boats were equipped. One Surgeon on a boat wrote Jane Stuart Woolsey a letter expressing the importance of the sustenance:

> Our friend, Surgeon Smith, went down with the truce fleet. Perhaps you will let me quote a sentence or two from his letter... "I have just received 560 poor, wretched, miserable sufferers. All their being, all mind, seems to be absorbed in the one idea of living...God help and pity them and take home the wretches that will die to-night. These living skeletons...are worse to see than any sight on battlefields.... Whiskey and hot strong broth are being served out rapidly.... The whiskey and broth, sweet soft bread and onions are working wonders. One poor skeleton said to me just now, 'Why, Major, I could but just crawl on board, and now I'm bully,' 'How is that?' Said I. 'Oh, it's the grub; I was starving to death.'[32]

Having women work on the hospital transport boats was a successful experiment, as they helped to organize the boats, and to assist in providing medical care to the soldiers. Certainly, the soldiers appreciated them.

The men were all patient and grateful. Some said, 'You don't know what it is to me to see you." "This is heaven, after what I've suffered." "To think of a Woman being here to help me!" One little drummer-boy thought he was going to die instantly. I said: "Pooh! You'll walk off the ship at New York."[33]

One practice followed in a number of hospitals during the war was that of differentiating the diets of the sick soldiers depending on their ailments. This was a practice that was instituted in a number of the Civil War hospitals and an innovation sometimes attributed to women in the hospitals. Certainly, a number of women wrote about the benefits of the practice. Fannie Beers detailed how it worked in Buckner Hospital in Gainesville, Alabama:

> For the sick, I had my own kitchen, my own cooks and other servants, my own store-room, and also liberty to send out foragers. Every morning I sent to each surgeon a list of such diet as I could command for the sick. With this in hand he was able to decide upon the proper food for each patient. Each bed was numbered. The head-nurse kept a small book, into which he copied each day's diet-list. He as also expected to have ready every morning a fresh piece of paper, upon which the surgeon wrote the numbers of the beds,

and opposite, F.D., H.D., L.D., V.L.D., or S.D. (full diet, half diet, light diet, very light diet, and special diet).[34]

While women working full time in hospitals may have saved the lives of hundreds, or even thousands, there were also individual women who cared for individual soldiers. Who can doubt that Mary Lawrence helped her husband's recovery when she traveled from Massachusetts to nurse her husband day and night through the amputation of his foot in a hospital in Washington. She reported spooning beef tea down his throat, and buying, cooking, and serving him steak. He survived, while men in the same ward with similar operations who had no such personal care did not.[35]

Hospital and Medical Work

But women provided far more than food as they helped out with the hospitals, either as occasional visitors, regular volunteers, or, in some cases, by traveling from home and dedicating a portion of their lives to living and working in the hospitals full time. The most common experience was that of women who volunteered when they could at hospitals in their local communities. Sarah Jane Full Hill, reported on activities in St. Louis:

> The women's Soldiers' Aid Society had been organized and I offered my services which were gladly accepted and I was a busy woman those dark days of the winter of '61 and '62. A large vacant block of stores on Fifth and Chestnut streets was taken by the government for a hospital, and the store rooms on the ground floor were used as Headquarters of the Medical Corps. The three upper stories were used for the hospital.... At first there was little system or order in our work, each and every woman doing what she could, our main object being to help the sick soldiers, and we found plenty of work. Of course we were all giving our time and labor to the cause. The doctors and surgeons availed themselves of our help, and everyday we women gathered at the rooms and scraped lint, tore and rolled bandages, knitted socks. We solicited donations of delicacies for the sick. Many boxes were packed and sent to the soldiers in the field hospitals. We were called on to assist the surgeons in their operations and to nurse the patients. There were no regular nurses then and volunteer nurses were scarce...mother spent much time making soups, broths and dainties, for she had much experience in cooking for the sick. My sister and I would visit the hospital three or four times a week, always carrying a well-filled basket of broth and delicacies. These we would distribute ourselves among the patients who had come under our notice...we were frequently called on for nurses, for there was great lack of help in that line.[36]

Some women set aside their daily lives to answer a call for full time nurses who would travel to whatever location the military had established hospitals. Miss Katherine Wormeley traveled to Washington, DC and worked on hospital transport boats and in hospitals far from her home during the war.

> ...As far as I can judge, our duty is to be very much that of a housekeeper. We attend to the beds, the linen, the clothing of the patients; we have a pan-

try and store-room, and are required to do all the cooking for the sick, and see that it is properly distributed according to the surgeons' orders; we are also to have a general superintendence over the condition of the wards and over the nurses, who are all men. What else, time and experience will show, I suppose.[37]

Women wrote marvelously detailed accounts of the many tasks they performed in the hospitals, showing the many ways in which they met the human needs of the soldiers.

I ate a few bites...and then laid down [and] fell asleep. A rap at the door brought me up quickly. It was the sergeant, come to say he wounded were on their way, and we must get ready. Some of the nurses were away, and the way I took shirts, drawers and stockings out of the boxes, the young doctor, tearing off the covers, was up to the top of my speed. ...we laid out a piece of each upon every bed till the end of our supply, then sent to the church across the street for enough to make 150 pieces.... When we ran down the main hall stairs, such a sight met our eyes as I hope you will never witness. From the broad open entrance into the hall, to the base of the staircase, there bent, clung, and stood, in dumb silence, fifty soldiers, grim, dirty, muddy and wounded.... I stood by the doctor as he took the name of each and handed each his bed with a ticket. Then they were led or lifted up over the great staircase, winding along, some to the ballroom, others to the banqueting room. When all were up, we each took our portion and commenced to wash them. We were four hours. Everything they had on was stripped off — and, weak, helpless as babes, they sank upon us to care for them. With broken arms and wounded feet, thighs, and fingers, it was no easy job to do gently. One quite old man, sick every way, and a bullet hole through his right hand, called me 'good mother' when I laid his head on his pillow, and soon he slept as though he had come to the end of the war, unto a haven of rest. That was the experience of...5th of July, 1862.[38]

Prior to the Civil War, the author of this account, Hannah Ropes, had been an ardent abolitionist. When her son joined the army she left her daughter Alice (to whom this letter was written) to serve as a full time nurse. Hannah died in service January 20, 1863.

The logistical tasks associated with running the massive hospitals needed during the Civil War included far more than simply making beds and signing in the soldiers. More than tending to wounds, changing bandages. More than procuring, cooking and feeding meals to the soldiers. Behind all these activities were those associated with the hospital laundry. Fannie Beers, who worked in a number of Southern hospitals, reported on organizing the laundry service at Buckner Hospital in Gainesville, Alabama:

Everything relating to the bedding, clothing, and the personal belongings of the sick and wounded I found in a fearful state...it appeared to me impossible to bring any degree of order out of the chaotic mass of wet, half-dry, rough-dry, in some cases mildewed clothing lying everywhere about.... A "linen-master" having been detailed, a "linen-room' set apart and shelved, the articles were placed upon large tables to be sorted and piled upon the shelves.... Some of the clothes were torn and buttonless. My detailed men could not sew. The demands of the sick and the duties of general supervision left me not time. Taught by my experience of the devoted women of Virginia.... I resolved to visit some of the ladies of Gainesville, and to solicit their aid. The response was hearty and immediate. Next day the linen-room was peopled by bright, energetic ladies, at whose hands the convalescents received their renovated garments with words of warm sympathy an encouragement to cheer their hearts.[39]

In field hospitals, wounded soldiers were sometimes left in the relatively clean environment of a field or forest. Or, they might be transported into a building. In some cases these buildings were houses, but in others, they were barns and stables. Who can say how many complications resulted from laying wounded soldiers in environments where their wounds would be contaminated by animal waste? Individuals, community organizations, and the Sanitary Commission labored to provide hospitals with beds, or at least bedding, that were as convenient as possible to the sites of major conflicts. It is no exaggeration to say that removing soldiers to beds with clean sheets actually saved lives.

While some women provided soldiers food, clean laundry, and other housekeeping services to meet the human needs of the men, other women ventured into areas of providing for the surgical and medical needs of the soldiers. Hands-on medical care was usually reserved for surgeons and (male) nurses, but not always. Julia S. Wheelock reported her own experiences, being called upon to bathe wounds and change bandages:

> As we entered the building, oh, what a sight met our eyes! ... There lay the wounded, stretched upon the floor side by side, in close proximity, weltering in blood and filth.
>
> They were faint and hungry, some having only a short time before arrived from the battle-field, with wounds still undressed, their blankets and clothing saturated with blood and not unfrequently covered with vermin. It was a site well-calculated to appeal to the stoutest heart; but, nerving ourselves for the task, we went to work feeding these poor sufferers, bathing and dressing their wounds.[40]

"Aunt Becky" (Mrs. S. A. Palmer) reported that one surgeon encouraged her in providing "hands-on" medical care:

> The doctor hoped I would not hurt the man any more than I could help, and with this precautionary remark, ordered one of the nurses to assist me, and we went to the hard task. The rifle-ball had gone in at the back of his neck, tearing through, and coming out at his nostrils. As we syringed the cleansing preparation into his ear, it discharged at both apertures, and was a painful operation for us all, yet he bore it bravely. When he was made as comfortable as possible we found two more whose condition was as pitiable as his had been, and we washed and dressed their wounds also, and gave them something to eat.[41]

At the time of the Civil War, there were women doctors in the United States, and a number of them volunteered their services in various capacities. Dr.

Mary Walker earned a Medal of Honor for her service in providing medical care to troops. Dr. Elizabeth Blackwell organized and ran a program for training nurses who intended to work with the military. Dr. Esther Hill Hawks ministered to colored troops, and was eventually (though temporarily) placed in charge of a military hospital. Women had broken through the barriers blocking them from obtaining medical degrees nearly a decade before the Civil War.

Did the women's help — as doctors or nurses — meet the needs of soldiers? Mrs. S. A. Palmer, "Aunt Becky" related an incident in which she personally saved a life:

> As I looked from the upper window to shut out the terrible sight of blood and wounds, my eyes fell upon another still as dreadful, and appealing urgently to my heart for help. A soldier lay on the bare ground — his head raised upon a pile of stones, the hot sun pouring down upon his pallid face, in which was no sign of life. Some moments passed, and he stirred not — then I questioned a nurse who was passing, and he replied to my inquiry of "Is that man dead?" "No, but about as good as dead — he can't live."
>
> I never paused till I reached his side, and seeming to gather supernatural strength I helped to bring him into the house, after feeling his pulse, and ascertaining that there was life still in the body.
>
> I gave him brandy, and in an hour he opened his eyes, and seemed to be a little conscious of what was going on about him. While striving to revive him the Doctor passed that way, and paused, asking, 'What are you doing with that dead man?'
>
> 'Going to raise him for myself,' I replied very deferentially, and he went his way, muttering about "calico nurses" being such plagues in a hospital, ... I saw my patient — who had been left to die, and would have died soon but for the help he had — made comfortable, and tended him daily, till he was sent to the General Hospital, and had the satisfaction of knowing that he fully recovered. I saw him afterward in Washington.[42]

Were these roles for women significant to the soldiers? By most accounts, the answer is a resounding "yes:"

> Their [the nurses'] presence was proof that [people] cared for us, and were willing to brave danger, and come even within range of the fearful shells to minister to those from whose wounds the warm blood was still flowing. In their presence, men could suffer with more fortitude, and die with more resignation. If we could not look upon our dear ones at home, we could upon their representatives.[43]

Social Support

Encouragement, clothing, ammunition, food, and medical care, are not all the things that soldiers wanted and needed. In some instances, they simply wanted female companionship or the companionship of a particular female. During the long winter encampments when there tended to be few campaigns and battles, and soldier housing often transformed from canvas tents to semi-permanent huts, some women stayed in the camps. The following is an excerpt from a letter written home by a woman living in such a camp with her husband:

Camp Cochran
Washg, Dec 25th 1861

It is Christmas evening and the first Christmas I have ever been absent from my home....

Last evening we had a grand time here...with the assistance of some officers [we] dressed the Marquee with greens, festoons, wreaths, lights[?], colors, colored lanterns etc. and in the evening had a fancy dress soiree. I wore a Chasseur jacket, red sash over the shoulder. My balmoral skirt with dress festooned up over it balmoral boots and black feather and ornaments out of the regimental hat in my hair.

...I would say we had some very amusing costumes. Lt. Bernard was dressed as an Indian Chief. Lt. Roome as a female. Had on a pair of my pantalets and all the other female accoutrements complete throughout. We had a French count, a Chinese Mandarin and a big boy. [illeg] big mucks. And I forget the rest now. Whiskey punches — as usual — dancing, singing & theatricals were the order of the evening. We had a grand time, I assure you.

Tell [Ma] not to be so worried about my keeping myself comfortable that although the cold is intense (not in tents) & the wind roars & blows about us almost turning our tent inside out all that troubles me is the noise & sympathy for those who are compelled to be on guard. We wrap ourselves well in the blankets cover our heads & go to sleep — I tell you I am getting to be quite a soldier....[44]

Some have proposed that staying in a military encampment could not have been consistent with maintaining the modesty and lifestyle necessary for a proper lady and that all women living in and around military camps must have been prostitutes. There are too many accounts of officers who boarded their wives in or near the camps to make this a credible argument. As a further note, the letter quoted above was written by a young lady to her father.

However, it is also true that not all women visiting military encampments were of impeccable virtue. There were, of course, women who did prostitute themselves and the officers and armies dealt with these problems in a number of ways. In one grand experiment, Major General Benjamin F. Butler created a structure for the licensing, and regular medical examinations of prostitutes in and around April-May of 1862 in New Orleans, Louisiana. He was able to show the value of his arrangement in reduced rates of venereal disease among both the prostitutes and the soldiers. It was not, however, a program that was widely copied.

Colonel (later Brigadier General) Thomas R. R. Cobb felt compelled to respond to some hearsay that had bothered his wife, assuring her that his regiment had no "vivandieres' attached to it. "I have never heard of such appendages on this peninsula," he wrote. "the Louisiana and No[rth] Ca[rolina] regiments had some camp-women who were said to be soldier's wives. But I confess I asked no questions."[45]

It is interesting that Colonel Cobb felt that the term "vivandiere" was a euphemism for a prostitute and responded accordingly. Vivandiere is in fact, a term given to female soldiers who accompanied (primarily Zouave) troops in the Crimea and other wars. "Cantiniere" is a term given to women who served as water carriers for the troops. Few American units used either term, though photographic evidence indicates that at least a couple women adopted uniforms similar to those of the French vivandieres. These uniforms generally consisted of a shirt with a tailored jackets worn over it and a full, knee-length skirt, which was, in turn, worn over relatively lose ankle-length trousers.

The costume itself is not necessarily an indication of a vivandiere or cantiniere, as it is quite similar to the costumes often used to symbolize "Daughters of the Regiment." A "Daughter of the Regiment" could be a female of any age from toddler to adulthood. She was usually the daughter of an officer of the company and her post was largely ceremonial. Often the Daughters of the Regiment marched with troops when they paraded through their hometown.

> [Irene] was at that time four years of age; her dress was...red pants, a white blouse with embroidered ruffle at neck and wrists; over this a zouave jacked of red, a small three-cornered hat of the same, warm hue, with ribbon rosettes bearing the colors of the southern standard.[46]

(Left) The uniform on this actress is either a real uniform borrowed for the occasion or a better-than-average theatrical costume. Author's collection

(Right) The Daughter of the Regiment costume in this photograph is nearly identical to those worn by Clara Kellogg in the title role of "Daughter of the Regiment." Author's collection

When the troops left for war, the Daughter of the Regiment generally returned home. Some few of the older Daughters continued on, serving as nurses for "their" troops. The term, "Daughter of the Regiment," became a ceremonial title that soldiers bestowed on women who provided especially valuable service to them. There is quite often a disconnect between finding a woman who referred to herself as the "Daughter of this or that regiment" and finding any regimental paper indicating that the title was officially recognized.

Finally, both the vivandiere-like costume and the title "Daughter of the Regiment" were used in an operetta that was performed in many locations during the war. Photographs of various actresses in theatrical costumes were published and widely distributed and provide further confusion for people looking for evidence of vivandieres and female soldiers in the Civil War.

Soldiers, Spies and Scouts

That there were women who served as soldiers is indisputable. That doing so was contrary to the prevailing culture is also indisputable. The cultural norms that divided the sexes were strong ones, as evident from Sarah Morgan Dawson's efforts to even try on the garb of a man:

> If they attack I shall don the breeches and join the assailants and fight, though I think they would be hopeless fools to attempt to capture a town they could not hold for 10 minutes under the gunboats. How do breeches and coats feel? I am actually afraid of them. I kept a suit of Jimmy's hanging in the armoir for six weeks waiting for the yankees to come, thinking fright would give me courage to try it (what a paradox) but I never succeeded. Lilly one day insisted on my trying it, and I advanced so far as to laying it on the bed, and then cried my bed out — I was ashamed to let even my canary see me; — but my courage deserted me. I have heard so many girls boast of having worn men's clothes; I wonder where they get the courage.[47]

But some did get the courage, and cut their hair, and enlisted in the army, and camped, and marched, and fought side-by-side with soldiers, or at least did their level best to try. It was the general practice of the armies to prevent these efforts by women and to throw out of the military women they found to be perpetrating this fraud.

Charles Moulton worked in the Provost Marshall's office in Harpers Ferry during the war, and recorded a number of instances in which such women were discovered:

> We sent away to Fort McHenry today another of the "questionable characters" in the personification of a female woman clad so snugly in a soldier's uniform. There are 5 more of the same class still loitering about, who will be "nabbed" as speedily as the committee discovers their whereabouts. This one delighted in the sobriquet of Maggie Simpson and was by no means an "ornament to her sex." On the whole, she was rather a scaly looking specimen of the human frame, has a face similar to a crocodile and a voice as sweet as a cracked fiddle or an old cow bell or bellows![48]

Were their contributions significant? A critical view might conclude that these transvestites seemed to have worried — and acted — more on their own needs and desires than those of the soldiers or the armies. If, on the other hand, we accept that they were soldiers, then in meeting their own needs, they were meeting the needs of at least one soldier and, like other soldiers, they risked their lives to do it.

The female soldiers were not the only ones who risked life and limb. There is solid evidence of some women who passed information or acted as spies during the War. In some cases, their activities were formally acknowledged after the war. In general, though, researching women who spied for the military is problematic.

We may have a dearth of information because; presumably, the most successful spies are not caught, and do not leave behind evidence that is easily traced by historians.

We may have false information; those who were charged with being spies were sometimes selected based more on politics and convenience than on solid evidence of their deeds. Every woman charged, imprisoned or exiled on a charge of spying during the war was not necessarily guilty.[49]

We may have fictional information; as a number of individuals admittedly exaggerated their own accounts of acting as spies during the war. Emma Edmonds claimed to disguise herself not just as a male but as a black male contraband in her spying.[50]

There were perhaps even more women involved in smuggling as in spying. Adelaide Stewart Dimitry included in her book on the war information about smuggling activities by a "Mrs. Smith:"

> Mr. Smith secretly bought and shipped ammunition, guns, etc., while his wife continually made purchases of small articles — medicines at different drug stores, tea, coffee, pins, needles, etc....and smuggled them to friends in the Confederacy. Having quilted her purchases into a petticoat, she was ready for a ride. Mrs. Smith's horse had been trained at a given signal to run away. On arriving at the guard house, Mr. Smith would engage the officer in pleasant talk. Presently, his wife's horse becoming more and more restive, would suddenly dash forward, vault the fence and bear its rider away with the speed of the wind. The objective point was an old stump well known to the boys in gray. Reaching it, she would quickly dismount, remove from her thick coils of hair small packages of drugs, unloop her quilted skirt stored with good things and correspondence that might not have passed muster at the city post office. Quickly concealing all within the stump, she would spring into the saddle and on her mad gallop homeward probably meet her husband and an anxious Federal officer coming in search of her.[51]

Spiritual Support

As historians view the painting, they may notice, here and there, a poignant scene of a soldier who is clearly dying. But as his life-sustaining blood spilled onto the ground, no amount of medical assistance could save his life. In these instances there was little that any man or woman could do for that soldier. Or was there?

Many thousands of women recognized that soldiers needed care for their souls, as well as their bodies. Women at home prayed fervently, by day and night for the safe keeping of their soldiers. Organized religious organizations opened their doors and transformed convents and other church buildings into hospitals. They also sent religious into the field on some occasions to minister to the soldiers. One minister related an experience representative of the way in which the prayers of women did, indeed, matter to the soldiers:

> "Now, Chaplain," said the young man, "I want you to kneel down by me and return thanks to God."
> "For what?" I asked.
> "For giving me such a mother.... And thank God that by his grace I am a Christian. Oh, what would I do now if I wasn't a Christian? Thank him for the promised home in Glory. I'll soon be there where there is no war, nor sorrow, nor desolation, nor death..."[52]

In addition to the male ministers who traveled to the field, nurses and nuns found themselves ministering to the spiritual needs of the soldiers. Fannie Beers related her own experiences in this area:

> Two soldiers in particular attracted my attention. One was an Irishman...fast passing away, ...earnestly desired to see a priest. There was none nearer than twelve miles... Finding the poor fellow, though almost too far gone to articulate, constantly murmuring words of prayer, I took his prayer-book and read aloud the "Recommendation of a soul departing" also some of the preceding prayers of the "Litany for the dying." He faintly responded and seemed to die comforted and satisfied. Afterwards I never hesitated to use the same service in like cases.[53]

Was it significant to the soldiers? More than forty years after the war's end, a soldier read about the illness of a nun he had observed during the Civil War. He penned a tribute to Mother Gonzaga:

> No poet could describe, no artist could faithfully portray on canvas the scenes at the deathbed of a soldier, that could convey to those not having witnessed them the solemnity of the quiet kneeling, the silent prayer, a murmur faintly heard as a whisper, a Sister of Charity paying her devotion to Him on high, and consigning the spirit of the dying soldier to His care.
> As one of many thousands under her care I shall always think of Mother Gonzaga as one of a constellation of stars of the greatest magnitude... We soldiers cannot forget the service they rendered.[54]

Burial and Mourning

But the "services they rendered" — the needs they met — extended even beyond the death of a soldier. Fannie Beers touched briefly on her efforts to attend the burials of soldiers who had died in her care:

> For months after entering the service I insisted upon attending every dead soldier to the grave and reading over him a part of the burial service. But it had now become impossible. The dead were past help; the living always

needed succor. But no soldier ever died in my presence without a whispered prayer to comfort his parting soul.[55]

Katherine Wormely reported on tasks associated with the deaths of soldiers.

Beside the letters we write and send off for the men, we have many from friends inquiring after husbands, sons, and brothers who are reported wounded. Such letters will never cease to be a sad and tender memory to us. One came last week from a wife inquiring after her husband, but none of us could attend to it until to-day. 'Give him back to me dead," she says, "if he is dead, for I must see him." Mrs. Griffin remembered the name; he was one of the men whose funeral she attended ashore one Sunday evening. So to-day I went up and found him under the feathery elm-tree. I made a little sketch of the place and sent it to her, — all I could send, poor soul.[56]

Was it significant to the soldier that even after his death women mourned him? They were certainly sustained by thoughts and prayers of those at home and by the knowledge that they were remembered by the ones they left behind. "Aunt Becky" related one incident in which a soldier expressed the peace he felt in that knowledge:

I said honestly, "I think you can live but a short time," and sighing, he replied slowly, "Well, I am not sorry that I came here, even if I have got my death, but it will be very lonely for her." He seemed to dwell upon the thought very calmly and went on saying, "If the country forgets me, she always remembers me; there will be a monument raised in her heart to my memory, and it will always live." He died as peacefully as a child goes to its slumbers — dropped away silently without a struggle.[57]

Were these roles significant? Who can place a value on dying peacefully?

Other Activities

Women helped with even more than food, shelter, clothing, arms, ammunition, medical sanitary, social and psychological needs, or as soldiers, spies and scouts. Wherever and whenever they discovered other needs of soldiers and armies, they worked to meet those needs.

Let us not forget the women who stayed at home, and, quite literally, "kept the home-fires burning." For many a soldier, the memory of that woman at home gave him something to fight for and someone to come home to. He knew when he returned that his job might be gone and his community changed beyond recognition, but so long as there was a familiar face that longed to see him, come home a hero, he would fight on.

Elizabeth Thorn was married to the caretaker of the cemetery in Gettysburg, Pennsylvania. Despite being pregnant, she labored alongside men, digging graves and burying soldiers in the days following the Battle of Gettysburg. Her efforts are both remarkable and representative of the roles of women and are being recognized with her depiction in the Gettysburg Women's Memorial.

During the war women worked for the government in some roles that had been open to them prior to the war (such as lighthouse keepers, clerks and copyists) and in some newly-created positions (such as government telegraph operators).

Elisa B. Rumsey agreed with her friend John A Fowle that the soldiers stationed in and around Washington DC had too much free time on their hands and needed intellectual stimulations. Together, they established a Soldiers Free Library. In the end, with a total cash expenditure $1,200, they managed to establish and run a 6,000 volume library, housed in its own building.[58]

Authoress Grace Greenwood traveled to and stayed in the winter camp of the First Division, Second Corps at Brandy Station while she gave a lecture (or lecture series) to troops encamped there.[59]

Intellectual stimulation included religious topics, as well. Esther Hill Hawks was a medical doctor who served in, and was briefly in charge of, a military hospital. But in addition to that, she found an avocation in teaching both contrabands and soldiers.

> January 15th 1865
>
> Our Sunday-school is large and very interesting. To-day there were a hundred pupils present. I have a large class of soldiers — about fifteen in all — good readers bright — and quick. We take a chapter in the Testament have it read and then talk it over. I find them very ready with answers![60]

Susie King Taylor and her husband knew that many of his fellow soldiers in the U.S. Colored Troops could not read and write. Susie and her husband both gave lessons:

> I taught a great many of the comrades in Company E to read and write, when they were off duty. Nearly all were anxious to learn. My husband taught some also when it was convenient for him. I was very happy to know my efforts were successful in camp, and also felt grateful for the appreciation of my services.[61]

Mrs. Taylor found other ways to help, as well:

> I learned to handle a musket very well while in the regiment, and could shoot straight and often hit the target. I assisted in cleaning the guns and used to fire them off, to see if the cartridges were dry, before cleaning and reloading each day. I thought this great fun. I was also able to take a gun all apart, and put it together again.[62]

But it was not all great fun. Mrs. S.A. Palmer ("Aunt Becky") suffered qualms of her conscience at leaving her daughters behind to volunteer in the war efforts:

> I thought of the two little girls I was leaving motherless, I felt a wild desire to return — shrinking from the duties which I had undertaken — a shrinking from the duties which I had undertaken and sickened at the thought of dressing bloody wounds, of combing out hair tangled and matted with the thick gore... Then better feelings took possession of me, and I knew if they could suffer so much, and die for their country, I could at least give some years of my poor life in the attempt to alleviate their sufferings; and I took up my burden of duties again.[63]

Hannah Ropes recorded her strong feelings that women had a duty to support the war efforts:

> Now is the judgment of his world. Each man and woman is taking his or her measure. As it is taken even so must it stand — it will be recorded.... Let us be loyal and true, then if the great world never hears a word about us one shall not fear, even though the waves of war's uncertain tide swallow us in the general wreck![64]

And these efforts continued long after the war ended. Individuals and Ladies Aid Societies turned their attentions to the needs of veterans, orphans and widows, raising money for prosthetic devices, and establishing and funding Orphanages and Homes for those left unable to maintain their own households. They paid for the removal and reburial of soldiers and for gravestones and memorials erected in the memory of the soldiers. They advocated for the continued remembrance of the soldiers through the establishment of Memorial Day. They supported and helped to fund organizations like the Confederate Memorial Literary Society which was established to collect and preserve artifacts and documents related to the war. And it is through supporting those same efforts that women (and men) carry on to this day the roles of women in the Civil War.

Having examined the scope of women's roles in the Civil War, we find some that are visible to the observer of major, minor, political and military events of the war. These include women who procured, provided, presented, and then preserved flags and banners for the troops, women who assisted the wounded and dying and even burying the dead, and women who served as spies, scouts, smugglers and soldiers. We pay appropriate homage to the contributions of these women. And then we turn our attention "behind the scenes" to the needs of soldiers and the vast legions of women and the countless roles they played providing food, shelter, clothing, ammunition, accoutrements, encouragement, social, spiritual, psychological, medical, monetary, mourning, and memorial support. Without this support could they, would they, have fought the same war? Without supporting canvas, the portrait of war would be far different.

Endnotes

1. Wormeley, Katherine Prescott, *The Other Side of War With the Army of the Potomac*, Boston, Ticknor & Co., 1889, page 3.

2. Rood, H. W., *Company E and the Twelfth Wisconsin in the War for the Union*, Milwaukee, 1893, pages 17 & 48. Quoted in Huren, Ethel Alice, *Wisconsin History Commission: Original Papers No. 6: Wisconsin Women in the War*, Wisconsin, Wisconsin History Commission, 1911, page 5.

3. Hill, Sarah Jane Full, *Mrs. Hill's Journal — Civil War Reminscences*, Chicago, The Lakeside Press, 1980, pages 39-40.

4. Welch, Spencer Glasgow, *A Confederate Surgeon's Letters to His Wife*, Marietta, GA, Continental Book Company, 1954 (originally published 1911), page 55.

5. Gay, Mary A. H., *Life in Dixie During the War, 1861-1862-1863-1864-1865*, Atlanta, The Constitution Job Office, 1892, page 16.

6. Watkins, Sam R., Co. Aytch: *Maury Grays First Tennessee Regiment*, Wilmington, NC, Broadfoot Publishing Co., 1994 (originally published 1882), pages 88-89.

7. This conclusion is made after examining the pay records of women at the Richmond and Atlanta Depots. One some pages fully 70% of the signatures are represented by "X." I am indebted to Les Jensen who has reviewed pay records.

8. "Miss Abby's Diary," January 20, 1864, quoted

in Dyer, Thomas G., *Secret Yankees: The Union Circle in Confederate Atlanta*, Baltimore, The Johns Hopkins University Press, pages 158-159.

9. Wormeley, page 186.

10. Les Jensen's research into records of the Staunton Depot indicates the Mrs. Blackburn cut hundreds of garments in a three or four month period in 1864.

11. Joslyn, Mauriel Phillips, *Charlotte's Boys: Letters of the Branch Family of Savannah*, Berryville, VA, Rockbridge Publishing Co., 1996, page 23.

12. Wormeley, pages 5-6.

13. Bacon, Georgeanna Woolsey, and Howland, Eliza Woolsey, eds., *My Heart Towards Home: Letters of a Family During the Civil War*, Roseville, MN, Edinborough Press, 2001 (originally published 1898), page 42.

14. Crabtree, Beth Gilbert, and Patton, James W., eds., *Journal of a Secesh Lady: The Diary of Catherine Ann Deveraux Edmonston, 1860-1866*, Raleigh, Division of Archives and History of Cultural Resources, 1995, page 282.

15. Gay, pages 42-43.

16. Beers, Fannie A., *Memories*, J. B. Lippencott Co., Philadephia, 1888, page 54.

17. These are almost surely inflatable rubber mattresses. An 1856 advertisement for George N. Davis & Brothers' rubber goods includes an illustration of an inflatable mattress with the caption "Air Beds and Pillows." Pictured in Woshner, Mike, *India-Rubber and Gutta-Percha in the Civil War Era*, Alexandria, VA., O'Donnell Publications, 1999, page 116.

18. Bacon & Howland, page 36.

19. Pember, Phoebe Yates, *A Southern Woman's Story: Life in Confederate Richmond*, Ballantine Books, NYC, 1959, page 40.

20. Anonymous, *Minute Book of the Bellingham Methodist Sewing Society, Organized March 15th 1853*, manuscript in the collection of the author.

21. Wormeley, page 6.

22. Smith, Rev. Edward P., *Incidents of the United States Christian Commission*, Philadelphia, J. B. Lippincott & Co., 1869.

23. *Ibid.*, page 5

24. Wormeley, page 62.

25. Stegeman, John F., *These Men She Gave: the Civil War Diary of Athens, Georgia*, Athens, University of Georgia, 1964, page 59.

26. Welch, page 66.

27. Anderson, John Q., ed., *Brokenburn: The Journal of Kate Stone 1861-1868*, Baton Rouge, Louisiana State University Press, 1972, page 339.

28. Beers, p. 95

29. Beers, p. 44

30. Goodrich, Frank B., *The Tribute Book: A Record of the Munificence, Self-Sacrifice and Patriotism of The American People During the War for the Union*, New York, Derby & Miller, 1865, pages 419-420.

31. Based on research presented by Steven Roca, "Permission to Come on Board: Women Nurses on the *USS Red Rover*," presented at the 1997 Conference on Women and the Civil War.

32. Bacon and Howland, page 373.

33. Wormeley, page 21.

34. Beers, pages 65-66.

35. Rollins, Rachel, "After the Battle of Antietam: Letters from a Hospital," *Atlantic Monthly*, May, 1876, Boston, H. O. Hoighton & Co., pages 575-588.

36. Hill, pages 49-52.

37. Wormeley, page 67.

38. Brumgardt, John R., *Civil War Nurse: The Diary and Letters of Hannah Ropes*, Knoxville, Univ. of Tennessee Press, 1980, pages 52-53.

39. Beers, pages 66-67.

40. Wheelock, Julia S., *The Boys in White: The Experience of a Hospital Agent in and Around Washington*, New York, Lange & Hillman, 1870, page 197.

41. Palmer, S. A., *The Story of Aunt Becky's Army-Life*, Aurora, NY, Talbothays Books (originally published 1867), page 96.

42. *Ibid.*, pages 56-57.

43. Locke, E. W., *Three Years in Camp and Hospital*, Boston, George D. Russell, 1871, page 184.

44. Letter in the collection of the author.

45. Stegman, pages 45-46.

46. Anonymous, *Confederate Women: Arkansas in the Civil War*, United Daughters of the Confederacy, 1907, page 157.

47. Dawson, Sarah Morgan, *A Confederate Girl's Diary*, Boston, Houghton Mifflin Co., 1913, page 120.

48. Drickamer, Lee C., and Drickamer, Karen D., eds., *Fort Lyon to Harper's Ferry: On the Border of North and South with "Rambling Jour,"* Shippensburg, PA, White Mane Publishing, 1987, page 215.

49. Elizabeth Lindsay Lomax asserted, even in her private diary, that her daughters were entirely innocent of spying charges leveled against them. Lomax, Elizabeth Lindsay, *Leaves from an Old Washington Diary 1854-1863*, New York, E. P. Dutton & Co., 1943.

50. Edmonds, Emma E., *Nurse and Spy in the Union Army: The Adventures and Experiences of a Woman in Hospitals, Camp, and Battlefields*, Hartford, W. S. Williams & Co., 1865.

51. Dimity, Adelaide Stuart, *War-Time Sketches: Historical and Otherwise*, New Orleans, Loui-

siana Printing Co. Press, undated, pages 53-54.

52. United States Christian Commission, *Christian Work on the Battle-field*, London, Hodder & Stoughton, 1902, pages 229-230.

53. Beers, page 85.

54. J. E. MacLane quoted in Barton, George, *Angels of the Battlefield: A History of the Labors of the Catholic Sisterhoods in the Late Civil War*, Philadelphia, The Catholic Art Publishing Co., 1897, page 115.

55. Beers, page 83.

56. Wormeley, page 121.

57. Palmer, page 75.

58. Lovett, Robert W., "The Soldiers' Free Library," *Civil War History*, March 1962, State University of Iowa, pages 54-63.

59. Greenwood, Grace, *Record of Five Years*, Boston, Ticknor & Fields, 1867, pages 166-212.

60. Schwartz, Gerald, ed., *A Woman Doctor's Civil War: Esther Hill Hawks' Diary*, Columbia, University of South Carolina Press, 1992, pages 103-104.

61. Taylor, Susie King, *Reminiscences of my Life: A Black Woman's Civil War Memoirs*, New York, Markaus Wiener Publishing, 1988, page 52.

62. *Ibid.*, page 61.

63. Palmer, page 4.

64. Brumgardt, page 113.

The Editor

Eileen Conklin began researching women's service in the Civil War over twenty years ago when she was a Licensed Battlefield Guide at Gettysburg National Military Park. Having come across so many women mentioned in primary sources while studying that battle, she embarked on a ten year research project culminating in her book *Women at Gettysburg—1863*. The volume contains stories of over forty women from Maine to Louisiana who served in various capacities on the field of Gettysburg.

She has written articles for *Military Images*, *The Gettysburg Magazine*, and *The Journal of Confederate History*. Conklin has lectured on women in the Civil War to audiences at battlefields, colleges, museums and libraries and has addressed historical, military and women's groups. She is the co-founder of the Conference on Women in the Civil War, past president of Women in the Civil War, Inc., and president of In the Company of Women, Inc. Eileen is the recipient of the Delaware Valley Civil War Round Table's 1998 Award of Merit.

Conklin's second book, *Exile to Sweet Dixie*, is based on the life and war experiences of Euphemia Goldsborough of Baltimore, a Confederate nurse and smuggler. She edited Rose Greenhow's book, *My Imprisonment and the First Year of Abolition Rule in Washington*, for a book on tape which was released in 2000. She organized and edits *From the Home Front to the Front Lines*, a journal on women in the Civil War. Eileen is currently working on a novel and a screenplay.